The Seminole Wars

The Florida History and Culture Series

UNIVERSITY PRESS OF FLORIDA
STATE UNIVERSITY SYSTEM

Florida A&M University, Tallahassee

Florida Atlantic University, Boca Raton

Florida Gulf Coast University, Ft. Myers

Florida International University, Miami

Florida State University, Tallahassee

University of Central Florida, Orlando

University of Florida, Gainesville

University of North Florida, Jacksonville

University of South Florida, Tampa

University of West Florida, Pensacola

The Seminole Wars

America's Longest Indian Conflict

John Missall and Mary Lou Missall

Foreword by Raymond Arsenault and Gary R. Mormino, Series Editors

University Press of Florida
Gainesville · Tallahassee · Tampa · Boca Raton
Pensacola · Orlando · Miami · Jacksonville · Ft. Myers

09 08 07 06 05   6 5 4 3 2

Missall, John, 1949–
The Seminole wars : America's longest Indian conflict / John Missall
and Mary Lou Missall ; foreword by Raymond Arsenault and Gary R. Mormino.
p. cm. — (Florida history and culture series)
Includes bibliographical references and index.
ISBN 0-8130-2715-2 (cloth : alk. paper)
1. Seminole War, 1st, 1817–1818. 2. Seminole War, 2nd, 1835–1842.
3. Seminole War, 3rd, 1855–1858. I. Missall, Mary Lou, 1949– II. Title. III. Series.
E83.817.M57 2004
973.5-DC22   2003070522

Frontispiece: Tukose Emathla, Seminole chief. Drawing by
James G. Clark, 1843. Courtesy of the Florida State Archives.

The University Press of Florida is the scholarly publishing agency for
the State University System of Florida, comprising Florida A&M University,
Florida Atlantic University, Florida Gulf Coast University, Florida International
University, Florida State University, University of Central Florida, University
of Florida, University of North Florida, University of South Florida, and
University of West Florida.

University Press of Florida
15 Northwest 15th Street
Gainesville, FL 32611-2079
http://www.upf.com

To our parents, Lee J. and Ramona, Chester P. and Ruth.
Though only one of you is still with us in person,
your memories remain. Thank you for the guidance.

To our brothers and sisters and their spouses, Paul and Connie,
John and Pearl, and Effie. Thank you for the companionship.

To our daughter, Shelley, and grandson, Justin.
Thank you for the future.

Contents

Figures

Maps

Foreword

During the past half century, the burgeoning population and increased national and international visibility of Florida have sparked a great deal of popular interest in the state's past, present, and future. As the favorite destination of countless tourists and as the new home for millions of retirees and other migrants, modern Florida has become a demographic, political, and cultural bellwether.

Unfortunately, the quantity and quality of the literature on Florida's distinctive heritage and character have not kept pace with the Sunshine State's enhanced status. In an effort to remedy this situation—to provide an accessible and attractive format for the publication of Florida-related books—the University Press of Florida has established the Florida History and Culture series.

As coeditors of the series, we are committed to the creation of an eclectic but carefully crafted set of books that will provide the field of Florida studies with a new focus and that will encourage Florida researchers and writers to consider the broader implications and context of their work. The series includes standard academic monographs, works of synthesis, memoirs, and anthologies. And, while the series features books of historical interest, we encourage authors researching Florida's environment, politics, literature, and popular or material culture to submit their manuscripts as well. We want each book to retain a distinct personality and voice, but at the same time we hope to foster a sense of community and collaboration among Florida scholars.

In *The Seminole Wars,* John and Mary Lou Missall reexamine one of the seminal developments in Florida history. Stretching across five decades, the three Seminole Wars of 1817–18, 1835–42, and 1855–58 played a pivotal role in Florida's transition from a Spanish colony to a U.S. territory and state. Regrettably, as the Missalls point out, many modern

Americans, including most Floridians, have little sense of the Seminole Wars' significance. Despite several fine monographs by historians such as James Covington and John K. Mahon, public consciousness of the complexities and far-flung ramifications of these interrelated conflicts has dimmed. Reduced to a few disconnected anecdotes about Andrew Jackson, Osceola, and Billy Bowlegs, the ongoing confrontation between the Seminoles and the American government occupies a marginal position in the history and memory of both state and nation.

In an effort to remedy this unfortunate situation, the Missalls have constructed a richly textured narrative that pays proper attention to both text and context. Drawing upon a wide variety of secondary and primary sources, they retell the story of the Seminole Wars in vivid detail. But, perhaps even more important, they recapture the meaning of the wars, placing them in the broad flow of nineteenth-century American history. The expansion of slavery, the displacement of native peoples, the dictates of racialist ideology, the quest for national security, the ebb and flow of imperial rivalries, and the consequences of land hunger and unrestrained territorial expansion are themes that run through the length and breadth of the Seminole Wars. How these wars were fought and justified and how they ended had lasting consequences not only for Floridians but also for those who lived well beyond the state's and even the nation's borders. For better or worse, the use of military force to bring about a political and cultural reconfiguration of the Seminole borderlands represents an important part of our past, a contingent episode that merits serious consideration and sober reflection.

Raymond Arsenault and Gary R. Mormino, Series Editors
University of South Florida, St. Petersburg

Preface

It should be the question game-show hosts ask when they do not want to give away that million-dollar prize: What was the longest, most expensive Indian war fought by the United States? Few people know the correct answer. The Second Seminole War lasted seven years (1835–42) and cost about $30 million, a sum that was greater than the entire federal budget for just one of those years. The Seminole Wars dwell among many skeletons in our nation's closet, but not many Americans have heard the rattling of the bones. Perhaps it is time the closet door was opened.[1]

There were three Seminole Wars. The first was a punitive excursion into the Spanish colony of La Florida in 1818, led by Andrew Jackson. The second war was fought in the Territory of Florida and was part of the tragic Indian removals of the 1830s. The final war took place in the new state of Florida on the eve of the Civil War and was an attempt to remove the last remnants of the Seminole Nation from their homes in the Everglades.

Today these conflicts are all but forgotten. Except for a paragraph or two in some textbooks, they are rarely mentioned in history classes at any level. With the exception of one man, Osceola, few of the participants are remembered. Andrew Jackson, a driving force behind the conflicts, and Zachary Taylor, the wars' only white "celebrity," are remembered for other deeds. Indeed, if not for the name of Osceola, the Seminole Wars would be an even more obscure footnote in the history of this nation.

Why is this? One can easily blame geography. Everyone "knows" that the great Indian wars were all fought west of the Mississippi after the Civil War. The very thought of an Indian war in Florida is an alien concept. Also, few people are aware of the fact that Florida's first large industry was cattle production and that Florida remains one of the top cattle-producing states in the Union. In its earliest days, Florida had more than its share of cowboys and Indians. More than a century of Wild West tales have obscured the fact that natives and settlers fought just as desperately in the eastern United States.

When we think of Indians east of the Mississippi, a few disconnected names come to mind: Pocahontas, the Iroquois, the Cherokee, or the last of the Mohicans. If not for their distinctive haircuts, the Mohawks might be completely forgotten. We are often left with the erroneous impression that the Indian tribes of the East were more passive than those of the West: they could be invited over for Thanksgiving dinner or would allow themselves to be herded west over the Trail of Tears. The "wild" Indians all seemed to live out west.

Those who have taken the time to study Native American history know better. As we look into our nation's past, we often see signs of the Indians' presence: The French and Indian War, the purchase of Manhattan, the wives of mountain men and fur traders, some mythical acquaintances of Daniel Boone and Davy Crockett. We often know more about the Indians who were conquered by the Spaniards than we do about the Indians who confronted the English on North American soil.

We might blame other events for eclipsing the Seminole Wars, especially the First and Third, which were much smaller affairs than the Second. The Mexican War, which quickly followed the Second Seminole War, captivated the nation's imagination. Then, of course, there was the Civil War. All other conflicts were soon forgotten. At times it appears as if everything that happened between 1815 and 1860 took place solely for the purpose of leading us into a civil war.

The idea that other events overshadowed the Florida War, as the Second Seminole War was known, does not stand up to scrutiny. Wasn't the nation more concerned with the extremely divisive issue of slavery? Yes, it was, but as we shall see, the problem of slavery was one of the major causes of the war. What about foreign relations? What did the Seminole Wars have to do with America's national security? More than one might expect. The Seminoles had been allies of both the English and the Spanish. They were a "hostile nation" within our borders, occupying a territory that would be easily accessible to the fleets of unfriendly European nations.

To the people of the time, the Second Seminole War was an important event—not necessarily the most important subject for discussion, but one everyone knew about and concerning which many had strong opinions. For seven years, the matter came up before Congress and was reported in the press. Thousands of young Americans from all over the nation went off to fight under the worst conditions possible, and many did not return. To their families, the Seminole War was not a minor affair. In the national press, more space was devoted to the Seminole War than to any other single subject in the years 1836–39. Indeed, for the first two years of the conflict, news of the war commanded front-page coverage.[2]

We wonder what motivated the Seminoles to take up arms against a large, vigorous nation. The mystery compounds when we realize that a large number of these Florida Indians were not actually Seminoles, were not born in Florida, and were not truly Indians. Yet Florida was their chosen home and they struggled heroically to remain within its borders. Militarily, the Second War was an embarrassment. There were no great victories, no parades for the returning soldiers. The United States and its powerful army were repeatedly humiliated by a relatively small band of warriors whom most whites derided as nothing more than "savages." The honor and glory that were supposed to accompany civilized warfare were almost totally absent. For those who had fought in the war, there was little about which to go home and boast; it was an experience few of the participants wanted to talk about, and very few did.

For the nation as a whole, the war was often seen as a moral failure. The Indians were considered desperate underdogs, defiantly attempting to defend their homes against a heartless and greedy aggressor. Many of them were taken prisoner while negotiating under a flag of truce, and Seminole villages and farms were burned, leaving women and children to scavenge for food in the inhospitable swamps. The Indians, of course, committed their own atrocities and treacheries, but many people felt they were driven to it. When the war ended, these painful and troubling thoughts were easily put aside.

Because the Seminole Wars were so quickly forgotten, the American public never learned some valuable lessons. Later conflicts with the Indians of the West proved no less satisfying. The parallels with our experiences in Vietnam and the Middle East are often very striking, which may be one of the reasons the tale is so relevant. Perhaps if we Americans had understood what had happened in our nation's infancy, we might have been better able to avoid the pitfalls that have entrapped us in our present day and age.

The purpose of this volume is *not* to rewrite the history of the Seminole Wars. Those who are familiar with the subject will find little that is new. Although the three conflicts have been largely ignored, there are several excellent volumes that examine them in minute detail. These works are listed in the bibliography, and we heartily recommend each of them to anyone interested in delving deeper into this subject. As with all histories, some of these works cover an entire conflict while others look at only a single individual or event.

What we as authors felt was missing was a volume that adequately covered all three wars and the years leading up to them. We also wanted to look at the larger picture. How did these wars fit into American history in general? What forces in American society influenced events in Florida and how did the wars affect the nation as a whole? Each Seminole War was entangled with many other issues taking place at the time. Newton's laws of action and reaction apply to history as well as to physics: a seven-year war does not take place for no reason at all, nor does it pass without leaving a trace. History is never as simple as we would like it to be.

If there is one thing missing in this work, it is the Seminole side of the story. There are two reasons for this. First, and most obvious, is the fact that the Seminoles left very little of a paper trail. White Americans wrote all the documents, official and unofficial. Even when the Seminoles spoke, their words were recorded by white transcriptionists. Second, we do not feel qualified to tell the Seminole side. Quite properly, that is for the Seminoles themselves to do.

We do not, however, feel this comparative lack of Seminole input to be a problem. The American Indian is as complete a human as any other American. He or she will respond to the world in the same manner as any of us might. We can put ourselves in their moccasins and try to imagine how they felt and why they reacted as they did just as easily as we can put ourselves in a soldier's boots. In any given instance our interpretation may be in error, but we will still learn something in the process. In addition, it must be remembered that the primary focus of this work is an attempt to understand why the United States government and certain of its citizens acted as they did. Unfortunately, it often seems as if the Seminole Nation was the nail being pounded by the hammer of American policy. What interested us most was why the hammer was swung in the first place.

This project is a direct offshoot of Mary Lou's master's thesis. In a quandary as to a subject for the paper, she began to ask friends for ideas. A business acquaintance suggested looking into some aspect of the

Seminole Wars. We were intrigued; the only thing we knew about the Seminole Wars was that our hometown of Fort Myers had been founded during one of the conflicts. Initial research brought up myriad questions, but two stood out: What were the causes of the Second Seminole War? Why had it lasted for seven years?

In the process of proofreading and helping edit the thesis, John also became wrapped up in the project. We both discovered the advantage of studying a subject about which we had no previous knowledge: everything was a surprise. In one sense, this volume is a catalog of those surprises. There were, of course, big disadvantages. Because Mary Lou had a deadline for the thesis, we had to take in and digest an abundance of material in a short amount of time. Full-time jobs did not help the situation. Evenings and weekends were given over to sifting through old newspapers, military reports, and diaries. Weekend outings and vacations were restricted to watching Seminole War battle reenactments, trips to sites associated with the conflicts, or to what can best be termed "writer's retreats." While the thesis was completed on time, we felt that it had only scratched the surface.

As our research progressed, two recurring themes seemed to float throughout the history of the Seminole Wars. First, triumphs seemed less satisfying to the winners than they should have been. All too often the victors had little to cheer about. The old saying "Be careful—you might get what you ask for" seems especially appropriate when applied to the Seminole Wars. Second, the sheer determination of the participants was to be marveled at. The government was as determined to remove the Seminoles as the Seminoles were to resist that removal. Individuals on both sides endured unbelievable hardships in the struggle. We were humbled by their examples of moral and physical fortitude.

A note on ethnic identification. In this book we refer to the white citizens of the United States as "Americans." We realize that Seminoles and blacks are also Americans, but we see little use in confusing what is already a complex story. We do not mean to imply that they were any less deserving of citizenship than their white counterparts. In some ways, they were more deserving. Also, we have rarely used the term "Native American," primarily because we feel it improper to use a modern designation when referring to a time period when that term did not exist. We do use the term "native" when referring to groups originally occupying an area *at a given time,* but once that time has passed, the designation no longer seems to apply. We do feel comfortable using the term Native American when used in the same sense that we might use African American or Polish American.

Although we had each other to rely upon while writing this book, we required the assistance of many others. The first note of thanks should go to Annette Snapp for suggesting the Seminole Wars as a topic for Mary Lou's thesis. Thanks also go to the research staff of the Fort Myers–Lee County Library for their assistance over the years. No matter how obscure the document or how inaccessible the microfilm, they always seem to come through.

Inspiration and encouragement came from all corners of the Seminole Wars "community." Some of us write books; others are living historians who re-create the past with amazing fidelity to fact and detail. All of us seek to share some of what we have learned, and among the living historians a few stand out as true inspirations. Foremost are Earl DeBary, his wife, Bettie, and their son, Jeremy. We thank them for the many wonderful hours spent beside the campfire. By the same fire usually sat Christopher Kimball, to whom we are much indebted both for his friendship and for the valuable information gleaned from his detailed chronology of the Seminole Wars. More than anyone else, Kent Low showed us what the life of a Seminole War–era soldier was like. Reenactors are, in truth, actors, and like the finest thespians, they bring life to a time and place that few of us are familiar with.

As a nation, America had the unfortunate luxury of being able to forget the Seminole Wars. The same cannot be said for the Seminoles. They live daily with the consequences of those long-past conflicts and are among the most generous and gracious people one could hope to meet. A note of appreciation must go out to all the Seminoles we have come into contact with over the years and to the whites who are associated with them. Most notable among them is Billy Cypress, executive director of the Ah-Tah-Thi-Ki Museum, along with museum director David Blackard and operations manager Brian Zepeda. We also thank Patsy West, curator of the Seminole/Mikasuki photo archives, for her kind words of encouragement.

Initial (and continued) inspiration came from John K. Mahon, who provided the groundwork for nearly all Seminole War studies during the past half century. Without his work, the rest of us would be fumbling in the dark. Perhaps the greatest inspiration came from our dear friend Frank Laumer and his wife, Dale. We doubt that we will ever stop apologizing for taking Frank's two excellent volumes on the Dade Battle and condensing them into two inadequate pages. The inevitable choices over what to include and what to exclude produced the most difficult moments in writing this book.

Other excellent authors also provided us with a starting point for our research. David and Jeanne Heidler are the acknowledged experts on the First Seminole War, and our copy of *Old Hickory's War* is getting well worn. Likewise, James Covington's works on the Third Seminole War and the Seminoles in general are benchmarks we relied upon heavily. A special note of thanks must go out to Joe Knetsch, both for introducing us to the Seminole Wars community and for the unselfish manner in which he shared his time and resources.

We had the privilege of working with some members of the Seminole Wars community more closely than others and cherish the hours spent in their company. A four-hour dinner in Washington, D.C., with Alcione Amos will always be fondly remembered. We thank Terry Weik for the opportunity to assist him at the excavation of Peliklikaha. We are also greatly indebted to Dave Porfiri and his wife, Linda, for their friendship and their faith in our work.

We also received a tremendous amount of support from our friends in the Seminole Wars Historic Foundation. Thanks go out to Henry Sheldon, Brent Weisman, and Lt. Col. Greg Moore, who welcomed us into the foundation and allowed us to share in their work. Artists Jackson Walker and William Temple brought the wars alive on canvas, giving us images that helped inspire our thoughts. Support and encouragement also came from Barbara Roberts-Webster, Richard Procyk, and James Cusick. We would also like to thank William and Sue Goza, whose collection of period newspapers proved invaluable.

While there may be some writers who can pen the perfect book the first time around, we do not consider ourselves among that group. Friends, editors, and reviewers offered indispensable advice and insight. Among those are Jerald T. Milanich and the anonymous readers at the University Press of Florida. We must also thank Meredith Morris-Babb and the staff at the University Press of Florida for a most professional and courteous relationship.

Gathering illustrations was one of the more difficult parts of this project. We are deeply indebted to Jeff Falzarano for the many hours spent in preparing the maps used in this book. Especially gratifying was the aid of several descendants of Gen. Duncan Clinch, notably Clinch Heyward,

Carter Morris, Duncan Belser, and Mrs. A. C. Heyward, Jr. We must also express gratitude to the staffs of various archival institutions, including the Florida State Archives, the U.S. Military Academy, and several branches of the Smithsonian Institution.

Friends and family provide the moral support so necessary to the completion of a task such as this. They may not understand what we are doing or why we are doing it, but they are always behind us. Our parents made us who we are, and we regret that not all of them are here to share in the joy of our accomplishments. Special thanks go out to Paul and Connie Missall, Alan and Susan Lee, and Gail and Bill Grant for their continued enthusiasm for our work. To our daughter, Shelley, and to our grandson, Justin, we simply say thank you for being the wonderful people they are. We also express our gratitude to our employers, Heinz and Roxanne Bührig and Jeffrey Cooner, who graciously accepted the inconvenience of an occasional absence when we needed to work on the book.

Perhaps the greatest encouragement came from our good friends Richard and Maggie Blizzard and Maggie's parents, Phil and Anne Payne. Their faith in our abilities, gifts of research material, and tokens of support touched us greatly. Thanks to you all, and to the countless others who did their little bit along the way.

1 Newcomers

▲▲▲▲▲▲▲▲▲▲▲▲▲▲▲▲▲▲

In the winter of 1855, a wave of fear and panic spread throughout the thinly settled Florida frontier. This widespread anxiety was brought on by news that the Seminole Indians had once again taken to the warpath. In preparation for the anticipated hostilities, the federal government had reactivated numerous posts within the peninsula and had begun to gather the material needed for a major campaign. In Tallahassee, Governor Broome called out as large a militia force as the barren state treasury could afford. Throughout the frontier, isolated families frantically fled to the safety of the larger fortified towns. The cause of all this? Barely a hundred reclusive warriors led by a short, middle-aged chief with the somewhat laughable name of Billy Bowlegs.[1]

It was no laughing matter. The people of Florida and the United States military had faced these determined warriors before, suffered bitterly at their hands, and had not forgotten the painful lessons learned nearly twenty years earlier. The entire nation recalled the day when more than 100 soldiers were killed in a matter of hours. The army remembered how their finest generals had returned from Florida in frustration, embarrassment, or dishonor. The people of Florida could not forget the smell of burnt homes or the sight of women and children cruelly slain by the tomahawk and the scalping knife. And thousands of Seminoles sadly recalled the forced migration that had led them to an unfamiliar land west of the Mississippi.

From a twenty-first-century perspective, the Seminole Wars seem improbable. How could a small group of displaced natives have hoped to stop the unrelenting tide of American expansion? It was a hopeless undertaking in which the Seminoles, to their credit, were marginally successful. What was so different about the situation in Florida that made the Seminoles fight so much harder to remain in their homeland? Our puzzlement becomes greater when we realize that they, like those they fought against, were relatively recent immigrants to Florida. The tale of where the Seminoles came from and how their nation evolved sheds light on why they fought a series of wars that, in reality, no one would win.

The story commences long before recorded history. Twelve thousand years ago, when humans first set foot in Florida, the climate was drier and the sea level much lower. The shallow waters that now cover the continental shelf were gone, leaving a peninsula twice as wide as the one we are familiar with today. Living in Florida were creatures that have long since gone extinct, including mammoth, mastodon, sabertooth cats, and giant ground sloths.

As millennia passed, the sea level rose and the climate moistened. The population of Florida slowly increased as sustainable, seasonal foods were discovered. As the art of cultivation was learned, nomadic camps became permanent villages. Complex societies developed, along with the political and spiritual systems that supported them. Cloth weaving, cord braiding, and pottery making provided the people with valuable new tools. Tribes that flourished became powerful nations, engaging in wars with their neighbors or conducting varied forms of trade in times of peace. Florida, now much warmer and with a mixture of wetlands and woodlands, was a good place to live.

On the southwestern coast of the peninsula were the powerful Calusas. To the east, where now stands the ever-spreading metropolis of Miami–Fort Lauderdale, were the Tequestas. In northern Florida, the various tribes were linguistically related and are known today as the Timucuans. In the eastern Panhandle, the dominant people were the Apalachees. Five hundred years ago, there may have been as many as 350,000 Indians living in the land we now call Florida, a level of population that would not be reached again until the 1880s.[2]

Within 200 years of the Spaniards' arrival, virtually the entire population of aboriginal Floridians was gone. The first wave of death came with the arrival of the Narváez expedition in 1528, followed by the de Soto expedition in 1539. For nearly all concerned, the quest for glory proved fatal. Narváez and de Soto died, along with most of their men. Left behind were more than rotting bones and rusting weapons. Wherever the

Spaniards went, the diseases they carried infected the local population. Entire villages were wiped out or abandoned. The social structures that supported the native cultures began to crumble. They would never recover.

The conquest of Florida became a reality with the founding of St. Augustine in 1565. Chronically short of labor, Spanish authorities conscripted the natives into the harsh service of the Crown. Those who resisted were either killed or sold into slavery. Those who submitted spent the remainder of their lives toiling to feed themselves and most of the Spanish population of Florida. New shiploads of missionaries, soldiers, and colonists brought their diseases with them. One of the final blows came from the English colonists in the Carolinas, who raided northern Florida in search of Indians to enslave. By the early eighteenth century, the aboriginal population of Florida was all but extinct.

This is, of course, a tale of the Seminole Indians, yet before the eighteenth century, the Seminoles did not exist. Initially, it seems odd that the Indian group that fought hardest to remain on its land was not native to it. Yet one of the lessons American history teaches us is that "home" is often defined more by dreams than by memories. Many present-day Floridians have a "home town" in the North, but their hearts and futures are in their new southern home. Our whole national saga of migration and expansion is a testimony to the power of hope. Why should the Indians have felt any different?

One of the things that separates the Seminoles from other Indian nations is the fact that there exists historical records of the tribe's formation. The genesis of any nation is an evolutionary process, and with the Seminoles, we are fortunate that it happened recently enough for outsiders to have observed and recorded some of those evolutionary events.

Ironically, we are forced to admit that, to a large extent, the Seminoles were a European invention. Consider the following: The decimation of the native population by the Spaniards made Florida available for new Indian settlers. Conflicts with the English caused Indian bands from other parts of the South to move into the peninsula. The need for new hunting grounds to satisfy the European deerskin trade lured bands of hunters into Florida, where, eventually, many brought their families to live. Even the term "Seminole" was European in origin, and its application was strictly for white convenience. Finally, it was war with the

United States that forged a nation from many scattered, sometimes antagonistic, tribes. As we shall see, without the Europeans and their descendants, there would be no Seminoles.

Through it all we must remember that these Indians were making their own decisions, reacting to strange, often dangerous, situations as best they could. Having no better foresight than any of us alive today, these people weighed their options and took their chances in the same manner we all do. Under extreme pressure from the much more powerful white societies surrounding them, the Indians that came to populate Florida created a new identity for themselves, embraced a name they did not create, and thrived in a portion of the world others considered uninhabitable.

As would happen throughout early Florida history, the politics of Europe determined events in this remote New World outpost. Florida was not a profitable colony for Spain. Mineral poor and generally unsuited to a plantation economy, the area was always viewed as a drain on the Spanish Royal Treasury. To reach Spain, treasure ships from the Caribbean and South America had to follow the trade winds and the gulf stream, both of which ran up the East Coast of North America. The narrow Straits of Florida, which separates the peninsula from Cuba and the Bahamas, were the favored hunting grounds of pirates and rival European warships. Places like St. Augustine were of extreme importance to the protection of Spanish shipping. Profitable or not, Spain needed Florida.

The people who would eventually make up the Seminole Nation had their origins among the tribes of what would become the Southeast United States. Decimated by European-introduced diseases and warfare, the southeastern Indian societies had been in a state of flux for much of the seventeenth century. Old groupings fell apart and new ones were formed. Faced with an array of names such as Alabamas, Apalachicolas, Chiahas, Hitchitis, Koasatis, Oconees, Yamassees, and Yuchis, among others, we can easily understand the longing of English traders and officials to impose some order upon the chaos. The name that finally stuck was "Creeks," derived from the fact that traders paddled up creeks to meet with the Indians. Although these different native groups saw little or no unity among themselves, it did not deter the British from imposing the term upon them.[3]

As much as the English may have wanted it, these Indians could not become a united nation. The most important division among the Creeks was a linguistic one. Although the vast majority spoke a language derived from the Muskogee family of languages, the differences in those languages were often great enough to make many of them unintelligible to one another. In the end, the Creeks fell into two distinct groups, labeled "Upper" and "Lower" by the whites. Although these divisions appear very neat and orderly, we must remember that they were artificial and never well defined. They are generalities that, like all generalities, should be viewed with a degree of suspicion but, in practice, cannot be abandoned.

The tribes that made up the Lower Creeks normally settled into what is now southwestern Georgia, primarily along the Flint and Chattahoochee Rivers. Their principal language was Hitchiti, though other tongues were certainly present. In contrast, the Upper Creeks lived primarily in what is now eastern Alabama, mostly along the banks of the Coosa and Tallapoosa Rivers. They usually spoke Muskogee, a language that was considerably different from Hitchiti. Although both groups were supposedly part of a greater Creek Confederation, the confederacy often existed only in the minds of the whites who had to deal with them. Long-standing animosities among the individual Creek tribes could not be easily erased and often led to violence and bloodshed among the different groups.

By the end of the first decade of the eighteenth century, the Spanish had more or less abandoned North Florida between Pensacola and the St. Johns River. With the exception of St. Augustine, Pensacola, and a fort at St. Marks, the land was nearly deserted. To the north, in what is now eastern Georgia, tensions were building between the British of South Carolina and the Yamassee tribe. War broke out in 1715, and the defeated Yamassees were forced to retreat into Florida, where they became allies of Spain. A steady wave of migration into northern Florida had begun.

Throughout the eighteenth century, the migration continued. Most were Lower Creeks who, for various reasons, saw the opportunity for a better life south of the border. Some were refugees who had been displaced by the whites. Others were lured south by the Spanish, who had finally begun to see some advantage in having what they considered "savage" Indian allies as opposed to docile Indian subjects. Others were more concerned with simply getting away from the whites.

Two groups, both Lower Creek and both speaking the Hitchiti dialect, stand out in particular. The first were the Mikasukis, who settled around the lake of the same name, just east of present-day Tallahassee. For them,

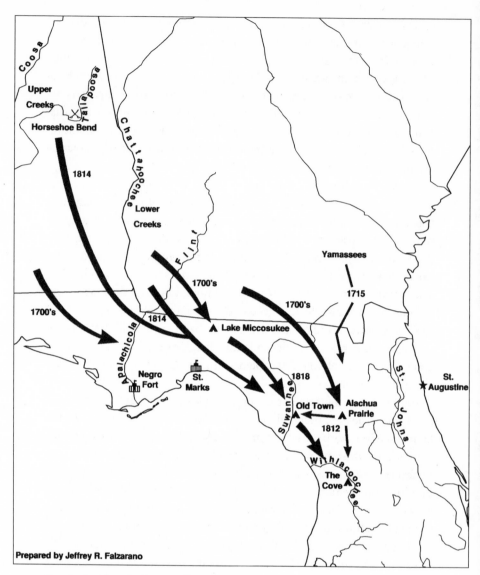

MAP I. Seminole migration, 1700–1820.

it had been no great migration, simply an expansion to the south. Still, as the decades passed, their community grew and the tribe became prosperous. Ties with other Creek towns lessened, and a separate identity developed. From the eighteenth century through to today, the Mikasukis have considered themselves a people apart.

The other prominent group was led by a chief known as "Cowkeeper." Along with missions, the Spanish had maintained several large cattle ranches in northern Florida. One of the most successful had been La Chua, located near a large, fertile prairie south of present-day Gainesville. The area became known as the Alachua Prairie and was considered the best land in the peninsula. In addition to good land, there was also an abundance of free-ranging cattle, let loose when La Chua was abandoned. As their wealth from cattle ranching increased, Cowkeeper's tribe became a powerful force, at times antagonistic to both the Creeks and the Spanish.

As Cowkeeper's band became more influential, it came into greater contact with the Spaniards, who soon felt the need to create a name for this newly evolved tribe. Perhaps because of their ferocity or independence, the Spanish took to calling them Cimarrones, which is generally taken to mean "wild ones" or "runaways." Such a term could have had any number of connotations and was originally applied to any Indian not living near one of the Spanish missions. At any rate, the term was eventually corrupted to the present-day Seminole.

While the term may have originally referred only to the Alachua Indians of Cowkeeper's band, as years passed and the Florida Indian situation became more confused, "Seminole" came to refer to all Indians living in Florida. Up until the time of the Second Seminole War, however, the Indians did not generally see things that way. As far as they were concerned, they were Alachuas, Mikasukis, Tallahassees, Apalachicolas, or members of some other tribe. In an attempt to lend some clarity to this rather confusing situation, we will, in this text, stick to the convention of using "Seminole" to denote any Indian living in Florida. When necessary, we will call the individual tribes by their proper names, using "Alachua Seminoles" as a designation for the descendants of Cowkeeper's band.

The politics and conflicts of the Old World soon brought changes to the lives of Floridians of all races. The year 1763 saw an end to the Seven Years' War, better known in America as the French and Indian War. During the conflict, the British had occupied Havana, the centerpiece of Spain's Caribbean empire. In order to regain possession of the Cuban capitol, Spain was forced to turn over Florida to England. Two hundred years of Spanish rule had come to an end, and what would come to be known as the "English period" began.

For the Indians, the change of ownership generally proved to be a good thing, primarily because of the extensive trade in deerskins and other animal hides. The size of this trade was staggering. The largest trading houses could expect to export about 100,000 deerskins annually. The whole industry was exceptionally well organized, with agents, known as factors, in every sizable village. With the British now in control of all eastern North America, it was also an exceptionally well regulated trade. Competition was limited, prices were fixed, and factors kept meticulous track of the number of skins each warrior brought in, crediting the Indian's account against European goods purchased.[4]

We might tend to assume that the deerskin trade was viewed by the Indian as a way to turn his favorite pastime into a part-time job that provided him with the extra cash needed to purchase a few European luxuries. That would be a highly erroneous assumption. No longer were these natives simple hunter/gatherers. They were now professional hunters and subsistence farmers. Gone were the days of hunting with bows and arrows and stone-tipped spears. Rifles were a necessity, and firearms required lead and gunpowder. Efficient skinning required the use of steel knives. Pottery was replaced by metal cookware, and mill-woven fabric took the place of buckskin clothing. Nearly everything the Indians had once made by hand had been replaced by manufactured goods. They simply *had* to have them.

They also *wanted* them. It is somehow comforting to see that these supposedly "savage" people were no less materialistic and status conscious than we are today. A great hunter would gain status and respect in his society just as a great athlete or successful businessman does today. He could buy a better gun, a more ornate tomahawk, exotic ostrich feathers for his headdress, a gift for his wife, a doll for his daughter, slaves to work his fields, or bright silver ornaments to show off his hard earned status. They needed these things no more than we need luxury cars and designer clothing. They were also just as willing to go into debt to get them.

The key to the success of the British trading houses was credit. A warrior would purchase his ammunition and other goods *before* the hunt. The factor would keep track of each warrior's purchases, then apply credit to the account when the skins were turned in at the end of the hunt. Sadly, it was just as easy to fall into debt in the eighteenth century as it is in the twenty-first. All too often, the number of skins brought in was not enough to cover the cost of the purchases made earlier. For many a hunter, it seemed as if there was always a negative balance on the books.

As we might expect, intensive hunting led to a decline in the deer population close to home. As their debts grew larger, hunters had to go farther afield to find enough deer to meet their self-imposed quotas. The time spent on hunting trips went from weeks to months. This need to find new hunting grounds helped bring a new wave of Indian settlers into Florida. With deer becoming scarce in other parts of the Southeast, Creek hunters began to move farther south into Florida. At first they occupied temporary hunting camps, but as the trips grew longer and the distance away from home grew greater, many warriors brought their families with them and established new villages. Some of these people were Upper Creek, some were Lower. Some integrated into the existing Florida tribes, while others kept to themselves and retained their old tribal designations. Other groups created new identities. One can sympathize with the Englishmen who simply gave up trying to keep track of it all and began to apply the term "Seminole" to any Indian living in Florida.

Although the Seminoles had separated from the Creeks, they still retained much of the Creek culture. Life centered around clans, which bore such names as Alligator, Bear, or Wind. Chiefs were chosen from a hereditary line that ran through the female side of the family. Under such a matrilineal system, succession did not pass from father to son but might go to a brother or the son of a sister. A warrior lived with his wife's family, and if the marriage dissolved, children and household effects remained with the woman.

While the head chief of a village might be chosen for reasons of lineage, other titles were generally conferred by merit. For the most part, merit was earned in warfare. Titles often replaced names, and many of the names that are remembered from the Seminole Wars are, in truth, titles. The most common of these were Micco (head chief), Emathla (war party leader), Tustenuggee (village war leader), and Hadjo or Fixico (fearless or heartless warrior).[5]

Seminole life also centered around the town, although "town" is a rather misleading term, bringing forth visions of a cluster of buildings all confined within distinct boundaries. A Seminole town was much more than a geographic entity. Indeed, a significant portion of the population might live some distance away from the town center in remote villages or camps. The town was the community to which an individual belonged. The clan might be the primary social unit, but the town was something to which many clans belonged. The town was the ceremonial and political center of the Seminoles' world, the place where they would gather in times of celebration or danger.

Ceremonies, rituals, and religious beliefs played an important part in the lives of the Seminoles. The most significant ritual was the annual Green Corn Dance. Like "town," "dance" can be a bit misleading. True, the members of the tribe spent a significant portion of their time chanting and moving in rhythmic patterns around the central fire, but it was much more than simple recreation. The dances had meaning, conveying tribal history, philosophy, and mores. Dancing helped bring a continuity to the Indians' lives, bringing them closer to the world in which they lived and to the lives of their ancestors.

Just as important were the activities that took place while the Seminoles were not dancing. Tribal courts, in which crimes were either forgiven or punishment decreed, were held. More important, purification and cleansing took place. Ritual fasting and blood letting were practiced, along with the taking of the "black drink," a strong tea brewed from the leaves of the cassina tree, known to induce vomiting. Not all activities were so unpleasant. Fasts were broken by feasts, and a lacrosse-like ball game helped settle disputes and release tensions. By the end of the four-day ceremony, the tribe was spiritually renewed and prepared to face the challenges of the coming year.

The most unusual of the numerous groups that made up the Indian population of Florida were not "red" men. They were black. Throughout the colonial period, the imaginary line drawn between Florida and Georgia meant little to the Indians. Yet to the slaves toiling on the English plantations in Georgia and South Carolina, the line meant something very real: freedom. Once an escaped slave crossed the border into Spanish Florida, he or she was essentially a free person.

Up until the transfer of Florida to the English in 1763, most escaped blacks lived near the Spanish settlements. The Spanish governors, chronically short of soldiers and settlers, learned to welcome the blacks. Eventually, free blacks had their own settlement near St. Augustine, complete with their own militia and a small fortification. This community, centered around the fort, was known as Fort Mose. With the coming of British control, however, came the prospect of being returned to slavery in the other English colonies. Most black people departed for Cuba with the

Spaniards, but for those who remained, the safest refuge was among the Seminoles. For new runaways, it was virtually the only choice.

Freedom, of course, comes in varying degrees. Since long before the coming of the Europeans, Indians had kept Indian slaves. In Florida, runaway blacks who found themselves among the Seminoles might find themselves reenslaved; it depended on the circumstances. At one Indian camp they might be taken as slaves, while at another they might be welcomed as free men and women. Other blacks were actually purchased. Indian chiefs had often observed that the most respected white men were also slave owners. If owning blacks increased a man's status, then a great chief should also be a great slaveholder.

Slavery, like freedom, also comes in varying degrees. Most white Europeans, believing in a God-given superiority, looked down upon other races. From the point of view of many whites, blacks deserved to be slaves; they were created by God for the purpose of mindless labor. With such a mindset, it was easy to abuse the blacks and to disregard their feelings. For the most part, the Indians did not possess such a strong prejudice. To the Indian, a slave was not an inferior being but a less fortunate one. The unpredictable fortunes of life could easily turn a great warrior into a humble servant. The Indian who held slaves today could become one tomorrow.

For most blacks, being the slave of a Seminole was nearly equal to being free. There were no overseers, no whips, no families torn asunder. True, the slaves were not free to leave their masters, but where would they have gone if the opportunity had arisen? There was, indeed, no safer or more promising place within walking distance. Compared to life on a southern plantation, being a slave to a Florida Indian was perhaps the best life an English slave could hope for.

Congressman Joshua Giddings, in his 1858 book dealing with the treatment of the black Seminoles, commented on the relationship, saying, "They held their slaves in a state between that of servitude and freedom; the slave usually living with his own family and occupying his time as he pleased, paying his master annually a small stipend in corn and other vegetables. This class of slaves regarded servitude among the whites with the greatest degree of horror." Oddly enough, it might have been a disadvantage to be free black Seminole. An unowned black could, by the white man's law, become enslaved. Being a slave to an Indian offered a certai. degree of legal protection.[6]

Over the years, many blacks became assimilated into the Indian culture. They spoke the Indians' language, dressed in Indian clothing, and even rose to positions of leadership. Experienced in agriculture from their years on the plantations, they were generally more accepting of an agricultural life than their Indian counterparts. The Indians appreciated the surplus this provided, for it gave them more time for what they considered the important things in life: hunting trips and war parties. The blacks were also valued as interpreters. Rarely did an Indian speak English or Spanish. Whites who spoke either of the Creek tongues were just as rare. A person who understood both cultures was bound to be of value. By the time of the Seminole Wars, perhaps 15 percent of the warriors were black.[7]

No matter how rich and ancient the Creek/Seminole culture might have been, and no matter how intelligent the Indian leaders were, European civilization was still foreign to them. Surveyed boundaries, colonial governments, and global empires were imperfect concepts to the Indians. As anyone would, native peoples were forced to do the best they could within the circumstances they were given and with the knowledge they had. Survival often meant cooperating with the whites, while at other times it meant fighting them. It all depended on the situation.

For the Indians of Florida, dealing with the various colonial governments must have been at times frustrating. The policy in St. Augustine would be determined in Seville or London and was dictated by priorities in the Old World. Alliances in Europe could change as often as the wind, and with about as much warning. Today's designated foe could be tomorrow's trading partner. First there had been the Spaniards, then the English. Starting in 1776, there was a new force to be reckoned with: the Americans.

The American Revolution was not the Seminoles' war, but they soon became embroiled in it. The English, quick to exploit any advantage, recruited the Seminoles and some Creeks as allies. War parties, armed with British muskets, raided into rebel Georgia, laying waste to frontier settlements. Runaway slaves, increasing in number due to wartime confusion, joined the Seminole ranks. Unfortunately, the Seminoles picked the losing side. By the end of the Revolution, the victorious Americans looked upon the Seminoles as mortal enemies.

The end of the Revolution brought about another political change in Florida. During the war, Spain had allied itself with the United States and had retaken West Florida from the English. By stipulation of the Treaty of Paris, which ended the American Revolution in 1783, all of Florida was returned to Spanish control, thus ending the twenty-year English period. For the diplomats in Paris, the concerns of the Seminoles were not a factor. Florida was strategically important. Even though Spain could not afford the colony, the idea of simply letting the Indians have it probably never came to mind.

Because of the vast wilderness between St. Augustine and Pensacola, the English had divided Florida into two separate colonies, East and West Florida. Upon regaining Florida, the Spaniards saw the wisdom of this division and maintained it. East Florida consisted of the entire peninsula but did not include the Panhandle. West Florida extended from the Apalachicola River to the banks of the Mississippi. Although remnants of the old King's Highway still ran between St. Augustine and Pensacola, it was virtually unused by whites. It was easier (and safer) to get from one colonial capital to the other by taking a ship all the way around the peninsula.

The Spaniards, having troubles with restive populations throughout their empire, sent minimal garrisons to St. Augustine, St. Marks, and Pensacola. Initially, they felt they had little to fear from the Americans. The nobility of Europe was of the opinion that a democratic republic was doomed to failure. They could not imagine how any nation could survive without the strong hand of royalty to keep things under control. It would not take long, they felt, for the thirteen states to have a falling out among themselves. Perhaps, in the ensuing chaos, Spain might even increase its holdings in North America.

Even without the American presence, Spain soon found itself ill-equipped to administer its vast New World holdings, which also included the immense Louisiana Territory. As Europe fell into disarray due to the French Revolution, Spain found its military budget strained beyond capacity. For the Americans, inspired by their victory over the English and their ability to restrain their own potential anarchy, a grand vision of the future was emerging. Sooner or later, Spain and the United States would have to come to some sort of agreement about Florida. Whatever that agreement was, the Seminoles would have no choice but to live with it. They may have been the colony's primary residents, but their future was in someone else's hands.

2 **Americans**

▲▲▲▲▲▲▲▲▲▲▲▲▲▲▲▲▲

For the young United States, dealing with the various Indian tribes was a vexing problem, but certainly not the most important one it faced. The formation of a stable government, paying off massive Revolutionary War debts, relations with sometimes hostile foreign nations, and the development of the vast territories west of the Appalachians were all matters of great concern. All too often, difficulties with the natives were ignored until they reached the crisis stage. With hundreds of thousands of Indians living in the undeveloped territories, it was a crisis that never went away. The tide of white immigration was a slow-moving, unstoppable flood, and whatever peace existed between settlers and Indians was only temporary. The natives were a proud people who had a strong sense of homeland; they were not going to simply disappear.

For high-minded Americans, steeped in the ideology of Jefferson, there were serious questions to be answered. The precise status of the Indian tribes was difficult to define. How did you deal with a sovereign nation residing within your own borders? In the history of civilized diplomacy, there was no precedent for the situation. The subsequent policies of the United States show the confusion and ambiguity. In the early years of the Republic, the Indian tribes were dealt with through the War Department, not the State Department. Normally, it would have been the province of the State Department to negotiate with sovereign nations, since the job of the War Department was exactly what its name implied. This policy indicates that the nation expected to have to fight for much of the continent.

Were the Indian nations actually hostile? It was a moral dilemma that many Americans felt uncomfortable with, for it was not until whites began to encroach upon Indian land that problems arose. The difficulties were multiplied by the character of many border-dwelling whites. Shifty traders fleeced unsuspecting Indians, while greedy speculators laid claim to vast tracts of land that Indians had occupied for generations. Unprincipled squatters and certain criminal elements also pressed upon the Indian lands. Americans knew that if the Indians went on the warpath, white intrusion was often at the root of discord.

Capt. John T. Sprague, a participant in and the first historian of the Second Seminole War, understood the problem very well: "Upon this, as upon all Indian borders, there is a class of men destitute of property and employment, who for excitement and gain, would recklessly provoke the Indian to aggressions, and in the midst of which, escape detection and punishment, leaving the burden to fall upon the honest and industrious."[1]

Although this lawless element may not have been in the majority, enough of them existed to create continuous problems for both sides. When wrongs were committed against an Indian, violent retribution was often his only recourse. Sprague knew that equality under the law did not apply to the natives. "No rights were conceded to the Indians, and every act which interfered with the designs of individuals crowding within the Indian limits in all quarters, was regarded as the commencement of hostilities," he wrote. "Personal abuse was heaped upon them, their property and persons disregarded; no law shielded them, and no protection was given, other than that which was sought by the untiring exertions of the agent."[2]

The Indians were not simply facing an undisciplined horde of opportunists. In reality, they were up against a nation that was on "a mission from God." From the Pilgrims and Puritans onward, Americans had seen themselves as part of a providential grand plan. In the eyes of the early Americans, the New World was the Promised Land. God had provided it as a place where Christian reformers could establish the perfect society that had been so often prophesied. This new land was to be cultivated, built upon, and put to its most efficient use. It is an attitude that persists to this day. Only recently, with the birth of the environmental movement, have we begun to question the wisdom of such a policy.

To most early Americans, the Indians were not using the land in accordance with God's plan. Because the Indians did not practice intensive farming, because they did not build large cities or employ the latest technology, and because they did not seem to have the divinely inspired "purpose" the whites possessed, they were looked upon as not conforming to God's will. It was, in the end, all too easy for the colonists and their successors to justify the taking of Indian land as a moral right endorsed with a heavenly stamp of approval.

Lewis Cass, who was secretary of war when the Second Seminole War began, held those same beliefs: "There can be no doubt . . . that the Creator intended the earth should be reclaimed from a state of nature and cultivated; that the human race should spread over it, procuring from it the means of comfortable subsistence, and of increase and improvement." Missouri senator Thomas Hart Benton, a strong proponent of Indian removal, believed that whites had a superior right to the land because they "used it according to the intentions of the Creator."[3]

A promised land requires a "chosen people." In general, early Americans were a deeply religious folk, convinced they had a decisive role to play in Christ's plan of redemption. Jonathan Edwards, a leader of the Great Awakening, remarked, "This work of God's Spirit, so extraordinary and wonderful, is the dawning or at least a prelude of that glorious work of God so often foretold in Scripture, which in the progress and issue of it shall renew the world of mankind." After the United States won its independence from England, Americans were convinced that God was on their side.[4]

The prominent theologian Ezra Stiles preached in 1783 that "this will be a great, a very great nation, nearly equal to half Europe. . . . Before the millennium the English settlements in America may become more numerous millions than that greatest dominion on earth, the Chinese Empire. Should this prove a future fact, how applicable would be . . . the text, when the Lord shall have made his American Israel 'high above all nations which he hath made,' in numbers, 'and in praise, and in name, and in honour.'"[5]

This feeling of "anointment" easily crossed from the ecclesiastic to the secular side of society. John Adams reflected in his diary, "I always consider the settlement of America with reverence and wonder, as the opening of a grand scene and design in Providence for the illumination of the ignorant, and the emancipation of the slavish part of mankind all over the earth." In his inaugural address, Thomas Jefferson said, "I shall need . . . the favor of that Being in whose hands we are, who led our fathers, as Israel of old, from their native land and planted them in a country flowing with all the necessaries and comforts of life." Jefferson also boasted that the "rising nation" was "advancing rapidly to destinies beyond the reach of mortal eye."[6]

There was, of course, the legal question of who actually owned the land the Indians had occupied for countless generations. The Indians had never faced that problem. Illiterate societies do not have deeds and titles. For them, occupation was synonymous with ownership. Creek land was land that was occupied or used by Creeks. If the Creeks abandoned a certain parcel and the Cherokee moved in, then it was Cherokee land. As has been the case throughout the history of both the Old World and the New, ownership of valuable land was usually determined militarily. Both the Indians and the white men understood the concept of conquest.

What really separated the two cultures were the issues of who owned *unoccupied* land and the concept of *individual* ownership. The Indians generally believed that if no group exercised control over a certain parcel, it was free to be used by whomever was willing to put forth the effort to use it. Unoccupied land belonged either to the Great Spirit or to no one at all. For white society, that was not an option. Since feudal times, European society had existed with the notion that *someone* had to own every piece of land, whether or not it was desirable land. If an individual or corporation did not own a particular parcel, then the government did. No spot of land, no matter how valueless, could be allowed to remain unowned.

This difference in cultural philosophy is apparent during the Seminole conflicts. When the Indians moved into Florida, the land they occupied had been abandoned by the aboriginal natives. As far as they were concerned, it was now Seminole land. White society did not agree. From a European point of view, the Seminoles had taken up residence in land that belonged to either the English or the Spanish. Throughout the Seminole Wars, Americans generally felt that the Seminoles were not as "native" to their lands as other Indian tribes. In a way, the Florida Indians were seen as "squatters" without a legal right to their land.

Equally as foreign to the Indians was the idea that an individual could somehow claim a portion of the earth as his personal property. A man might own a gun, a prized blanket, or even a slave, but the earth itself was beyond ownership. These were deep-seated philosophical differences the two cultures were never able to fully resolve.

After the United States had gained its independence, the Seminoles lived in comparative peace for the better part of thirty years. Viewed through the distorted lens of history, thirty years may not seem like a long time. It was, however, long enough for a new generation of Seminoles to be raised. Many of the Indians who had been born in the Spanish colony were now in positions of leadership, and most Seminoles had ancestors who were buried in Florida. Enough time had passed for them to now consider Florida their home.

It was, at best, an unquiet peace between the Florida Indians and their white neighbors to the north. The Seminoles, not party to the Treaty of Paris, had little respect and no need for this imaginary line that ran between Spanish Florida and the United States. Several Seminole and Mikasuki towns were actually situated north of the line. Conversely, white squatters often set up housekeeping south of the border, perhaps unaware of exactly where the line was.

The relative stability of Indian life was broken by events that were largely out of their control. Since gaining its independence, the United States had coveted Florida. A quick glance at a map will explain why. For a nation that felt destined to rule the continent, this large foreign appendage on the southeast border was both an embarrassment and a liability. Many people felt that Florida belonged to the United States simply because it was physically attached to Georgia. The Louisiana Purchase of 1803 only intensified those feelings.

There were practical reasons for wanting Florida as well. The most outstanding motivation was an economic one. The areas that are now Alabama and southern Georgia, as well as parts of Tennessee and Mississippi, were all drained by rivers that emptied into the Gulf of Mexico through West Florida. Therefore, Spain controlled, to some extent, the commerce of the South. For the southern states, this was an intolerable situation. Another reason the United States coveted Florida was one of national security. With its long coastline and deep harbors, Florida was vulnerable to invasion by foreign armies. What was to stop a large British or French force from landing at St. Augustine, then working its way into the southern states? For a young nation just free of European domination, this was a very real fear.

By 1810, the Madison administration was ready to acquire Florida. Unfortunately, as a "civilized" nation, the United States was bound by certain rules. An armed seizure of Florida would be a serious violation of international law. Spain would certainly consider such a thing an act of war, as might Great Britain, Spain's ally. If, however, the residents of Florida were to stage a "revolution," set up their own government, then ask to be incorporated into the American nation, the United States could, with questionable justification, honor that request.

Complicating the situation were a pair of major disputes. The first dealt with the matter of who owned the territory west of the Perdido River near Pensacola. The United States claimed that it had been included with the Louisiana Purchase. Spain and France, who had done the selling, insisted that Spanish West Florida extended all the way to the Mississippi. The second dispute centered on exactly who ruled Spain. The Napoleonic Wars were raging throughout Europe, and the French had conquered the Iberian Peninsula, setting up their own puppet government. The legitimate king was backed by the English, who were attempting to oust the French. In the New World, Spanish officials supported their legitimate rulers but were more or less left to their own devices. Caught in the middle of all this were the Seminoles, no doubt very interested, but no doubt very confused by it all.

At first, the American plan to seize Florida proceeded better than expected. Residents in and around Baton Rouge held a convention, formed their own government, and easily took control of the neglected Spanish fort. A plea went out for U.S. protection, and President Madison quickly issued a proclamation that annexed the area to the Louisiana Territory.[7]

The government then cast its eye toward the remainder of West Florida. Feeling the pressure and perhaps miffed at the lack of support from the his superiors in Havana, West Florida Governor Vicente Folch sent a letter to Washington stating that he would hand over the colony if he did not receive aid from Havana. Elated, President Madison appointed former Georgia governor George Mathews as an agent to deal with Folch. By the time Mathews reached Pensacola, Folch had rescinded the offer. Evidently Folch had made his point in Havana.[8]

Mathews then headed to the East Coast, where he hoped to convince the locals to stage a "revolution" similar to the one that had taken place in Baton Rouge. The people of East Florida would have none of it. Engaged in the lucrative business of smuggling slaves and embargoed goods into the United States, they had no desire to upset the status quo. Mathews would not give up. If the real local residents would not stage a revolution, he would import his own revolutionaries. In response to promises of free land, volunteers from Georgia were recruited, forming a force known as the Patriots. To make the force somewhat legitimate, John McIntosh, a Georgian who owned land in Florida, was placed at the head of the group.

By March 1812, the Patriots had formed a government and were ready to start their "revolution." With the aid of several U.S. Navy gunboats, the Patriots quickly took the town of Fernandina then headed for St. Augustine. The Spaniards, secure within the stone walls of Castillo de San Marcos, refused to surrender. In Washington, President Madison was becoming distracted by other matters, primarily the upcoming war with England. Mathews was recalled.[9]

Mathews, unaware of his removal, had spoken with the Seminoles and refused their aid. He also told them to stay out of the conflict. Perhaps the sight of black warriors had made him uneasy. The Spaniards, on good terms with the Seminoles, were not above asking for assistance. Late in July, the Indians began to attack the Patriot army, their supply lines, and the homes of their supporters. The Patriot War, as it came to be known, soon ended.

Aiding the Spaniards did the Seminoles little good. In the eyes of the Georgians, the Indians had gone from annoyance to menace. In addition, black Seminoles had fought against the Americans and had reignited an old fear. If blacks banded together, they might mount an invasion of the southern United States, destroying countless plantations and freeing thousands of slaves. There was little proof on which to base these worries, but for those who had designs on Florida, it was a fear that could be easily exploited.

In September 1812, a company of Georgia volunteers under Col. Daniel Newnan moved against the Seminole heartland in the Alachua prairie, but were driven back. Five months later, a larger force again invaded Florida, once again striking the Alachua region. This time, the invaders were able to drive the Seminoles from their villages. Before returning to the United States, the Americans destroyed hundreds of Seminole homes, killed or confiscated thousands of their cattle, and destroyed whatever supplies they could find. The cross-border animosity was quickly turning to hatred.

The War of 1812 helped stop the American advance on Florida, but only temporarily. In the summer of 1814, English forces arrived in Pensacola and elsewhere in West Florida. The Spanish governor, caught between two powerful antagonists, could do nothing to prevent the intrusion. In full control of the situation, the British occupied several Spanish installations and began to recruit Indian allies. Not far to the west, in Mobile, the U.S. Army took notice and was preparing for action. The American general had little love for the British, the Spanish, or the Indians. He was Andrew Jackson.

Most Americans now assume that Andrew Jackson came to national prominence following his victory over the English at New Orleans. In truth, it was an earlier triumph that had made him a national hero. In the early months of 1813, the Creek Nation was on the verge of civil war. The Lower Creeks of Georgia had come under the influence of the whites, while the Upper Creeks of Alabama were growing increasingly resentful of that same power. The more militant of the Upper Creeks, known as Red Sticks, began to call for a return to a more traditional way of life. They had heard the call of the great Shawnee leader Tecumseh and had been inspired by the message of his brother, the "Prophet." Harsh words eventually led to escalating bloodshed, which culminated in the massacre of about 350 whites and Lower Creeks at Fort Mims, Alabama, on August 30, 1813. What started out as an internal Creek problem became a serious concern for southern Americans.[10]

The governor of Tennessee, fearing a spread in Indian hostilities, dispatched Maj. Gen. Andrew Jackson of the Tennessee Militia to deal with the Indians. After several sharp battles that were costly to the Red Sticks but failed to conclude the conflict, Jackson came upon approximately 1,200 Red Sticks at a curve in the Tallapoosa River known as Horseshoe Bend. It was a location the Indians had chosen specifically for the purpose of making a stand. The meander of the river had formed a wide peninsula with a relatively narrow neck. Believing the river would serve as a protective moat, the Creeks completed their defenses by erecting a double barricade that zig-zagged across the neck of the peninsula. To them, their position seemed impregnable.

On March 27, 1814, Jackson proved them wrong. By the end of the day, Jackson's force of approximately 5,000 men had crossed the river and breached the wall. In terrible close conflict, the soldiers came over the top or tore down the wall. The Indians, surrounded, would not give up. At first they fought bravely against the overwhelming odds. Almost 600 fell on the battlefield. Those who sought to escape fared no better. More than 250 died in the river, victims of snipers stationed along the opposite shore. Very few of the warriors survived, and only darkness put an end to the slaughter. In the morning, 350 prisoners were counted, almost all of them women and children. Officially, the Creek civil war was over. In truth, it would move farther south, into Florida, where the Seminoles would become involved.[11]

The Lower Creeks, with the aid of the Americans, may have won the civil war, but in the process, they lost most of their land. Jackson, as a reward for his victory, was made a major general in the regular army and given command of the Southern District. He was also given authority to negotiate a new treaty with the entire Creek Nation. In the resulting Treaty of Fort Jackson, more than half the Creek territory, both Upper and Lower, was taken. Encompassing more than 20 million acres, the ceded territory included the bottom third of Georgia and the eastern half of Alabama.[12]

There were several reasons for taking such a large amount of territory. First, there was the matter of national security. By taking all the Creek land along the Florida border, Jackson hoped to remove the Indians from foreign influence. Second, there was the matter of simple greed. White southerners wanted the Creek land, and Jackson had gained the opportunity to seize the best of it with one quick stroke of the pen. Third, Jackson knew the terms of the treaty would drive many Creeks, both Upper and Lower, into Florida. Trouble would soon follow, thus giving the United States an excuse to invade Florida and take it under American control. Jackson, pointing out the significance of the transaction, said the cession "will secure to the U.S. a free settlement from Georgia to Mobile and cuts off (as soon as settled) all foreign influence from the Indians and gives to the U.S. perfect security." He also considered it "the best unsettled country in America."[13]

The stunned Lower Creeks had no choice but to accept the provisions of the treaty. They had seen the ruthless manner in which Jackson waged war. They had thrown their lot in with the Americans and were now paying the price. One of the more immediate results of the Creek civil war was an influx of Creek immigrants to Florida. They understood that it was useless to argue or to ask for more lenient terms. With Andrew Jackson as the negotiator, there would be no compromise.

Jackson's decisive, merciless victory over the Creek Indians at the Battle of Horseshoe Bend created the image of a "hard-bitten Indian hater." "Indian hater" may be too harsh a term for Jackson. It implies that all his venom was reserved for Indians and no one else. In truth, he seems to have hated anyone who did not hold the same values he did. Whites, be they British, Spanish, or conservative Americans, were equally despised. Anyone, of any ethnic background, who crossed Andrew Jackson found themselves saddled with an enemy for life.[14]

Like most Americans, Jackson seems to have been sympathetic to the Indians only when it was convenient. In general, as long as the Indians did what whites thought they ought to, their presence was tolerated. When violence erupted, however, the best of friends could easily turn into the worst of enemies. In this respect, Jackson was no different from his contemporaries. When on the warpath, the Indians became the enemy, and Jackson always dealt harshly with enemies. Yet the same Andrew Jackson raised an orphaned Indian as his own son and became infuriated when the Georgia militia attacked Chehaw, a Creek village that had been friendly to Jackson. As with most people, especially those who are touched by a certain greatness, Jackson was much more complex than his legend would lead us to believe.[15]

Andrew Jackson's victory at Horseshoe Bend had a profound effect upon American history in general and Seminole history in particular. Most notably, the victory destroyed Creek power and, by extension, helped to reduce all Indian power in the Southeast. Because of his triumph and subsequent promotion, Jackson was put in charge of the defense of New Orleans, which led to his becoming the prominent political figure of the period. For the Seminoles the results were not as immediate, but no less telling. Jackson, more than anyone else, proved to be the Seminole's greatest enemy.

As the Creek conflict was winding down, British plans for the Gulf Coast were beginning to come into place. In May 1814, Capt. George Woodbine of the Royal Marines landed at the mouth of the Apalachicola River and began to distribute arms to the local Seminoles, refugee Creeks, and runaway slaves. He also began the construction of a fort farther upriver at Prospect Bluff. In August, Maj. Edward Nicholls arrived, stepping up the effort to recruit the natives into a force that would hopefully attack the southern United States. He also moved his base of operations to Pensacola, disregarding the muted complaints of the Spanish governor.

In September, the British and their Indian allies moved against Mobile. The small American force at Fort Bowyer was ready, having been warned of the attack by disgruntled British traders. In the subsequent battle, the English were beaten back and suffered the loss of one of their ships. Mobile was saved.

As the fall of 1814 progressed, Jackson gathered his forces. In early November, he crossed the Perdido River and advanced upon Pensacola. The British, outnumbered and unsure of their Indian allies, quickly boarded ship and departed the city, destroying its defenses as they left. On November 7, Pensacola surrendered. A few days later Jackson received belated instructions from Washington ordering him not to invade Spanish territory. Having no further use for the Spanish town, Jackson gave it back to its rightful owners and headed for New Orleans and his place in history.

For the Seminoles of Florida it was a time of excitement, stress, and change. The Creek civil war had forced hundreds of new immigrants into their midst, all of whom held a fierce animosity toward the Americans. British encouragements had also lured runaway slaves into the Florida territory. The genesis of the Seminole Nation was nearing its conclusion. At the same time, Andrew Jackson, the nemesis of the Seminole Nation, was impatiently awaiting the day when he could finish the task he had started at Horseshoe Bend and Pensacola.

The War of 1812 is sometimes called the Second War for American Independence. For the nation, the war had been a rite of passage. America had been tested, and it had survived. The nation's institutions had remained intact, despite the capture and destruction of Washington. The navy had done well, bettering the "invincible" Royal Navy on several occasions. After a number of miserable attempts to invade Canada, the army, under the command of a new generation of officers like Winfield Scott, Edmund Gaines, and Alexander Macomb, had scored several brilliant victories along the northern border. Jackson's stunning triumph at New Orleans ended the conflict on an especially high note. America had proven something to itself and the world. No, the United States was not yet a world power, but it could no longer be considered an infant nation incapable of taking care of itself. People on both sides of the Atlantic came to realize that the United States and its "experimental" form of government were here to stay.

The end of the war signaled the beginning of what came to be known as the Era of Good Feeling. The future seemed limitless. More than ever, Americans felt compelled to continue work on "God's Plan." If the British were unable to stop the United States, who could? Once again, it was not difficult to see the hand of Providence at work. Americans felt that sooner or later, the entire continent would be theirs. Americans were also aware that a large portion of the continent remained in the hands of England and Spain. Considering the outcome of the late war, not much could be done with respect to Canada. Spanish North America, however, was another matter. To the west were Texas, New Mexico, and California, sparsely populated and chafing under colonial rule. Closer to home was Florida—another Spanish possession, no better explored than the land beyond the Mississippi, and to many Americans as intriguing as California.

The situations that had prompted the attempts to annex Florida before the War of 1812 had not changed. Spanish governors still controlled the waterways that drained the South. Slaves continued to flee to the freedom Florida offered. Foreign control over a territory so close to the nation's heartland still made Americans nervous. There was also the problem of the Indians. They had aided the British during the War of 1812 and were still causing trouble. The war was over, but the English influence had not completely disappeared.

In the latter months of the war the British had completed the fortification at Prospect Bluff on the Apalachicola River. At war's end the British departed, all except for Royal Marine major Edward Nicholls. Under

Nicholls's direction, British warships offloaded cannon, muskets, and ammunition aplenty at Prospect Bluff. Nicholls also stirred up the Indians with reports that the Treaty of Ghent had guaranteed that the United States would return all Indian lands taken during the war, including those lost as a result of the Creek civil war.[16]

By the summer of 1815, Nicholls was ready to leave Florida, but only temporarily. Boarding a British naval vessel, he headed for London, accompanied by Josiah Francis, a Red Stick who, like Tecumseh's brother, was known as the "Prophet." Their mission was to secure English aid and support for the Indians, both militarily and diplomatically. They failed. The British Foreign Office, having less need of the Seminoles than of peace with the United States, turned a deaf ear. The Florida natives would be on their own.

In truth, the British had left the Seminoles a considerable amount of aid at Prospect Bluff. Thousands of muskets were available, along with the powder and lead necessary for their use. The fort itself was no meager gift. Well armed with artillery, it was a formidable structure indeed. Unfortunately, the Seminoles had little use for a fort. Their security would be better served by fleeing an invader, rather than fighting one. The lesson of Horseshoe Bend was not easily forgotten.

Runaway blacks were of a differing opinion. They saw strength in numbers and the fort as a gathering place for others in the same situation. As the Seminoles began to return to their villages, blacks, at the urging of Major Nicholls, moved into the fort. Nervous whites to the north soon began to refer to the installation as the "Negro Fort." As news of the fort spread throughout the plantation houses of the South, word also filtered down to the fields and the slave quarters. For those slaves inclined to run away, the all-important question of *where* to run had been answered.

The presence of the Negro Fort served to heighten the fear of a slave insurrection. The famous English actress Fannie Kemble, finding herself the mistress of a large Georgia plantation during the years of the Second Seminole War, commented upon the fears of southern slave holders, "I know that the southern men are apt to deny that they do live under an habitual sense of danger, but a slave population, coerced into obedience, though unarmed and half-fed, *is* a threatening source of constant insecurity, and every southern *woman* to whom I have spoken on the subject, has admitted to me that they live in terror of their slaves."[17]

The combined fears of economic loss and a slave revolt caused southerners to push for the elimination of the Negro Fort. There was, however, one serious complication: the fort was in Spanish territory. Because *Spanish* slaves were also fleeing to the Negro Fort, the governor of West Florida would have liked to have destroyed the fort himself. Unfortunately, the forces at his disposal were insufficient for the task. The governor was also aware that the United States might use the presence of the Negro Fort as cause to invade and take over the colony. Sadly, there was little the Spanish governor could do about it.

The problem of dealing with the Negro Fort was taken up by the one man who was most anxious to do something about it: Andrew Jackson. As major general in charge of the Southern Division of the army, Jackson was the man whose responsibility it was to protect the southern frontier. Without any specific orders from Washington, he began to plot the fort's destruction. To lead the effort, Jackson chose his loyal supporter and second in command, Brig. Gen. Edmund Pendleton Gaines.

For Secretary of War William Crawford, things were progressing faster than he would have liked. Concerned about the growing strength of the fort, he wrote to Jackson, "The Negro Fort . . . has been strengthened . . . and now occupied by between two hundred and fifty and three hundred blacks, who are well armed, clothed, and disciplined. Secret practices to inveigle negroes from the frontiers of Georgia, as well as from the Cherokee and Creek nations are still continued by the negroes and hostile Creeks. This is a state of things which cannot fail to produce much injury to the neighboring settlements, and excite irritations which may ultimately endanger the peace of the nation." Possibly fearing Jackson's impetuosity, Crawford then reminded the general that the Negro Fort was, in the first place, a Spanish responsibility, and failing that, it was up to President Madison to decide what course of action to take.[18]

Jackson, as was his lifelong habit, paid little or no attention to his civilian superiors. Although a staunch defender of the Constitution, Jackson would repeatedly ignore the parts of that document that gave Congress the sole authority to declare war and the State Department the responsibility to handle foreign policy. In those early days of the Republic, even the most fundamental aspects of governmental authority were open to question. Two centuries later, we still have not determined where to draw the line between "war" and "police action" or between "self-defense" and "aggression." Ironically, having the "Father of the Constitution" sitting in the president's chair seems to have made little difference. At any rate, Jackson was not the sort of man to be bothered by technicalities.

In April 1816, Jackson dispatched an aide to the Spanish capitol at Pensacola. In a letter to the governor, Jackson announced that if the Spaniards did not eliminate the Negro Fort, the United States would. The governor responded that he could do nothing without aid or authority from Havana.[19]

It was the responsibility of General Gaines to devise a plan to destroy the fort and up to Col. Duncan Clinch to actually accomplish the feat. Gaines's plan was innovative, in the sense that it allowed the United States to claim, for political purposes, that it had been acting in self defense. Gaines had ordered Clinch to erect Fort Scott along the Flint River, just north of the Florida border. Gaines then announced that the fort would be supplied from New Orleans, which meant bringing supplies up the Apalachicola, past the Negro Fort. Writing to Jackson, he remarked that "if such an intercourse could be opened down the Apalachicola, it would enable us to keep an eye upon the Seminoles, and the Negro Fort. The negro establishment is (I think justly) considered as likely to produce much evil among the blacks of Georgia, and the eastern part of the Mississippi territory." If the Negro Fort fired upon the supply convoy, it would provide the excuse needed to destroy the fort.[20]

The exact purpose of the planned action was masked by continued references to the "Indian menace." Clinch reported that the Seminoles were preparing for war and planning attacks upon white positions in Georgia. Considering the number of American soldiers moving into the vicinity, the Seminoles may very well have been preparing for hostilities. It would have been the prudent thing to do. Clinch wrote to a fellow officer that the objective was to "capture the negroes within the fort, and restore them to their proper owners." Once again, the Seminoles were being caught up in something with which they had little concern.[21]

On July 10, 1816, a small fleet of supply ships arrived at the mouth of the Apalachicola. The convoy consisted of two supply schooners and two navy gunboats under the command of Sailing Master Jarius Loomis. Under orders to await word from Clinch, Loomis anchored his vessels and waited. A week later, Loomis sent a small boat ashore to locate some fresh water. The boat never returned. Later in the day, the dead body of one of the sailors was found, and later still, a lone survivor was found stranded on a sand bar. He reported that two others had been killed and a third taken prisoner.[22]

Clinch, meanwhile, had left Fort Scott with more than 100 men. He soon caught up with a force of 150 friendly Creek warriors also headed toward the Negro Fort. The combined army arrived in the vicinity of the Negro Fort on the twentieth, where Clinch immediately dispatched Indian messengers to Loomis. The naval officer, perhaps suspicious after the loss of four men, requested a squad of soldiers be sent down to guide him up the river. Clinch complied, and on the morning of July 27, the two gunboats tied up opposite the fortification.[23]

Without the navy, Clinch could have done very little. Having no artillery of his own, he could not respond to the occasional volley fired from the fort. Other than surrounding the fort to prevent any escape, he was almost powerless. Against his force of less than 300 were an almost equal number of defenders, but most of them were women and children. Also within the fort were a small number of Choctaw Indians. The defenders, well armed and secure within their fort, had no intention of surrendering. They were no doubt aware of the fact that any survivors of the assault would be immediately returned to slavery. Many of them had risked everything to reach the Negro Fort. For such people, freedom meant more than life itself.[24]

Afterward, Clinch described the fort to a friend: "It stood on the east side of the river, about twenty-five miles from the bay. . . . The parapet was about fifteen feet high and eighteen thick, and defended by one thirty two [pound cannon], three twenty fours, two nines, two sixes, and an elegant five and an half-inch howitzer. It was situated on a beautiful and commanding bluff, with the river in front, a large creek just below, a swamp in the rear, and a small creek just above, which rendered it difficult to be approached by artillery."[25]

One might have thought that the small naval vessels would have been sitting ducks, but such was not the case. In order to hit a sitting duck, one must know how to shoot. While no doubt brave and determined men, the gunners of the Negro Fort were not trained artillerymen. What did they know of elevations and of powder charges? The blacks fired but did no real damage.

Loomis's sailors, on the other hand, were experienced at their craft. Some may have fought against the Royal Navy during the War of 1812. With calm professionalism, they began to fire on the fort, refining their aim with each shot. By the eighth round, they had found the mark. The ninth round was something different. It was a "hot shot," a cannonball that had been placed in a fire to make it red hot when loaded into the gun. The glowing ball, fired by Sailing Master Basset of gunboat number 154, landed squarely in the fort's powder magazine. In one massive explosion, heard more than 100 miles away in Pensacola, the Negro Fort was leveled.[26]

The carnage was appalling, even to hardened veterans. One soldier wrote to his father, telling him that bodies were "stretched upon the plain, buried in the sand and rubbish, or suspended from the tops of the surrounding pines. . . . Here lay an innocent babe, there a helpless mother, on the other side a sturdy warrior, on the other a bleeding squaw." Clinch saw a higher purpose to his victory: "The war yells of the Indians, the cries and lamentations of the wounded, compelled the soldier to pause in the midst of victory, to drop a tear for the sufferings of his fellow beings, and to acknowledge that the great Ruler of the Universe must have used us as instruments in chastising the blood-thirsty and murderous wretches that defended the fort."[27]

Like Colonel Clinch, many Americans, already convinced of their "chosen" status, could easily believe that God had guided the hot shot to its mark. The logical inference was that God had intended the Americans to occupy Florida and that slaves were not meant to be free. Some Indians may also have seen the hand of a higher power at work. If so, it must have given the Seminoles reason to worry. Why would the Great Spirit have done such a thing? What was He trying to say?

There had been perhaps 320 people within the fort. Over 250 died instantly, their dismembered bodies blown in every direction. Others soon died of their wounds, despite the best efforts of Clinch's staff surgeon, Dr. Buck, and the ordinary soldiers who did what they could to relieve the suffering. The few surviving blacks were bound and guarded, soon to return to a life of slavery. To Clinch's dismay, few of the surviving blacks were the property of white Americans. Most were either escaped Spanish slaves or the property of Creeks from Georgia and Alabama. Most of the blacks belonging to white southerners had fled the area, making for villages located farther south, hopefully out of the reach of the U.S. Army. For southerners expecting an end to the black refuge in Florida, the destruction of the Negro Fort would prove somewhat meaningless.[28]

As the smoke cleared, the looting began. Despite the destruction, there was plenty of valuable property left undamaged. Most of it consisted of rifles, pistols, gunpowder, and swords. As payment for their services, Clinch had promised his Creek allies the lion's share of the booty. After the Indians had taken what they wanted, the army selected its own spoils. Loomis's sailors, who had done all the work, were left with the scraps. Today, the site of the Negro Fort is preserved as part of the Apalachicola National Forest.

The shock wave from the Negro Fort served to quiet the frontier for some time. No doubt fearing a similar fate, the Seminoles wisely restrained themselves. Blacks who had not been at the fort fled the area, most of them going to villages along the Suwannee River.

The army, having done its duty, was ordered away from the Florida-Georgia border, and into the newly created Alabama Territory. There, as settlers rushed into ceded Creek lands that had yet to be vacated, the army was needed to keep the peace. Along the Florida border, unrestrained squatters and outlaws raided into Spanish territory, killing Indians, stealing slaves, and rustling cattle. There was, in truth, no one to stop them. The army was gone, the Spanish were too weak, and the Indians were too few and scattered. The destruction of the Negro Fort brought about an uneasy peace that would soon be shattered.

3 The First Seminole War

▲▲▲ ▲▲▲▲ ▲▲▲▲ ▲▲▲ ▲

The destruction of the Negro Fort did not bring lasting peace to the Florida-Georgia border lands. The root causes of the cross-border tension had not been addressed and would eventually result in armed conflict. Particularly troublesome was the matter of cattle theft. Florida abounded in good range land, and the Seminoles excelled at animal husbandry. Backwoods whites, coveting the Indians' herds and grazing land, seized every opportunity to steal Seminole cattle. The Indians, feeling a need for just retribution, stole white cattle. Unprotected by the Spaniards and abandoned by the English, the Florida Indians found it difficult to defend themselves. A frustrated chief complained:[1]

> The white people have carried all the red people's cattle off. . . . I sent to all my people to let white people alone, and stay on this side of the river; and they did so; but the white people still continue to carry off their cattle. . . . The whites first begun, and there is nothing said about that, but great complaint made about what the Indians do. This is now three years, since the white people killed three Indians. Since that, they have killed three other Indians, and taken their horses, and what they had; and this summer they killed three more; and very lately they killed one more . . . but there is nothing said about that. . . . The cattle that we are accused of taking, were cattle that the white people took from us; our young man went and brought them back, with the same marks and brands.[2]

By February 1817, the Seminoles had suffered one too many indignities. The older and wiser chiefs attempted to restrain their hot-blooded young warriors, but it was a hopeless cause. In southeastern Georgia, near the St. Marys River, the isolated home of the Garrett family fell to their wrath. With her husband away, Mrs. Garrett could do little to protect herself. Shot, stabbed, and scalped, she was joined in death by her two children, one a toddler, the other an infant. Nervous and angry frontiersmen called out for revenge. The murderers may have felt justified in their actions, but the raid would gain nothing for their people.

Farther to the west, at Pensacola, General Gaines became involved in a war of words with José Masot, the Spanish governor of West Florida. Fort Crawford had been erected in southern Alabama, just north of the Spanish capitol. Gaines requested permission to bring his supply vessels up the Escambia River, through Spanish territory. Masot agreed but insisted that the vessels pay duty. Angry letters flew between the two commanders, but Masot held his ground. Gaines bristled but paid the duty. To American minds, it was simply another reason to remove the Spaniards from Florida.[3]

Not only was Gaines bothered by hostile Indians and difficult Spaniards, he was also concerned about a renewed British presence in Florida. This presence was not the least bit supported by London, but neither Gaines nor the Seminoles seemed to care. The Indians were being threatened by the Americans and needed any ally they could get, while Gaines, like most Americans, harbored a special hatred for the British. Gaines had nearly died from wounds received during his heroic defense of Fort Erie in 1814.

This new British presence in Florida existed in the persons of former Royal Marine George Woodbine, who had helped lead British intrigues in Florida during the War of 1812, and Alexander Arbuthnot, an aging Scottish trader from the Bahamas. Woodbine appeared to be up to no good, but Arbuthnot was in Florida simply to make a profit. Dismayed by the treatment of the Seminoles at the hands of their northern neighbors, he wrote letters to both British and American officials on the Indian's behalf.[4]

The letters brought a measure of notoriety to Arbuthnot but did nothing to help the Seminoles. Rumor had it that the Scottish Bahamian was selling guns to the Indians and preparing them for war. That he was selling them guns should have come as no surprise: the Seminoles' major commodity was deerskins, and killing deer required the use of a firearm. The idea that he was inciting the Indians to violence seems less likely; it would have been bad for business. Still, the Americans, seeing a British bogeyman, cast a worried eye south.

There was another Englishman on the scene who appeared even more sinister. Robert Ambrister had been a lieutenant in the Royal Marines

FIGURE 2.
Maj. Gen. Edmund
Pendleton Gaines,
by Mathew Brady.
By permission of the
Florida State Archives.
Image #RC01681,
DBCN#AAM-3830.

and an acquaintance of George Woodbine. In the spring of 1817, Woodbine sent Ambrister to Florida to engage in some unspecified trouble-
making. Arriving in full military attire, Ambrister was able to convince
the Seminoles that he represented a new British alliance. In truth, he
was nothing more than an agent for Woodbine, who had concocted
dreams of a personal Florida empire protected by black and Seminole
warriors. Fanciful as it was, Ambrister fell for it and became part of the
plot. Between the Indians, the Spaniards, and the British, Gaines had a
right to be concerned.[5]

In Washington, President Monroe and his Cabinet were decidedly inde-
cisive about the Florida situation. Everyone in the administration wanted
Florida, but nobody wanted to ruffle any European feathers. Secretary of
State John Quincy Adams was involved in delicate negotiations with the
Spanish and did not want the boat rocked. In the meantime, troubles
along the frontier were crying out for a solution.

In the minds of Generals Gaines and Jackson, the solution was clear: a large force should enter Florida, destroy the Seminoles, and put the colony under U.S. control. If the Florida Indians were causing trouble and the Spanish authorities could not control them, the United States had the right to take care of the situation. Unlike Monroe and Adams, Gaines and Jackson would not have to face angry ambassadors and indignant congressmen.

Sadly, the Seminoles were playing right into Jackson's hands. By violently reacting to lawless incursions, the Indians were giving the Americans an excuse to take Florida from Spain. Cooler heads among the Seminole leadership no doubt saw the danger but could offer no real solution to the problem. If the Indians did not respond to attacks by marauding whites, the incursions would continue. If they did respond, it could lead to a devastating war.

While the politicians and diplomats in Washington fretted over what to do about Florida, General Gaines realized that there were things that could be done without encroaching upon Spanish territory. Several Mikasuki villages existed in southwestern Georgia on land that had been ceded to the United States at the end of the Creek civil war. Gaines possessed the authority to remove any Indians not legally residing in the ceded territory but had seen no good reason to do so. Now he had one. Forcing the Seminoles out of Georgia would send a strong message to their cousins living south of the border.

Foremost among the Seminole villages in Georgia was Fowltown, located about fifteen miles from Fort Scott on the opposite side of the Flint River. As the Fort Scott garrison's activities grew, Neamathla, headman of Fowltown, let his displeasure be known. In a proud but foolish gesture, he informed the commander of Fort Scott that the army was not allowed to cut timber on the east side of the Flint. He pointed out that the land was his and that "he was directed, by the powers above and below, to protect and defend it." Gaines was incensed at the chief's blatant disregard for U.S. sovereignty.[6]

At the heart of the matter was a simple question with a very complex answer: Whose land was it? It was the same question that had been asked since Jamestown and Plymouth Rock. To Gaines, the answer was simple: Fowltown was in Georgia and therefore on United States soil. To make matters even more conclusive, Fowltown was situated in an area that had been ceded to the United States by the Creek Confederation at the end of the Creek civil war. Neamathla and his Mikasukis were of a differing

FIGURE 3.
Neamathla, a
Seminole Chief.
By permission of the National
Museum of the American
Indian, Smithsonian Institu-
tion. #P27766.

opinion. They had, after all, been living on the land long before there even *was* a United States. The Indians also held a different point of view concerning the Creek cession. The Mikasukis and other Seminoles did not consider themselves Creeks and had not taken part in the civil war. In their eyes, Fowltown and the surrounding areas were not Creek land to be given away. By the rules of their own societies, each man was right. As was sure to happen sooner or later, the time had come to decide the matter.

In order to chastise Neamathla, Gaines sent a force of 250 men across the river to seize the chief. On November 21, 1817, there was a sharp skirmish outside of Fowltown, and the Americans were forced to return to Fort Scott without having taken Neamathla captive. Infuriated, Gaines ordered another attack on Fowltown the following day. This time the Indians were driven from their homes, never to return again. By Indian custom, retaliation was called for. The First Seminole War had begun.[7]

For General Gaines and the men at Fort Scott, there were other problems besides Neamathla and the people of Fowltown. Foremost on their minds was the matter of food and clothing. Provisions were running low and the soldiers were anxiously awaiting a supply convoy that was scheduled to come up the Apalachicola from the Gulf of Mexico. In order to guide the convoy upriver, Lt. R. W. Scott and forty soldiers were dispatched down river to meet it. When Scott met the convoy, he found about twenty of the men in extremely ill health and in need of medical attention. It was decided that it would be best for the lieutenant to get them to Fort Scott as quickly as possible. In addition, there were seven soldiers' wives and possibly a number of children. Putting the dependents and invalids into one boat, Scott and twenty healthy men headed upriver for the safety of the fort. It was a week after the destruction of Fowltown.

Lieutenant Scott must have been apprehensive about the trip, for he dispatched a runner back to the fort to request an escort: "Mr. Hambly informs me that Indians are assembling at the junction of the river, where they intend to make a stand against those vessels coming up the river; should this be the case, I am not able to make a stand against them. My command does not exceed forty men, and one half are sick, and without arms."[8]

As the boat worked its way up the river, Scott and his companions scanned the shoreline with anxious eyes. Unaware of what had happened at Fowltown, they had no idea how hostile the Seminoles would be. The soldiers tried to keep to the center of the river, but the currents were strong and tended to drive them toward the water's edge. Fifteen miles below the welcoming walls of Fort Scott, their worst fears were realized. As the boat came close to the thickly wooded embankment, a deadly hail of rifle fire swept over the vessel. As soldiers fell dead or jumped into the water to flee, Indians leapt into the water and pulled the boat ashore. At close quarters, the tomahawk was put to work and the remainder of the soldiers slain. As the fighting ended, scalping knives were drawn and bloody trophies taken. Only one of the women, Elizabeth Stewart, remained alive (she was taken prisoner and would remain so for several months), and only six soldiers, four of them wounded, found their way back to Fort Scott. Almost fifty people had been in the boat.[9]

David Mitchell, former governor of Georgia and now the Creek Indian agent, was appalled at the whole affair. In response to questions from Congress, Mitchell dated the commencement of the war from the attack upon Fowltown and did not support Gaines's contention that the Indians were the cause of the hostilities:

The peace of the frontier of Georgia has always been exposed and disturbed, more or less, by acts of violence, committed as well by the whites as the Indians; and a spirit of retaliation has mutually prevailed. These petty acts of aggression were increased and multiplied by a set of lawless and abandoned characters, who had taken refuge on both sides of the St. Mary's river, living principally by plunder. I believe the first outrage committed on the frontier of Georgia, after the treaty of Ft. Jackson, was by these banditti, who plundered a party of the Seminole Indians, on their way to Georgia for the purpose of trade, and killed one of them. This produced retaliation on the part of the Indians, and hence the killing of Mrs. Garrett and her child.[10]

The Scott Massacre made open warfare inevitable. On December 2, before receiving word of the incident, the War Department advised Gaines that he was not to invade Spanish territory. A week later, the new secretary of war, John C. Calhoun, amended the policy, giving Gaines permission to intrude a short distance into foreign land. When news of Scott and his doomed companions reached Washington, Calhoun immediately gave Gaines orders to invade Florida and pursue the Indians wherever they might seek refuge. He was not, however, allowed to attack any Spanish installation.[11]

The orders may have been sent to Gaines, but the general was not there. Prior to the Scott incident, Gaines had been ordered to the East Coast to help the navy clear out a nest of pirates who had taken up residence on Amelia Island, just across the border in East Florida. Needing an immediate and powerful presence in West Florida, Secretary Calhoun called upon Andrew Jackson, commander of the Southern Division and Gaines's immediate superior.[12]

By late December and into January 1818, Jackson was busy in Nashville, gathering troops and planning his campaign. Calhoun, aware of Jackson's ambitions toward Florida, dispatched copies of the orders that had been previously issued to Gaines, including the one that had forbidden Gaines from attacking any Spanish installations.

Before receiving those orders, Jackson wrote a confidential letter to Monroe, informing the president that if the government so desired, Florida could be conquered within sixty days. All Monroe had to do was send approval through a confidential intermediary. Monroe never did. Just as significantly, the president never told Jackson *not* to take the Spanish

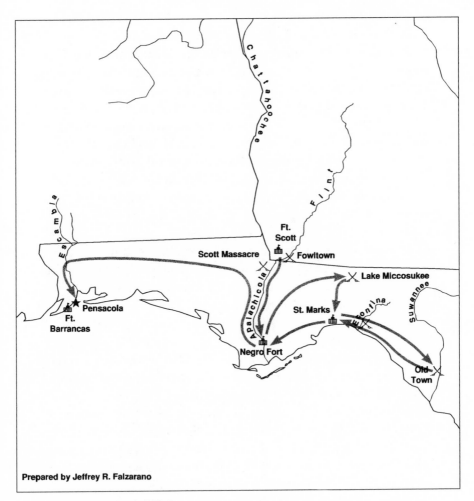

Prepared by Jeffrey R. Falzarano

MAP 2. First Seminole War, 1818.

forts. Fully aware of Jackson's reputation, motives, and ambitions, Monroe probably knew that, unrestrained, Jackson would do what he pleased. For the president, it was safer, politically, to say nothing. If things went wrong, Monroe could distance himself from the general's actions.[13]

Jackson arrived at Fort Scott early in March. Gathered at the fort was a formidable force. In addition to about 500 regulars, there were about 1,000 Tennessee volunteers and a considerable number of Georgia Militia. Also present were close to 1,400 Lower Creek warriors. These Indians were longtime enemies of the Upper Creeks who had fled to Florida after the Creek civil war. There was no force in Florida, Seminole or Spanish, capable of stopping such an army.[14]

On March 12, 1818, Andrew Jackson and his army departed Fort Scott, crossing into Spanish Florida the following day. The army moved swiftly down the Apalachicola, not so much in pursuit of the enemy as in pursuit of a good meal. Fort Scott had been in need of supplies at the time of the Scott Massacre; Seminole hostilities had prevented all but a few relief convoys from reaching the fort since the attack on Fowltown. The arrival of Jackson's army had depleted what little they had. For Jackson, there was no alternative; he needed to get his army to the relief boats or face starvation and desertion. Two days after entering Florida, the advance columns of the American army encountered the first of the supply boats.[15]

A few days later, Jackson and his men encamped at the site of the destroyed Negro Fort. While the men ate, rested, and filled their knapsacks, Jackson had them erect a new fort over the ruins of the old one. Supplies for the army were slow in arriving; a depot was needed to house and protect them. Jackson's army would be traveling light and living off the land. Before the war was over, those supplies would be needed.

The army left the newly erected Fort Gadsden on March 26, heading northeast toward the main Seminole towns at Lake Miccosukee. An advance party of Creek warriors under Maj. David Twiggs burned the deserted Indian town of Tallahassee on the thirty-first. The following day, Jackson attacked the town of Miccosukee, the largest in the area. An opportunity to capture almost the entire population failed when white troops mistook friendly Creeks for Seminoles and began firing upon them. In the resulting confusion, most of the Seminoles escaped.[16]

With the defenders gone, Jackson put his men to work destroying the Indian villages. More than 300 homes were burnt, and anything of value was taken or destroyed. The army rested for a few days, feasting on Seminole cattle and corn, then turned south, making for the Spanish fort at St. Marks.[17]

Jackson arrived at St. Marks on April 6 and immediately began to exchange pleasantries with the Spanish commander. In a friendly gesture, the Spaniards extended medical care to several ailing American soldiers. The Spanish hospitality proved useless; Jackson demanded the fort's surrender, even though the Spaniards had not been the least bit belligerent. The Spanish commander politely refused to surrender, but American soldiers rushed in before he could prepare a defense. Today, the remnants of the fortification are preserved as a state historic site.[18]

The capture of St. Marks also provided Jackson with several important captives. Alexander Arbuthnot, the seventy-year-old Bahamian trader, was a guest of the Spanish commander but soon found himself a prisoner of the American general. Also captured were Josiah Francis, the Red Stick called the Prophet, and Homathlemico, an important chief. Days earlier, the two chiefs had been lured out to an American naval vessel that had been flying the British Union Jack. Upon Jackson's arrival at St. Marks, the pair were taken ashore and immediately hanged. Weeks earlier, the Prophet's daughter, Milly Francis, had rescued, in Pocahontas-like fashion, a captive American soldier.[19]

After shipping off the Spanish garrison, Jackson pointed his army south, making for Bowlegs Town on the Suwannee River. On April 12, the army came upon a Red Stick village situated along Econfina Creek. The Red Stick warriors, engaged against their Lower Creek cousins, put up a stiff resistance but were overwhelmed. Nearly 40 warriors were slain and about 100 women and children taken captive. Entering the captured town, the victorious Creek warriors were surprised to find a white woman. It turned out to be Elizabeth Stewart, the lone female survivor of the Scott Massacre. She had not been harmed and had no idea why she had been spared in the first place.[20]

The army pushed quickly ahead, hoping to surprise the towns on the Suwannee before word reached the Seminoles of the Americans' advance. Jackson wanted not only to crush the Seminoles but also to take prisoner the many blacks who lived in the area. As had happened with the Negro Fort, pressure from slaveholders was helping drive government policy. The army arrived at the Suwannee on April 16 but found no one home. A small force of black Seminoles harassed the army, giving the women and children time to escape. For the next two days, Jackson's men rested, burning and looting the Seminole villages. They may have not killed or captured many Indians, but they had certainly made them destitute and homeless.[21]

Although few Indians had been taken, a more important prize soon fell into American hands. Robert Ambrister, the former Royal Marine who was pretending to be a British agent, somehow managed to stumble into an American camp, whereupon he was immediately seized. The fact that he was wearing his old British uniform sealed his fate.[22]

The stated goals of the war had been achieved. Jackson had destroyed the major Seminole towns and had left the Indians as refugees in the dense swamps. Declaring victory, Jackson dispatched the Georgia militia and allied Creeks to their homes. Moving north along the coast, the general, along with his Tennessee volunteers and the army regulars, retraced their path back to St. Marks.[23]

First order of business upon reaching St. Marks was dealing with Ambrister and Arbuthnot. A military tribunal was convened and both men were accused of aiding the Seminoles, inciting them to war, and leading them against the United States. Ambrister, young and honorable, threw himself upon the mercy of the court. Arbuthnot, maintaining his innocence, declared that he had only been conducting legal trade with the Indians and had actually worked for peace.

Ambrister's case should have been easier, but it proved more troublesome for Jackson. By throwing himself upon the court's mercy, the young man almost received it. The court initially sentenced Ambrister to death but then reconsidered. Perhaps it had something to do with his youth or his manner. At any rate, the court changed the punishment to fifty lashes and a year at hard labor. It was a noble but wasted effort. Acting as if he had a choice between two recommended punishments, Jackson chose to invoke the first one. On April 29, 1818, Robert Ambrister fell before a firing squad. Arbuthnot was hanged from his own ship's yardarm. Justice, according to Andrew Jackson, had been served.[24]

Leaving a garrison at St. Marks, Jackson and his men headed west to Fort Gadsden. Jackson had informed the War Department that the frontier was at peace and that he would be heading for Nashville. A week later, stating that he had received reports that Indians were gathering and being supplied by the Spaniards, he changed his mind and declared that he would march on Pensacola. Hoping to avert an attack, Governor Masot of West Florida told Jackson, "With respect to the Indians . . . the greater part of them were women and children . . . [and] these few unarmed and miserable men were not hostile to the United States." As before, the Seminoles had only been an excuse for aggression.[25]

The American forces, now reduced to about a thousand men, left Fort Gadsden on May 7, heading west. After getting somewhat lost in West Florida, Jackson arrived at Pensacola on May 23. Hopelessly outnumbered, Governor Masot and 175 men took up their posts at Fort Barrancas, several miles out of town. Without firing a shot, Jackson had taken the city. Fort Barrancas would be another matter. When Jackson called for the installation's surrender, Masot refused. For good measure, Masot quoted a copy of President Monroe's message to Congress that stated Jackson's purpose in Florida was strictly to deal with Indians and not to harass Spaniards.[26]

Jackson was forced into a siege. Even with better than a five-to-one advantage in manpower, Barrancas would be hard to take. On May 27, as they watched the Americans place their guns, the Spaniards opened fire. Having made his point, Masot offered to resume talks. Jackson offered the same unacceptable terms, and Masot again turned them down, re-commencing his fire on the American batteries.[27]

Unable to return an effective fire because of poor cannon placement, the Americans moved their batteries during the night. When the lobbing of cannonballs resumed the following morning, Masot must have real-ized that Jackson was serious. This time, the Spanish governor offered to surrender the fort on terms that were acceptable to Jackson. Masot had put up a token defense and could now surrender with a measure of honor.

The First Seminole War was over, at least as far as Andrew Jackson was concerned. Leaving Col. William King as military governor and Capt. James Gadsden as customs collector, Old Hickory headed home. He had gotten what he wanted and would let other people take care of the messy details.

The shooting war may have been over, but the political and diplomatic battles had yet to begin. Jackson's invasion had raised three major ques-tions. First, by what authority had he executed a pair of British subjects? Second, was the United States at war with Spain? And third, exactly who had authorized all this? A minor military excursion into a thinly inhab-ited swampland had turned into a major international incident while at the same time igniting a serious constitutional debate.

The matter of the executions of Ambrister and Arbuthnot seemed the most immediately threatening. Andrew Jackson may have harbored no fear of the British, but he was one of the few to hold that opinion. People not only remembered the recent burning of Washington, but merchants all along the eastern seaboard winced at the thought of another naval blockade. The military threat was not the only one. Industrial England was the largest purchaser of agrarian America's produce, and conversely, it was America's largest supplier of manufactured goods. A disruption of trade with England would severely derail the American economy. In addition, it had to be borne in mind that British Canada shared a very long and contentious border with the United States. In short, nobody in Washington wanted trouble with England.

It was not necessarily the same on the other side of the Atlantic. As Britons traveled throughout their far-flung empire, they expected, and generally received, the protection of the Crown. The execution of Ambrister and Arbuthnot deeply insulted the British lion's pride. Englishmen began to ask questions in both London and Washington, and the answers were not proving satisfactory. They demanded to know under what authority Jackson had executed two of His Majesty's subjects who had not even set foot on American soil. Jackson argued that the pair had given up the Crown's protection when they had taken up the Indians' cause. Could Lafayette or Kosciusko have claimed the protection of France or Poland had they been captured by the British during the Revolution? That interpretation, however, raised another argument, seemingly silly by today's standards. Jackson, in giving his reasoning, had called such a foreign agent "an outlaw and a pirate." Many congressmen recoiled at the idea of associating the hallowed name of Lafayette with those terms.[28]

Looking deeper, the House Committee on Military Affairs saw other, more serious irregularities. They started out by stating that they could "find no law of the United States authorizing a trial before a military court for offenses such as are alleged." They added, "In vain has your committee sought among the documents . . . for a shadow of *necessity* for the death of the persons arraigned before the court." If indeed these men were prisoners of war, why were they not treated as such? The committee also questioned Jackson's execution of Ambrister after the court had recommended leniency, then pointed out several errors in the way testimony was allowed in Arbuthnot's trial.[29]

Other questions resulted in no clear-cut answers. Had Ambrister and Arbuthnot been actively engaged against American troops? Neither had been caught with a gun in his hand, but both had strongly supported the Seminoles and supplied them with weapons. Had their alleged crimes been serious enough to warrant the death penalty? It is interesting to note that in American eyes, these two Britons were often seen as more responsible for the First Seminole War than the Indians themselves. The Indians were usually viewed as the hapless dupes of foreign instigators, too ignorant to know what they were doing. It was much easier to blame outside troublemakers than to admit that the Indians were reacting to American aggression.[30]

People in England began to talk of demanding reparations and of the need for some sort of reprisal. The *Christian Observer* wrote, "Mr. [Secretary of State John Q.] Adams not only excuses but justifies, not only justifies but eulogizes, the motives, the words, the actions of General Jackson. . . . We cannot doubt that every American will be anxious to remove from his country the stain imprinted upon it by the base and vindictive conduct of his agent. . . . Common consistency requires that the United States should disavow the proceedings of General Jackson."[31]

The hastiness of the trial, the flimsy evidence, and the severity of the sentences were all very embarrassing to the American officials who were called upon to defend the acts. It was going to be hard for Jackson to explain why an elderly trader and a young soldier of fortune were such a mortal threat to the United States.

In the end, he did not have to explain. By the time Parliament got around to discussing the matter, it was a cold issue. Official indignation had died down for the same reason Americans had considered trouble with Britain such a bother: The economies of the two nations were too tightly bound. English mills needed American cotton. English factories needed American customers for their finished goods. As a writer in the *Liverpool Mercury* put it:

> America is, of all other nations, the one whose friendship ought to be most assiduously cultivated, and whose enmity is most to be dreaded by Great Britain. It is in her power to injure us in the most vital manner. The extreme distress into which the manufactures of this country were thrown by the American non-intercourse acts sufficiently show how much we are interested in preserving an unrestricted intercourse with our transatlantic brethren. . . . The U. States is now become the most important market for the disposal of the staple manufactures of this country.[32]

Like Alexander Arbuthnot, the issue died a slow, agonizing death. Indeed, the executions were to dog Jackson the rest of his life, even after his retirement from office in 1837. A political cartoon from the 1844 election shows an angry Jackson with upraised cane threatening to "hang you all up . . . as I did Arbuthnot and Ambister [*sic*]!" Twenty-six years after the event, Jackson's enemies still equated those two names with the vindictiveness of Andrew Jackson.[33]

THE LITTLE MAGICIAN INVOKED.

FIGURE 4. "The Little Magician Invoked." Cartoon from the presidential campaign of 1844. Andrew Jackson (*left*) is saying, "By the Eternal! you old Hags! if I get hold of you, I'll hang you all up under the 7th section as I did Arbuthnot and Ambister [*sic*]!" Lithograph by H. Bucholzer.
By permission of the Library of Congress. LC-USZ62–91417.

The Spaniards had suffered even greater indignities. An American army had, with no provocation, attacked Spanish forces and taken a Spanish settlement. It was a clear act of war, and they demanded their property back, along with an explanation and the appropriate apologies. Secretary of State John Q. Adams had to walk a thin line over a deep chasm. He had just begun serious negotiations with Spanish minister Don Luis de Onís concerning the future of Florida and did not want them to fall apart. He also knew that to repudiate Jackson was politically unacceptable for the administration.

Wisely, Adams let the Spanish raise the required fuss. Talks were suspended but not entirely called off. Spanish sabers were rattled, but not very loudly. The empire was crumbling and Spain was in no position to go to war with the United States. Adams then went on the offensive with a carefully worded letter (accompanied by seventy-two supporting documents) that placed blame for the war on the British, the Indians, and corrupt Spanish officials in Florida. He then apologized, said that taking Spanish territory had not been American policy, and offered to return Pensacola and St. Marks to Spain.[34]

The foreign problems were troubling but faded with time. The domestic issues proved much harder to resolve. At the heart of the debate was the American public's attitude toward the military. Having suffered at the hands of the supposedly tyrannical George III supported by the overwhelming power of the English army, the founding fathers established a system they felt would prevent such abuses. The Constitution provided for civilian control over the military, and Congress, in full agreement with the policy, kept the size of the army ridiculously small. More than anything else, Americans dreaded the thought of a military coup. They had seen it happen in France at the hands of Napoleon, and it was happening repeatedly in Latin America. Americans were determined that it would not happen to them.

And therein lies the irony. Andrew Jackson had openly disobeyed orders from his civilian superiors by attacking the Spanish posts. By the same actions, he had also violated the constitutional provision that gave Congress the sole authority to declare war. He had, quite simply, usurped the powers of the duly elected officials. Left unchecked, such actions could have easily lead to a dictatorship. Even more alarming, because of his position in the army and his backing by the Tennessee militia, Andrew Jackson had the power to implement his own personal agenda. We would have expected Americans to be outraged. These were a people who were deeply concerned about any possible return to tyranny. Instead, the majority of Americans supported Jackson. Fortunately for the nation, Jackson was not a Napoleon. As self-centered as he was, above all else, he had a deep faith in the people of the United States and in the principles of democracy.

Still, there were plenty of people who saw the danger. Even a defender of Jackson, writing in *Niles Weekly Register*, felt uneasy about the situation: "Gen. Jackson appears unaware of the necessity of strict discipline and subordination, and being utterly fearless of responsibility himself, and always taught to believe that his personal liability would be a justification of his conduct, he does not sufficiently reflect how intimately the character of the country is associated with his own, now he is an officer; and that altho' he may freely offer his personal sacrifice, yet it places the government in a most delicate situation to accept it."[35]

As it happened, while the events of 1818 were unfolding Congress was not in session. Congress had adjourned in March and would not reconvene until December. By then, one might have thought that the matter would have died. It did not. Unlike Britain and Spain, who had nothing to gain by going to extremes against Jackson, political opponents in the United States felt they had nothing to lose. Jackson was quickly becoming the most powerful political force in the nation, and as such, he had no shortage of enemies. His opponents smelled political blood and were eager to spill more of it. The ensuing arguments lasted for several months, becoming the longest debate Congress had ever held up until that time.[36]

It was an odd time in the history of American politics. For the most part, the nation operated under a one-party system. In the early years of the Republic, there had been two loosely organized parties, the Federalists and the Democratic Republicans (Democrats). Washington and Adams had been Federalists. Fearing a strong national government, the people had elected Jefferson, a Democrat, as president in 1800. His successors, Madison and Monroe, were also Democrats. Having established a popular and stable form of government, the Federalists no longer had a cause, and the party began to die out. By the time of the First Seminole War, the vast majority of elected officials were Democrats.

A one-party democracy cannot long exist. Either the one party eliminates all opposition, thereby eliminating the democracy, or the party splits. It may be said that for the Democrats, the growing split widened in the early months of 1819. Conservatives, mostly from the Northeast and the more "aristocratic" parts of the South, lined up against Jackson's western liberals. It was not, however, a clean split, and a true opposition party did not develop until the 1830s. Jackson's personality became more important than the issues, and the line between conservative and liberal was, for the moment, blurred.

When Congress reconvened in December 1818, several resolutions were proposed that condemned the various actions of Andrew Jackson. The administration had attempted to wash its hands of the matter by approving whatever had been done, while at the same time saying it had not been government policy. If anyone was going to punish Jackson, it would have to be Congress, and a resolution would be the means by which they would do it.

As the debates commenced, Jackson's supporters admitted that some impropriety had taken place, but all for good reason. Jackson's opponents, led by Henry Clay of Kentucky, took the high ground, using the Constitution as their chief weapon. Clay warned, "Nations are often precipitated into ruinous war from folly, from pride, from ambition, and from the desire of military fame. . . . Beware how you give a fatal sanction . . . to military insubordination. Remember that Greece had her Alexander, Rome her Caesar, England her Cromwell, France her Bonaparte, and, that if we would escape the rock on which they split, we must avoid their errors. . . . Are former services, however eminent, to protect from even inquiring into recent misconduct?"[37]

Congressman Cobb of Georgia also saw the danger. "We become so infatuated with the *man* that we lose sight of the *principle,* and we are offering him our *worship,* before we are aware that we have made him a God."[38]

Jackson's supporters tended to dismiss the philosophical questions and instead appealed to the public's emotions or to the logic of expediency. Senator Johnson of Kentucky defended Jackson, saying,

> Considering the treacherous enemy he had to cope with, and the object of his measure, which was to give security to the frontier, and to save the wasteful expenditure of the blood, and even of the treasure of the nation; when I think on this. . . . I do not censure Gen. Jackson; but, as before my God, I give him my thanks. . . . Do you think you will ever stand in need of the arm of such a man again?— a man, sir, little understood—violent perhaps, in his enmities, and equally ardent in his friendships—but who, as an officer, is vested with all the energies of a Caesar, or a Napoleon—who meets with equal courage and conduct the Indians.[39]

Senator Tallmadge of New York challenged Jackson's foes to "go, count the bleeding scalps of your murdered countrymen, of all ages and sexes, found by Gen. Jackson—and then return, and tell to this house if this Seminole War was, on the part of our country, an offensive war."[40]

The arguments were good on both sides. In the end, Jackson's popularity made him invulnerable. As Senator Alexander Smith of Virginia remarked, "His name will descend to future times in a stream of light. Such is the man whom it is proposed to dishonor. . . . Let me assure you, sir, that the American people will not be pleased to see their great defender, their great avenger, sacrificed." The American people were creating their own Napoleon but refused to see it. For most members of Congress, it would have been political suicide to censure Jackson. The resolutions of condemnation failed. The representatives of the American people could not condemn Andrew Jackson, because Andrew Jackson had done exactly what the American people had wanted him to do.[41]

Jackson's exploits provided an example that did not go unnoticed by his fellow officers, both in and out of the army. In 1824, Commodore David Porter of the navy attacked and captured the Spanish fort at Foxardo in Puerto Rico. His justification for this attack on a friendly power was that the townspeople were aiding and abetting pirates. In his subsequent court-martial, Porter's primary defensive argument was that he had done precisely what Jackson had done in the First Seminole War. Porter equated pirates with Seminole war parties and the Spanish fort at Foxardo with St. Marks and Pensacola. If Jackson had received the backing of the administration and Congress, why shouldn't Porter? His fellow officers sitting in judgment did not agree. Not having to face reelection, they could afford to be more principled than Congress. Porter was punished and soon left the service.[42]

It is somewhat satisfying to find that Jackson did not get off scot-free. By the time 1819 ended, the nation had slipped into a deep financial crisis. Secretary of War Calhoun and Secretary of the Treasury William Crawford, both of whom were politically ambitious and antagonistic to Jackson, considered the poor economy a good reason to downsize the army. In 1821, cutbacks called for the elimination of one of the two major generals in the army. Andrew Jackson, having less seniority than Jacob Brown, who commanded the Northern Division, was forced into retirement.[43]

As we study the Seminole Wars, we are struck by how important Andrew Jackson is to the story. If General Gaines had been left in charge, history would have been considerably different. Although an able and courageous officer, Gaines did not possess the audacity and support that Andrew Jackson enjoyed. Gaines would not have had as large and loyal a force to command and would not have been able to destroy the Seminoles as completely as Jackson did. Before long, the Seminoles would likely have recovered. Jackson's victory was much more telling. Before the war, the Seminoles had been prosperous and relatively secure. The First Seminole War left the Indians destitute and homeless. Jackson dealt them a blow from which they were never able to recover.

More important, Jackson's capture of West Florida altered the history of the peninsula. Gaines, ordered not to molest the Spanish forts, would have obeyed those orders. Jackson openly disregarded them, unconcerned for the consequences. He felt that it was in the best interests of the nation that Florida be taken from Spain, and he did it. He felt that if he had defeated the British at New Orleans, he could defeat the Spanish anywhere. The Spaniards began to realize that he was probably right. Negotiations for the sale of Florida soon began in earnest.

What is most bothersome about the First Seminole War is the arrogance of the American government and its officers, especially Andrew Jackson. Dealing from a position of vastly superior strength, there was little need to pursue the Seminoles as far south as the Suwannee River. The executions of Arbuthnot and Ambrister seem excessive, the legality questionable. The forcible occupations of St. Marks and Pensacola appear as nothing more than pure aggression on the part of Jackson, with the unspoken approval of the administration in Washington. That the Spanish were unable to control the Indians seems obvious; that they were actually encouraging them against the Americans seems improbable today. To the American public of the time, it was easy and convenient to see Spanish complicity.

As in most conflicts, the price of victory was costly. True, the Seminoles were defeated, but they did not go away. The next war would prove much costlier to both sides. The conquest of Florida was only temporary; Pensacola and St. Marks were soon given back. One unnamed casualty of the war was the U.S. Constitution. Jackson's disregard for orders and for the authority of Congress to declare war proved that even with a system of checks and balances, a popular military leader could do as he wished and still maintain the support of the people. Finally, the arrogance of both sides cost many innocent lives. Neamathla's threats against the garrison at Fort Scott led to the destruction of Fowltown. General Gaines's destruction of Fowltown led to the Scott Massacre. Both leaders, anxious to protect their pride or eager for conflict, forgot that their primary responsibility was to keep the peace. Both men had failed.

4 Coming to Terms

▲▲▲ ▲▲▲ ▲▲▲ ▲▲▲ ▲

The return of Pensacola to the Spanish authorities allowed Secretary of State John Quincy Adams and Spanish minister Don Luis de Onís to get back to work on a treaty concerning Florida's future. The Spanish negotiator was dealing from a position of extraordinary weakness. There was very little he could ask for that the United States would be willing to give. If the price, in whatever form it took, was too high, the Americans would simply take the colony by force. In the end, Onís would have to settle for a deal that was primarily concerned with maintaining his nation's honor.

On February 22, 1819, Adams and Onís penned the treaty that would turn the two Floridas over to the United States. Contrary to popular belief, Spain was not paid $5 million for the colony. Instead, the United States agreed to assume payment for claims that American citizens held against Spain, up to but not exceeding $5 million. The major concession made by Adams was an acceptance that Texas was not part of the Louisiana Purchase.

Ratification of the treaty by the Senate was almost immediate. In contrast, the Spanish Cortes (legislature) was not so timely in their approval of the document. Having received no actual money for their colonies, the Spaniards probably felt they should get *some* sort of consideration. What they seemed to want most were assurances that the United States would not officially recognize the newly formed revolutionary governments of Latin America. Mollified by vague promises from the U.S. ambassador, the Cortes finally signed off in late October 1820. Because of the delay, a second ratification by the Senate was called for, which took place precisely two years after the treaty was originally signed.[1]

For what little it was worth, the Adams-Onís Treaty contained an article concerning the status of the inhabitants of the new Florida Territory. It guaranteed that those living in what had been Spanish Florida would become full citizens of the United States, enjoying all the rights and privileges of American citizenship. Some people felt this clause entitled the Seminoles and their black tribesmen the same status as white Americans. In reality, those groups were granted only those rights and privileges enjoyed by Indians and blacks in the rest of the union. In short, nonwhites had no rights.[2]

Among those interested in acquiring a piece of the new territory was one of the adjoining states. Alabama petitioned Congress to allow it to annex West Florida because several rivers that drained eastern Alabama flowed through the Panhandle. Among their arguments was one that was not very far-sighted: "The settlements of East and West Florida, separated from each other, (as they must always be,) by a long and narrow line of desert, or very thinly inhabited country, can scarcely ever be united." Many southerners agreed that Florida should be divided but were not in favor of giving part of it to Alabama. They preferred to see Florida enter the union as two slave states. Northerners were in obvious opposition to such a move.[3]

Now that the United States had possession of Florida, the problem of what to do with it arose. Andrew Jackson, appointed military governor in March 1821, seemed in no hurry to assume his post. Arriving in July, Jackson again found himself at odds with the Spaniards, but this time over legal matters having to do with the transfer of power. Although most of the assaults were verbal, Jackson did not hesitate to arrest the former Spanish governor when certain papers were not promptly turned over. By September, Old Hickory had tired of Pensacola and was ready to return to Tennessee. He formally resigned the office and headed home the following month.[4]

Those who envisioned a prosperous future for the new territory had little raw material with which to work. There were only two towns of any notable size and no roads of any great length. Except for the extreme north and the coastline, the territory was virtually unexplored. The climate, though pleasant in winter, was devastating in summer. From May to September, the elevated temperatures and high humidity drained a person's energy, while mosquitoes, flies, and sand fleas attacked incessantly. The land itself, mostly loose sand, was considered poor, and much of it was under water during the long rainy season.

Perhaps the biggest obstacle to settlement was the presence of the Seminole Nation. Whites were understandably hesitant to move into an area where potentially hostile natives were dwelling. The Indians may have been defeated during the First Seminole War, but they had not disappeared and generally held no love for the white Americans. In a territory where good farmland was scarce, the Seminoles occupied some of the best available and would not willingly move from it. Trouble was inevitable.

Even before Jackson took office, the government saw the need to open a line of communication with the Seminoles. On March 31, 1821, Jean Penieres was appointed as sub-agent to the Seminoles, though his qualifications for the position were questionable. A Frenchman, he had little command of the English language. Although he claimed to have spent two years living among the Indians of Arkansas, others in Florida were not impressed. Capt. John R. Bell, the provisional secretary of East Florida, complained to Secretary of War Calhoun that "the Sub Agent is useless, and so would any foreigner be who is totally unacquainted with the Indian Character and the liberal policy of our Government towards them."[5]

Penieres was not the only government official whose responsibility it was to deal with the Indians. As governor, Jackson was also superintendent of Indian affairs. Much of the work of dealing with the Indians fell to Captain Bell, who seemed willing to take up the task. On September 28, Bell was officially appointed temporary agent. During the first year of American ownership of Florida, the necessary officials were slow to gather at their posts and even slower to act upon their duties. Congress, who would have to appropriate the funds and confirm any appointments, had adjourned just as the territory was acquired and would not reconvene until December. In the meantime, the Departments of War and State administered the territory as best they could.[6]

For the Seminoles, the suspense was almost unbearable. They knew well enough that white settlers would soon be pouring into the peninsula and that troubles would inevitably follow. They also knew that some sort of line would be drawn between "Indian Territory" and land that would be opened up for white settlement. Their major concern was where those boundaries would be. Why plant the year's crops if you were going to be forced to move before they could be harvested? Curious as to their status, the Seminoles attempted to open communications through a pair of friendly whites. Jackson ordered the men arrested.[7]

As far as Andrew Jackson was concerned, the solution to any "Indian problem" was simple: ship them out of the territory. In his opinion, most of the natives in Florida were Upper Creeks who had fled to the Spanish colony following the Creek War of 1814 and should be repatriated. As for real natives, they seemed so few in number that moving them to some land in the West would be a simple task.[8]

By late 1821, the necessary elements for negotiations seemed to be in place. In September, Jackson met with Neamathla and two other chiefs and informed Secretary of War Calhoun that the Indians were pleased to know that land would be set aside for them and that they would be under the protection of the federal government. Further talks were scheduled for November but never took place. Within a matter of weeks, the white organization fell apart. Jackson resigned his governorship, Bell was court-martialed, and Penieres died of yellow fever. The Seminoles may have wanted to talk, but there was no one with whom to talk.[9]

For all parties, events moved slowly. Peter Pelham was appointed to replace the deceased Penieres in October, but as sub-agent, he lacked any real authority. Jackson left the territory in the fall of 1821, but his successor, William P. DuVal, was not appointed until April 1822. The following month, Gad Humphreys was appointed as the new Indian agent, replacing the suspended Bell. Despite the frustrations, the Seminoles remained peaceful. Going on the warpath would have done them little good.[10]

Few white men knew how many Seminoles there were in Florida and where they were located. Captain Bell, still acting as agent in early 1822, sent a crude census to Congressman Thomas Metcalf of Kentucky. Bell estimated there were about 5,000 Indians in Florida, along with about 300 of their slaves. Of those 5,000, he believed around two-thirds of them were refugees from the Creek war and held no claim to land in Florida, while the remainder, mostly Mikasukis, could justly claim a large portion of the northern part of the territory. Seminole settlements were small but numerous and extended from the Panhandle, mostly around the Apalachicola River, eastward to the Suwannee, then southeast to the rich Alachua Prairie, near present-day Gainesville, and south to the north of Tampa Bay.[11]

For those who assume that a smaller public administration is more efficient, a perusal of letters crawling between Florida and Washington would soon dispel such a notion. It was a time when the nation was run by men who felt that the government that ruled the least ruled the best.

Unfortunately, this policy of minimal government resulted in a Florida where no one seemed to know what was going on.

Much of this inefficiency could be blamed on poor communications. An exasperated Col. Abraham Eustis, temporarily in charge at St. Augustine, wrote to the secretary of war with a list of questions that asked for direction concerning the most basic aspects of his administrative duties. Secretary Calhoun penned his reply almost a month later. Getting word to and from Pensacola, where the governor resided, could take twice as long. At a time when most all mail traveled to and from Florida by sailing vessel, the time of transit could be affected by any number of variables. Wind, weather, ports of call, and the simple availability of a suitable vessel going in the right direction all added to the delay. Shipwrecks, not at all uncommon along Florida's treacherous coast, also contributed to the problem.[12]

There were other problems that made getting things done difficult. Sickness, especially in the summer, would often bring things to a standstill. A yellow fever epidemic that struck Pensacola in 1822 was particularly brutal; the two men who had been appointed commissioners to settle land disputes were forced to write Secretary of State Adams to apologize for not having gotten anything done: "Such has been the fury and fatality with which it raged, that very few Americans who were attacked, have survived. Out of a population of about 1,500 or 2,000, between 200 or 300 have fallen victims. . . . The population was flying in every direction. . . . Such was the general alarm and distress, that business of almost every description was suspended." Acting Governor Walton reported that "every one who could leave the city, fled from the pestilence . . . [and] many were obliged to live in huts and tents through the woods. . . . I was one of the last Americans to make my escape."[13]

The commissioners' and Walton's situations pointed to another difficulty: every little problem seemed to require an "act of Congress" to fix. Today, Americans use the term as a joke. In the early days of the Republic, it was no laughing matter. Ever fearful of tyranny, the American people, through their elected representatives, kept the power of the federal government as limited as possible. In order to continue their work past the deadline imposed by Congress, the commissioners would need approval from that body. Congress, of course, was not in session, nor would they be for another two months. A newly appointed judge, upon discovering that he could not be sworn in for another six months, wrote to Secretary of State Adams, requesting an Act of Congress to allow some other official besides the absent governor to swear him in.[14]

This remoteness from Washington seems to have brought out some of the best characteristics in the people working in Florida. Very often, officials would make large expenditures out of their own pockets or from funds that had been appropriated for other purposes, frequently with no assurance of repayment. If people were suffering or if a certain commodity was needed immediately, a responsible official often found it difficult to follow directions to the letter. It is heartening to note that, generally, officials in Washington were very understanding of the situation. On the other side of the coin, letters often contain numerous references to vouchers and receipts.[15]

These were problems that were not peculiar to Florida. Communications were slow throughout the nation, even along the populous East Coast. Along the far-flung frontier, word often moved at less than a snail's pace. The fear of a large government bureaucracy was a national fear, not a local one. The fledgling United States was still trying its wings; a clumsy flight was guaranteed. The people knew and accepted this. They were building a new nation and the blueprints were rather vague. What is inspiring is the spirit in which they tackled the project. A certain sense of adventure pervades the writing of the time. For most Americans, it was an exciting time to be alive.

Unavoidable delays and confusion were understandable, but other problems were not so easy to accept. One of the most aggravating problems concerned the absence of officials. Appointments often had to wait on the required act of Congress or the return of some higher official. Because the population of the territory was so small and included so many foreign nationals, many of the appointees came from elsewhere in the union. Due to cutbacks in the military, a number of positions were filled by former officers who had recently been thrown out of work. Although Americans had rid themselves of the monarchy, society still had a fascination with titles. Thus, many of these men, though no longer in the army, were referred to by their former rank.

The problem of having to recruit officials from outside the territory led to several inconveniences. The first problem was getting the man to his station. Arranging passage from New York to Pensacola could be an ordeal unto itself, and could include several unplanned stays in ports along the way. Because the man might not be returning home for quite some time, affairs at home would have to be well attended to, and good-byes to loved ones could be difficult. In East Florida, for example, the acting governor did not arrive until four months after the territory had been acquired, and the first judge did not show up until sometime later.[16]

Once an office holder made it to Florida, keeping him there was another problem. If someone took sick, which was not uncommon during the summer "sickly" season, the cure often involved spending considerable time in a more "healthy" climate. Personal problems might also call a man away from his duties in Florida. At the height of the yellow fever epidemic in the fall of 1822, Governor DuVal announced that he had to return to Kentucky to attend to personal business. He did not return until after the first of the year, and then only after being ordered back to work by the president.[17]

One of the other problems that plagued Floridians was the geographical and political separation within the territory. Since 1763, Florida had been divided into two colonies, first by the English and then by the Spanish. Although the United States called its newly acquired domain the Florida Territory, the land was still commonly referred to in the plural as the Floridas. Because of the vast wilderness between St. Augustine and Pensacola, people living near one center felt little kinship to those living in the other. The only common officials were the governor and a few aides, who spent most of their time in Pensacola and rarely visited St. Augustine. In the governor's absence, each half of the territory was ruled by a secretary, who then became the acting governor for his half of Florida. This division did not quickly fade, even after the establishment of a central capitol in Tallahassee. Until the admittance of Florida into the union in 1845, there was still a strong faction calling for two separate Floridas.

While government inefficiency affected everyone in Florida, the Seminoles seem to have been particularly neglected. They knew changes were coming but had no idea what they were. Worse still, the white officials who were supposed to know what was going on were either absent or uninformed. Seminole frustration and anxiety were high, but the Indian leaders kept control of their tempers.

Almost from the day the American flag was raised over Florida, officials in St. Augustine and Pensacola wrote to Washington expressing their concerns about the Seminole situation. Some of these letters expressed fear, while others showed a remarkable level of compassion. A

FIGURE 5.
Governor William
Pope DuVal.
By permission of the
Florida State Archives.
Image #N027085,
DBCN#AAB-7970.

letter from Captain Bell in August 1821 exemplifies the fears: "If something is not soon done to satisfy in some measure the apprehension of
those Indians, and to prevent the incursion of ill disposed whites and
Indian bands into their country we may expect difficulty with them. At
this time, almost any reasonable arrangement could be made on the part
of the Government, but if delay'd wars of extermination will take place."[18]

Just meeting with the Seminoles was proving to be an insurmount-
able problem. After the canceled "talk" of November 1821, little effort was
made to meet with any large body of Indians. By the summer of 1822,
Governor DuVal had realized he had a major problem on his hands. In a
June letter to Secretary Calhoun, DuVal noted that the "Indians . . . are
very uneasy . . . [and] are wandering over the Country in every direction.
They are in a wretched State, many of them have lost their Crops this
Season by the overflowing of the Rivers & Creeks. . . . I am confident they
are in a starving condition." DuVal also expressed a certain amount of
frustration at the lack of direction from Washington: "They are not ap-
prised who is their agent. . . . As I am not advised of my powers & duties

as superintendent of Indian affairs, I should be thankful to receive from you such Instructions as you deem necessary."[19]

On the other side of the territory, Colonel Eustis agreed to take over the duties of Sub-Agent Peter Pelham, who was forced to leave Florida for health reasons. In a letter to the War Department, Eustis said that Pelham "informs me that he has never received one line of instructions for his guidance either from your Department, or from Mr. Worthington the late acting Superintendent of Indian Affairs." Most of Eustis's problems had to do with trade. "There is not at this time a single *licensed* trader in East Florida, & in consequence, many of the Indians are compelled to bring their skins . . . to this place; & here they are abundantly supplied with spirituous liquor," he wrote. He also mentioned an unlicensed trader whose "whole stock in trade consists of Tobacco & Rum."[20]

It was the Indians who finally forced DuVal into scheduling talks. On the twenty-fifth of July, 1822, John Blunt and Tuskihadjo, two respected chiefs from the Apalachicola region, came knocking at the governor's door in Pensacola. Through their interpreter, Stephen Richards, they expressed their frustrations. As DuVal related it to Secretary Calhoun, "The Indians were becoming restless, with the uncertainty of their Situation." They stated that former governor Jackson had promised them that the Indian territory would be marked out in a few months but that almost a year had passed "and yet nothing has been done." They were well aware that things were getting dangerous. Already, two whites had been murdered near the Suwannee. The Indians simply wanted to know "when their Father the President would determine where they were to live."[21]

DuVal took time to think, finally giving the chiefs a "talk" on July 28. There was little he could do but apologize: "I am sorry your Great Father has not yet directed me where you are to live." His excuse was simple and honest: the people in Washington were too busy. "Our chiefs at Washington are few, that do all the business of the Great American nation . . . but be patient, all that is right, will be done for you in good time," he declared. He then lectured them on keeping the peace and demanded the surrender of the men who had murdered the two whites on the Suwannee. He set up a future meeting at St. Marks for the twentieth of November, the same date as the canceled talks of the previous year. There and then, hopefully, a treaty could be concluded, and the Seminoles would know what the future held in store for them. He next brought up a matter that would continually creep into negotiations with the Seminoles: if the

Indians would bring in all the runaway slaves living among them, "I will see that you shall be paid for your time and trouble."[22]

Surely, DuVal thought, three months would be plenty of time for the government to decide what it wanted to do. At first, it seemed as if all was going according to plan. On August 19, Calhoun approved of DuVal's plan to hold talks at St. Marks and sent a large packet of documents to aid the governor. DuVal, however, seemed to be having second thoughts. His first concern was where to settle the Indians. Although DuVal seems to have been genuinely interested in the Indians' welfare, he did not forget that the prosperity of *white* Floridians was his primary responsibility. After some investigation, he seems to have come to the realization that the lands presently occupied by the Seminoles were also the only good lands in the territory. As he told Calhoun, "It will be a serious misfortune to this Territory if the Indians are permitted to occupy this tract of Country." The United States owed more than $4 million on the peninsula, and the only way to come up with those funds was to sell the land to settlers and speculators. Giving the Indians the best part of Florida was out of the question.[23]

Like Andrew Jackson, DuVal believed the Seminoles rightfully belonged with the Creeks, but he knew of the opposition to such a move by both the Indians and the people of Georgia and Alabama. He then suggested that the Seminoles be sent to some land west of the Mississippi. At any rate, DuVal told Calhoun, no treaty should be made until the land set aside for the Seminoles had been well explored and the matter brought before Congress, which would not reconvene until December. He then added that because of the yellow fever epidemic, holding extensive talks at St. Marks in November was not a good idea. He would still order the chiefs to assemble on November 20, but only, it seems, for the purpose of putting them off once more. DuVal then closed his letter with the announcement that he was going to Kentucky to take care of some unspecified personal business.[24]

With the absence of DuVal, authority in Florida devolved to the secretary of West Florida, George Walton, who became the acting governor. Unfortunately, in his haste to leave, DuVal had left no instructions with Walton as to how to deal with the Indians. One would think the two men, both residing in the little town of Pensacola, would have taken the time to confer. In reality, neither man was at the capitol. Because of the epidemic, both had fled the city. Walton listed his address as somewhere in the woods "near Pensacola," while DuVal had moved to the home of Don Emanuel Gonzalez, fifteen miles from town.[25]

Walton was becoming extremely anxious. As far as he knew, the talks with the Indians were still scheduled for November 20, and it seemed his job to conduct them. It was now that the inefficiencies of staffing in the territory became embarrassingly apparent. Not only was the governor off on extended personal leave, but the long-awaited Seminole agent, Gad Humphreys, had yet to arrive in the territory and his whereabouts were unknown. Humphreys had been appointed in early May 1822 but would not arrive in Florida until December 24, and then only after receiving a threatening letter from Secretary Calhoun. In addition, the sub-agent, Peter Pelham, was off on lengthy sick leave.[26]

If that was not bad enough, Walton was unsure as to exactly what authority an acting governor had when dealing with the Indians. He would gladly meet and treat with the Seminoles, but he had no idea what the government's position was and what was expected out of the treaty. With the talks only a little more than two weeks off, he wrote to Calhoun, but could have had no hope of receiving a reply in time for the talks. He also was embarrassed by the fact that he had no funds with which to purchase any of the required provisions or presents that would be handed out at such a meeting. In the end, he decided the only thing he could do was dispatch a messenger to St. Marks to inform the Indians of the predicament, apologize, and let them know when new talks would be scheduled. He was aware that the natives would be "greatly disappointed, and it is to be feared, much dissatisfied. How far it may have an effect in exciting a spirit of hostility or interfer [sic] with any future effort at negociation [sic], I cannot certainly anticipate."[27]

Even Walton's effort to send a messenger did not work out. The messenger, army paymaster Maj. Thomas Wright, was prepared to leave Pensacola on November 18, but a severe storm postponed his departure until the twenty-first, already a day late for the talks. The weather must certainly have been disagreeable, for his ship did not arrive at St. Marks until the twenty-seventh. Normally, a trip between Pensacola and St. Marks would take a day or two, not a week. Upon arriving, Wright learned that several important chiefs had shown up on the twentieth, waited three days, then left in disappointment. Wright sent word to the closest chiefs, asking them to come to the fort to hear his "talk." Several of the chiefs responded, among them Neamathla, head chief of the Mikasukis. The Indians listened patiently to the embarrassed Major Wright, then Neamathla "assured me, that he, his chiefs and warriors, would remain peaceable and contented, until an authorized agent should arrive, for the purpose of establishing a definite and durable understanding between them and the government." Walton and Wright had done the best they could with what few resources they had. It was now up to the government to set things straight.[28]

As 1823 began, matters were moving, but at an extremely slow pace. Florida had now been a territory for two years, and the Seminole problem had yet to be faced, let alone solved. At length, the government decided to settle the Indians onto a reservation in the central portion of the territory. In April, James Gadsden and Bernardo Segui were appointed as commissioners to negotiate a treaty with the Seminoles. In June, Governor DuVal was added to the commission. Because Floridians of all races had entered the summer planting season, it was decided to postpone the meeting until later in the summer. By then, hopefully, many of the warriors who had gone off on long hunting trips would have returned to their homes.

The time chosen was early September 1823, while the place chosen was the landing at Moultrie Creek, a few miles south of St. Augustine. By the fifth of the month, most of the Indians had arrived. In the end, about 425 showed up for the talks. The logistics of gathering such a large body of Seminoles cannot be easily appreciated. The Florida Indians were not a unified tribe. Ever since the First Seminole War, the various bands had become more scattered and increasingly nomadic.

Before meeting with the whites, the Seminoles held a conference of their own. At this meeting, Neamathla was chosen as the primary Indian representative. The natives were well aware of the fact that they were not bargaining from a position of strength, yet they must have sensed that they were not totally powerless. Their most important strength was whites' fear of Indian attack. Very often a simple rumor of Indian hostilities was enough to clear the countryside of settlers.

From the Seminole point of view, nearly the entire peninsula still belonged to them. Unlike their neighbors to the north, the Florida Indians had never made large cessions of land to the whites. Indeed, the only territory they had given up was near St. Augustine, between the coast and the St John's River. That parcel had been handed over to the English in the 1760s. As far as the Seminoles (and sympathetic whites) were concerned, almost all of Florida still belonged to the Indians.

On the sixth of September, the negotiations got under way with much pomp and circumstance. Every chief needed to show off his importance to his followers and the other chiefs. Governor DuVal was present but did not feel well. Of the two other commissioners, James Gadsden did most of the negotiating. Although he spoke kindly, the strength of the American position was not well concealed: "The hatchet is buried; the muskets, the white man's arms, are stacked in peace. Do you wish them to remain so?"[29]

The Indians could argue the fine points, but the major thrust of the talks was not really open for discussion. The Indians were told that they must concentrate within a reservation in central Florida and surrender all claim to the remainder of the territory. They knew they were at the mercy of the United States, and were not too proud to ask for it. As Neamathla put it, "We are poor and needy; we do not come here to murmur or complain . . . we rely on your justice and humanity." Whether Neamathla was truly humble or simply putting on a performance is not clear. The old chief obviously had some clout. Attached to the final treaty was a second document, which allowed Neamathla and five other chiefs to remain on the Apalachicola instead of having to move south. Whether he simply drove a hard bargain or was bribed is difficult to ascertain.[30]

In the first article of the treaty, the Indians put themselves under the protection of the United States government and relinquished all claims to the lands in Florida, with the exception of the reservation they were about to be forced onto, which totaled some 4 million acres. The northern boundary ran just north of present-day Ocala, while the southern boundary fell even with the lower limits of Tampa Bay. Because the government feared the Seminoles would be influenced by contact with traders or agents from Cuba and the Bahamas, the eastern and western boundaries never came closer to the coast than twenty miles.

Succeeding articles spelled out what the government was going to do for the Indians. The United States agreed to take the Indians under its protection, provided the Seminoles remained peaceable and law abiding. In exchange the government promised to distribute farm implements, provide cattle and hogs, pay the tribe an annuity of $5,000 a year for twenty years, prevent white settlement and other intrusions into the reservation, compensate the Indians for losses and travel, and distribute rations for one year. There was also a provision for an Indian agent. Once under federal "protection," the government felt obligated to appoint someone to watch out for the Indian's interests. These articles also pro-

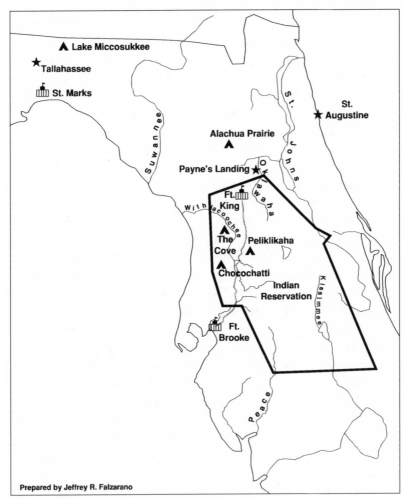

MAP 3. Seminole treaty lands, 1823.

vided for an interpreter, a school, and the services of a blacksmith, all for twenty years.

Besides remaining peaceable and law abiding, there were other obligations to which the Seminoles had to agree. They had to allow roads to be built through their reservation. Article Seven touched on the matter that was most important to many southerners. In it, the Seminoles agreed to apprehend any runaway slaves or other fugitives from justice, and provision was made to compensate the Indians for their trouble.

Was it a fair treaty? No, the difference in power between the two groups was too great. On paper, at least, the United States was about as generous as conditions and political pressures would allow. The Indians were given a large tract of land that, if needed, could be expanded. They were, to some extent, compensated for their losses, and provision was made to help them get started in their new homes. True, the Indians had given up claim to all of Florida, but what chance did they have of holding it? White expansion was unstoppable, and all parties knew it. By granting the Seminoles a well defined reservation and somehow keeping them separated from the whites, the negotiators hoped peace could be maintained until a permanent solution could be found. It was a hopeless cause, but the effort had to be made.

There were few alternatives. The most popular suggestion among whites was to ship the Seminoles west. The Seminoles were violently opposed to such an idea, and when the government eventually attempted a forced removal, a bloody war ensued. A proposal had been made to give each Indian family a tract of land and make them American citizens. Although it was a farsighted and humane suggestion, it was never seriously considered. Most whites of the time were not of a mind to treat the Indians as equals, while the Indians were not ready to abandon their culture. Reuniting the Seminoles with the Creeks had also been suggested but was politically unrealistic and was opposed by the Seminoles. Just leaving things as they were was also out of the question. Both sides knew that the only way to avoid bloodshed was to come to some sort of understanding as to who would live where. The best we can say is that the government tried to solve an unsolvable problem. The eventual failure to meet any of the treaty's goals shows how impossible the task was.

From a modern perspective, it is interesting to note the lack of national unity shown in the wording of the treaty. In it, the term "United States" is plural. "The United States *promise*" (not *promises*); "the United States . . . agree"; "the United States . . . stipulate." America was not one nation but twenty-four individual states acting as one. The Seminoles were even less unified. In fact, the term is not used in the treaty. Instead, they are referred to as the "Florida tribes of Indians." At that point (1823), the term was probably accurate. It took white pressure and warfare to bring the many disparate groups of Indians together.

The treaty of Moultrie Creek was forced upon the Seminoles because it was believed that large waves of settlers would soon be moving into the territory. A driving force that fueled much of American policy in the nineteenth century was *expansionism*. It was a new sort of nationalism, a strange mix of religious fervor, speculative greed, and racism. Were it not for the tragedy of the American Indian, the tale of the growth of the American nation would seem magical indeed. The Seminole Wars stand out because of the remarkable tenacity the Seminoles displayed in resisting this unstoppable force.

Many of us associate speculative greed with the stock market, and rightly so. Yet before the emergence of our industrial society, the primary road to wealth lay in the purchase and sale of large parcels of land. Peter Wraxall had written in 1754, "This hunger after Land seems very early to have taken rise in this Province, & is become now a kind of Epidemical madness, every Body eager to accumulate vast Tracts without having an intention or taking measures to settle or improve it."[31]

In order for God's "chosen" people to advance their civilization, it was seen as necessary for Americans to expand into the wilderness. Civilization required shops, churches, and schools, all of which required development and planning. The future great cities of America needed to be located in the most advantageous locations. If a particular location was especially well suited to agriculture or commerce, then people would surely settle there. They would, of course, pay good money for the best land. It soon became obvious that those who acquired the best parcels would stand to profit the most. The quest for honest profit often led to dishonest greed.

Postrevolutionary land speculation was seen by many as a means to get rich quick. Others saw the dangers. Theodore Dwight remarked, "On the ocean of speculation great multitudes of sober and industrious people launched the earnings of their whole lives, and multitudes became indebted for large sums which they never possessed." The duc de la Rochefoucauld described the effects of the "mania" in his *Travels*: "Every class of men, even watch makers, hairdressers, and mechanics of all descriptions, eagerly ran after this deception."[32]

By the nineteenth century, land speculation had become a national obsession. In the May 9, 1836 issue of *Niles' Register,* the headlines announced, "Speculation. Speculation. Speculation. We offer a selection of articles as to what is going on in the way of speculation. Verily, the people are mad." The speculative fever raged throughout the early 1830s, caused by the ability to buy on credit. The sale of public lands reached its highest point in 1836. That year, the receipts from public-land sales were $25,167,833, compared with $1,216,090 in 1830.[33]

Interest in Florida land was intense. A writer in the *National Intelligencer* could easily imagine the rosy portrayals that developers would use to lure their customers: "If the land be low and wet, it will suit for the culture of rice; if dry, it will be good for cotton; if marshy, excellent for manure; if a river be near, appropriate for trade; if the river be remote, secured from freshes; if woody, full of ship-timber; if pine barren, just the spot for health; . . . if near Augustine, how secure from invasion; if near Pensacola, how accessible to commerce; if inhabited, what an inducement to settle on it; if uninhabited, what a site for a colony."[34]

This is not to say that all speculators were greedy, evil men. Most were not. Although people today look upon many of their practices as illegal or immoral, such was not the case in the early nineteenth century. Making a fair though substantial profit was, and still is, seen as nothing more than the sign of a good businessman. It was only when unfair methods were employed that speculators were seen in an unfavorable light. Unfortunately, the wide open policies of the Jacksonian era gave speculators ample opportunity to cross over the line.

It is hard to say exactly what the Seminoles thought of the Treaty of Moultrie Creek. Being illiterate, the spoken word obviously meant more to them than the indecipherable black marks on the treaty. To them, what was *said* at the negotiations would have carried more weight. Even if they had a copy of the treaty in their possession, it would have taken a white man to read it. On the other hand, white society has no higher standard than to put something in writing. It was another cultural difference that could not easily be bridged.

Did an Indian truly believe that by putting an *X* on a piece of paper he was irrevocably signing away his home and his independence? Many Indians may not have understood the *finality* of a treaty. A chief might, in all sincerity, give his word concerning a certain subject but modify that promise at a later date, as circumstances changed and new knowledge became available. Did the collected chiefs actually understand that once they put their mark on that treaty, all further discussion on the matter was over?

The negotiations had taken place and the treaty had been signed. All parties went home, some satisfied, others not. Some people hoped for the best, others expected the worst. All probably felt they had done their best to resolve an impossible situation. Only time would tell if peace had been achieved or bloodshed would result.

5 Disagreement and Defiance

▲▲▲ ▲▲▲ ▲▲▲ ▲▲▲ ▲

The Treaty of Moultrie Creek had been signed, but the Indians did not simply pack up and move. The Seminoles occupied some of the finest land in the territory, had cleared large tracts, and had built homes. What incentive was there for them to give up what they had acquired and move to a new location where they would have to start all over again? For most Americans, migration meant moving to a *better* place. For the Indians, it usually meant going to a worse one.

For the most part, officials in Florida were doing their best to put the treaty into effect. Commissioner James Gadsden, the primary author of the document, had been ordered to remain in St. Augustine to see that it was properly carried out. In several letters to Secretary of War Calhoun, Gadsden repeatedly asked for the stationing of troops in Tampa Bay and for the occasional visit of naval vessels, all for the purpose of convincing the Seminoles that the United States meant business. In November 1823, Calhoun advised Gadsden that his wishes had been granted. Four companies of infantry under Col. George M. Brooke arrived in January 1824 and established Fort Brooke at a location chosen by Gadsden. Today the site is a parking garage in downtown Tampa.[1]

Showing sympathy for the Seminoles' impoverished condition, Gadsden requested that the reservation boundary be extended several miles northward. Gadsden recognized that the Indians were herdsmen, not intensive farmers, and that the lands he was recommending for inclusion were well suited to that purpose. He also pointed out that such an action would please several of the chiefs who were not happy with the treaty. Colonel Brooke, realizing the delicacy of his own position, informed the commanding general of the army that the Indians "will be treated with Kindness and respect but at the same time with determination and firmness."[2]

Despite their best efforts, things did not go well. In April 1824, Colonel Brooke reported, "The Indians appear to me, to be more & more displeased at the Treaty . . . and I am not unapprehensive of some difficulty. They have an idea that the nation is about to go to war with Great Britain, and was it to be the case, they would most certainly join our enemy." By June, Gadsden could also see trouble coming. The treaty was proving unworkable because it was one that had been forced upon the Indians; the terms had been dictated by politics, not by the realities of the situation. Gadsden pointed out that the Indians still held out hope for a renegotiation of the treaty, and he blamed "the unlicensed conversations of designing men" for giving them that hope.[3]

At first, Governor DuVal seemed somewhat optimistic that the Seminoles would follow through on their promises, but as time passed his mood changed. By April he had come to the realization that it was already too late to begin the migration, due to the fact that crops had been planted and hunting parties had gone off for the summer. Still, if the refugee Red Sticks would return to Creek lands (as some seemed inclined to do), and if Neamathla would be paid the $500 owed him, the migration might take place. On the other hand, some Indians were busy clearing land and building homes as if they had no intention of leaving. Weeks went by and the Indians were still unaware of where and when they were supposed to move. To make matters worse, white squatters, knowing the Indian land was soon to be vacated, began to set up housekeeping on parcels still being used by Seminole families.[4]

By July 1824, it appeared as if open conflict might break out. According to DuVal, the Indians had become "very insolent and made many threats . . . [and] had in some instances killed our cattle and hogs—they also had gone . . . to several of our settlers and ordered them off." Acting quickly, DuVal ordered the local volunteer militia into service. He then paid a visit to the chiefs from the Apalachicola region, who were inclined to be more agreeable to DuVal's authority. Caught off guard by the sudden movements, the dissatisfied Tallahassee and Mikasuki chiefs began to fall into line. Striking while the iron was hot, DuVal traveled to Neamathla's village accompanied by no one but an interpreter. There he found about 300 angry warriors. After giving them a stern "talk," DuVal ordered them to meet him at St. Marks on the twenty-sixth of July.[5]

Six hundred warriors gathered at the appointed time. The resolve of Governor DuVal must have astonished many of the Seminoles. After delivering "a talk that made considerable impression on them," DuVal appointed Tukose Emathla (John Hicks) leader of the tribes that would be heading south, a choice the warriors confirmed. DuVal also imposed a deadline of October 1, 1824, as the date when all Indians were to be on the new reservation. Neamathla, one of those who had obtained a private reservation and would remain behind, had begun to lose his influence.[6]

The October 1 deadline arrived and the Seminoles began to prepare to migrate. Getting them to actually do it was another matter. As an incentive, Governor DuVal began to pay them the compensation due for the improvements they were abandoning. He hoped the selling of their homes would make it abundantly clear that the time to leave had arrived. Being homeless also meant the Indians were going to be temporarily dependent upon the government for their sustenance. Knowing this, DuVal ordered that the promised rations be sent to Fort Brooke at Tampa Bay. If the Indians wanted to eat, they would have to go to Tampa to obtain their provisions. While the ploy produced the desired effect of luring the Indians to the south, it also created a problem: instead of setting up homes in the interior, the newcomers set up camp near the food depots.[7]

Incentives or not, the Seminoles were slow to get moving. In a letter to the secretary of war dated October 26, DuVal lamented that the "difficulty of reconciling the Indians to the late treaty; and to restrain them from outrage has not been inconsiderable, but to purswade [sic] and threaten them into a peaceable removal from this truly delightful country, required the exercise of uncommon patience, time, and prudence. I now believe confidently they will go without force, but evidently with reluctance."[8]

In anticipation of the growing number of Seminoles that would hopefully reside within the reservation, DuVal ordered Agent Gad Humphreys to select a permanent location for his agency. The establishment of a permanent agency would hopefully prevent unlicenced traders from selling rum and whiskey to the natives. Another sign that the Indians were in fact moving was the dismissal of the government interpreter, who refused to relocate to the new reservation. Humphreys, however, moved no faster than his charges, and did not select a site for his agency until September 1825.[9]

As could be expected, trouble slowly surfaced. Near St. Augustine, a group of warriors began to threaten certain plantation owners when three tribesmen came up missing. Jittery officials called out the militia, who gave chase to the Indians. Miscommunication added to the problem, and for a moment it looked as if hostilities might break out. Fortunately, the three missing warriors appeared and the volatile situation cooled.[10]

Being on the reservation and being happy there were two different things. A year after the migration began, a countermigration was reported by Acting Governor George Walton: "Those who formerly resided between the Rivers Suwannee & Appalachicola are on their return hither. They state to me as a reason . . . that they have always been furnished with a scanty supply of provisions only & which has sometime since ceased altogether; that they have no means of subsistence within themselves; that there is no game in their country; that it is moreover exceedingly unhealthy." Moving back, however, brought its own problems. As Walton pointed out, "This district . . . has been surveyed, in part sold, and is rapidly populating."[11]

In the meantime, changes had been taking place in Washington. John Quincy Adams had ascended to the presidency, replacing James Monroe, the last of the founding fathers. James Barbour was the new secretary of war, taking over from John Calhoun, who became Adams's vice president. A new part of Barbour's Department of War was the Office of Indian Affairs (later the Bureau of Indian Affairs). Thomas L. McKenney, head of the office, seemed unsure of what to do with the Seminoles. First he suggested feeding them forever, then extending both the northern and western boundaries of the reservation, then shipping them west, either as part of the Creek Nation or separate from it.[12]

By 1826, most of the Seminoles seem to have found their way onto the reservation. They were not, however, doing well. Resettlement is not a simple thing. For a new dwelling place to be prosperous, there needs to be planning, financial backing, and the place itself has to be chosen with some care. Above all, the residents of a new community have to possess hope, a feeling that they and their posterity will be able to prosper in this new home. For the Seminoles, few of those requirements were met.

For most of the Seminoles, the move had been disastrous. The government, to some extent, was sympathetic. In December 1825, Colonel Brooke wrote to the War Department expressing his concerns and asking for help: "The major part of the nation are, and have been, suffering for some time in extreme want. Some have died from *starvation*. . . . I can assure you they are in the most miserable situation; and unless the government assists them, many of them must starve." Brooke also pointed to a more practical reason for assistance: "others will depredate on the property of the whites, in the Alachua and St. John's settlement."[13]

In his letter, Brooke gave the reasons for the Indians' plight: "1st. The continued droughts, for two months, whilst their corn was tasseling. 2d. Those who removed within the new boundary line had to cultivate new lands, which would not produce the first year of planting; and 3d. Many did not come in till it was too late to plant."[14]

Colonel Brooke was not the only one trying to get help for the Seminoles. In January 1826, Governor DuVal pointed out that even the Indians who had been allowed to remain on reservations along the Apalachicola were not faring well. "Three times last year were their Corn fields and fences Swept by the uncommon rise of the river." Knowing that pleas on behalf of Indians often fell on deaf bureaucratic ears, DuVal hastened to point out that these were "good" Seminoles: "Until now they have never Solicited the aid of the Government for provisions. . . . These Chiefs and their warriors Served with Genl. Jackson during the Seminole war."[15]

Secretary of War Barbour handed these letters to President Adams with some of his own comments: "The correspondence with the department for some time past confirms the truth of Col. Brooke's statement." He also acknowledged the government's responsibility—"They are where they are by our seeking"—and had an eye to a possible permanent solution to the problem: "Being convinced that the country to which those Indians have emigrated is not suited . . . to their preservation, instructions were . . . forwarded to governor DuVal, to ascertain their dispositions in regard to a removal to lands west of the Mississippi."[16]

President Adams passed Barbour's recommendations on to Capitol Hill, where the required "act of Congress" was needed to fund the relief measures. Florida's delegate to Congress, Joseph M. White, had written a long letter to Secretary Barbour pushing for immediate removal. The whole matter proceeded to get caught up in the Indian removal debate, and by May, five months after Brooke's request for aid, the House and Senate were still arguing about feeding the starving Seminoles.[17]

Exactly why the Seminoles were starving was also up for debate. Colonel Gadsden, who had negotiated the treaty, took exception to the idea that the land allotted the Indians was not sufficient for their survival. He was willing to admit that the move had put them in a bad situation but felt that their continued poverty was one of their own making. Gadsden believed that the Indians had become too dependent on government rations. Whatever the cause of their distress, Gadsden pointed out that the Indians' plight might make them more agreeable to removal west of the Mississippi.[18]

In May 1826, a delegation of chiefs was taken to Washington. Among the party of seven were the three most powerful chiefs, Neamathla and John Hicks of the Panhandle tribes, and Micanopy of the Alachua bands. Most of the other large bands were also represented. Also present, serving as interpreter, was Abraham, the most influential of the black Seminoles. Unfortunately, Washington seems to have been unaware of their pending arrival. Seemingly miffed at the imposition, Indian Affairs head McKenney wrote a terse letter to DuVal, telling him the delegation should not have been sent. He then proceeded to deny all DuVal's requests for extra funding. Still, the chiefs were treated well and given their audience.[19]

Other than allowing both parties an opportunity to air their differences, the trip to Washington seems to have accomplished little. In a "talk" to the chiefs, the secretary of war was polite but blunt. The president would extend the reservation boundary, but only temporarily. The "Great Father" understood their present sufferings, was sending some help, but stressed that enough time had passed for them to get settled and to harvest their own crops; henceforth they were expected to take care of themselves. The Indians were also reminded that runaway slaves living among them were to be surrendered, while the agent would do what he could to reclaim slaves that had been stolen from the Indians. There was, of course, the stern admonition to keep the peace, and a strong suggestion to join the Creeks and move west.[20]

John Hicks, head chief of the Seminoles, gave a "talk" in reply. The chiefs seem not to have been impressed with what was told them, especially with the temporary extension of the reservation boundary. "This does not please us—The land we occupy, we expect will be considered our own property, to remain as such for ever," Hicks said. As to the matter of removal, the chiefs made themselves clear: "We have already said we do not intend to move again." As would happen again and again, the government refused to admit that the Seminoles would not allow themselves to be considered part of the Creek Nation. Hicks endeavored to put the matter straight: "We will not involve ourselves in the troubles of the Muscogees—We are a separate people and have nothing to do with them." He then pressed what he considered his rightful claim to the land. "We have heard that the Spaniards sold this Country to the Americans—This they had no right to do,—the land was not theirs, but belonged to the Seminoles."[21]

As to the matter of runaway slaves, the chiefs professed to be in agreement but did not consider themselves bound to turn over slaves who had escaped before the Treaty of Moultrie Creek was signed. They expressed happiness that Seminole slaves who were found in the possession of whites would supposedly be returned but doubted whether it would really happen: "We do not know if the white people will mind his [the agent's] talks when he demands our property, for they are not always willing to do right when they can avoid it—The laws of our nation are strong. . . . The laws of the whites, who have so much better sense than the red men, ought not to be less powerful and just." Finally, the Indians asked that the forever-promised school not be built. Literacy, they believed, was a white man's tool, and they wanted no part of it.[22]

For the most part, it seems the Seminole chiefs were trying to abide by the terms of the treaty, as were the white authorities. The biggest problem was with the people on both sides who could not be controlled. Among the Indians, the Mikasuki tribe seems to have been the major troublemaker. As Governor DuVal reported, "They are and have ever been the most violent and lawless Indians in all the South. They have set their own Chiefs at defiance. . . . The orderly Indians complain as much of them as the Whites." On the other side of the coin were lawless whites who preyed upon the Indians' defenseless position. Slaves, cattle, and other property stolen or falsely taken from an Indian would rarely be recovered, and crimes committed against an Indian person were almost never punished.[23]

As traumatic as the Seminoles' relocation may have been, they did seem to be adjusting to their new lives. In the last few years of the 1820s, serious white complaints about the Indians almost ceased. In the final weeks of 1826, an outlaw band murdered most of the Carr family near Tallahassee. Yet even while reporting the crime and calling out the militia, Governor DuVal had to admit that the main body of the Seminole Nation was not a party to the outrage. Indeed, it was General Gaines's old adversary, Neamathla, who finally brought the killers to justice.[24]

In response to the cries for protection that arose from the Carr murders, the army placed Col. Duncan L. Clinch in charge of all forces in Florida. After a tour of the territory with General Gaines, Clinch informed the War Department as to how he would deploy his men. One company would be stationed near Tallahassee, two would erect a new post near the Indian Agency (Fort King at Ocala), three would occupy Fort Brooke at Tampa Bay, one would be at St. Augustine, while the remaining three would stay at Pensacola. Within two months, Clinch was able to report that his men were in position, the Indians were on the reservation, and peace was being maintained.[25]

It was a fragile peace, but it managed to hold on for about five years. The Indians planted their crops and continued their hunts, usually managing to avoid unhappy contacts with the whites. For the most part, they stayed within the northern limits of the reservation, though they appeared to have wandered freely to the south of it. That, in itself, was no real problem; the few whites that lived south of Lake Okeechobee often made their living off the Indians. Seminoles caught in white territory were usually arrested and returned to their towns unmolested. Neither side liked the presence of the other, but neither side wanted to be the spark that would ignite hostilities.[26]

While the Seminoles could do nothing about the presence of the whites, the whites felt there was something that could be done about the presence of the Seminoles. Throughout these years of relative peace, the call for the removal of the Seminoles never died off. Sometimes the talk was serious, while at other times it was mostly wishful thinking. In February 1827, the secretary of war asked Delegate White to find out if the Indians were amenable to removal. Knowing that many Americans who were close to the Seminoles had a vested interest in keeping them in Florida, White sent special agents into the tribe to ascertain their true feelings. In June, White reported back: "I regret to say, there is a decided repugnance to it [removal], among all classes of the tribe, and I am satisfied that those who have written to the Department of War, suggesting their willingness to go, have consulted more their own wishes, that any correct knowledge, or information of the disposition of the Indians."

White then went on to list the reasons for this "decided repugnance": "1st—Their entire ignorance of the Country, to which it is proposed to remove them. 2nd—Their attachment to the land of their nativity, which operates more strongly on Savage than Civilized Communities. 3rd— Their fear of the Indian tribes in that quarter, and an apprehension that they would all be exterminated."

White added that although the reservation was large enough to support a population of whites equal to that of the Seminoles, with the Seminoles' "habits of life, and ignorance of the arts of husbandry and agricul-

FIGURE 6.
Brig. Gen. Duncan
Lamont Clinch.
Miniature in the
private collection
of the descendants
of General Clinch.
By permission of Duncan
Clinch Heyward.

ture, it is impossible that they can live within the present assigned limits." As happened with most Americans, he could not bring himself to believe that Indians could make good farmers, even though it was well known that they had once owned large herds of cattle and grown extensive crops. The delegate then hit upon a deeper problem: "It is exceedingly difficult to make them believe that any plan proposed by the Government is for their benefit. . . . They receive with great distrust any proposition . . . proceeding from our Government, and it will require something more than promises to convince them that the humane plan of colonization recommended . . . will be conducive to their improvement, and happiness."[27]

It was, perhaps, the most honest appraisal of the situation any official could have given. White seems to have sincerely felt that removing the Indians was in their best interests. He also knew it was in his constituents' best interests. Barely a month after penning the previous letter, White again wrote to Secretary Barbour, this time making a long and impassioned plea for removal. He may have known it was a waste of time, but it would certainly be well received when printed in the Tallahassee and St. Augustine papers. In the end, it was all a moot point. Unless Congress was willing to pay for removal, it would never happen.[28]

By 1828, the major point of contention between the Seminoles and their white neighbors centered around slaves. First, there was the continuing problem of runaways seeking refuge among the Seminoles. Bombarded by the conflicting claims of Seminoles and slave catchers as to the true ownership of several blacks, Delegate White requested the War Department provide some sort of system for settling the disputes. Knowing that Seminole slaves were a sore subject among the whites, Agent Humphreys asked permission to allow the Indians to sell their slaves through his agency. Permission was denied. Slaves were also on the mind of Governor DuVal. With each new plantation came a new batch of slaves. Between the threat of an Indian uprising and a slave insurrection, DuVal thought it a good idea that more troops be stationed in Florida.[29]

Unfortunately, the opposite was going to happen. In early 1828, Gen. Winfield Scott replaced Edmund Gaines as commander of the army's Western Department. Unlike Gaines, who was an old Indian fighter, Scott was an expert at the art of "civilized" European warfare. Finding Florida in a state of relative peace, Scott immediately decided Fort King was no longer needed and ordered the post closed. A letter of protest quickly came from Delegate White. Apparently, Scott did not realize that the troops at Fort King were there to keep the peace, not restore it.[30]

Slowly, the lack of troops at Fort King began to have its effect. This single company had been all that stood between Indian and white lands. Without the presence of the soldiers, both Indians and whites began to cross the line. By the end of 1829, the citizens of Alachua County were calling for the reopening of the post or the construction of another at the town of Micanopy. Colonel Clinch, still in charge in Florida, also called for the reoccupation of Fort King. Washington, however, would not supply the manpower.[31]

Another situation that was deteriorating was the Florida Indian Agency itself. In early November 1828, the secretary of war received a list of charges brought against Agent Gad Humphreys. These included dealing in slaves, preventing whites from obtaining runaways, and using government funds for personal business. A month later, the secretary recommended that President Adams remove the agent. A lame duck in the final months of his administration, Adams appointed Alexander Adair to go to Florida and investigate the charges.[32]

What Adair found was puzzling. None of the people who had made charges against Humphreys were willing to talk, yet supporters were hard to find. A memorial sent in defense of the agent seemed to support him only because the writers felt he could hasten the day when the Seminoles were removed. Humphrey's most critical opponent was Governor DuVal, who perhaps leveled the most dangerous charge: the agent had not supported Andrew Jackson for the presidency. Still, Humphreys managed to hang onto his job for more than a year longer.[33]

Whatever frictions may have existed, some white authorities were still intent on doing what they could for the Seminoles. In early 1830, the Office of Indian Affairs noticed that the $1,000 annually stipulated by the Treaty of Moultrie Creek for a school had never been spent. The reason had been simple: the Seminoles wanted no part of the white man's education and had refused the school. Still, the money had been appropriated and had to be used for the purpose designated. Director McKenney wrote to Governor DuVal, ordering him to send eight Seminole boys to a special school in Kentucky. Knowing there would be resistance to the idea from those living on the reservation, DuVal found his eight candidates from among the bands living along the Apalachicola River and promptly sent the boys on their way.[34]

Having done his duty, DuVal sent a bill for $1,000 to the War Department. One can only imagine his surprise when he received a letter informing him that the bill would not be paid because the treaty stipulated that the school must be on the reservation. We can easily understand the exasperation as DuVal politely informed his superiors that *they* had been the ones who told him to send the boys to Kentucky. Not willing to admit an error but needing a way out, the War Department informed DuVal that he must obtain permission from the chiefs to send their sons to a school off the reservation. The governor promptly did so, and the bill was paid.[35]

For the Seminoles, the presidential election of 1828 was an evil omen. Brought to power was their most hated enemy, Andrew Jackson. With a new administration came new people with whom the Seminoles would have to deal. John Eaton, a close friend of the president, became secretary of war. Other changes would also take place. In a matter totally unrelated to the election, Alexander Macomb replaced the deceased Jacob Brown as the commanding general of the army. Macomb was elevated past both Winfield Scott and Edmund Gaines, which only added to the bitter animosity between the army's top three officers. In early 1830, Agent Humphreys was finally removed from his position. Later in 1830, Thomas McKenney, head of the Office of Indian Affairs, was replaced by Samuel Hamilton.

The election of 1828 had been especially bitter, and had concluded the breakup of the party originally formed by Thomas Jefferson. Every president since Jefferson had been a Democratic Republican. The party had ascended by default; the old Federalists had simply died away. Still, the natural division between conservative and liberal had not died with it. An obvious split had become apparent in 1824, when the conservative Adams won the presidency by the narrowest of margins over the liberal Jackson. With the electoral vote tied, the winner was decided by the House of Representatives, where Speaker Henry Clay gave his support to Adams. By the time of the next election, there were clearly two competing camps: Jackson men and anti-Jackson men. There seemed to be no middle ground. Left out of normal Democratic circles, the anti-Jackson men became the conservative Whigs.

For Andrew Jackson, Indian removal was not a question, it was a certainty. The new president saw the Indians as an obstacle to national expansion and as a potential enemy to the American nation. As far as Jackson was concerned, the natives must be removed from the white man's path, voluntarily if possible, forcibly if needed. On May 28, 1830, the Indian Removal Act passed the House by a narrow margin of 101 to 97.[36]

Such a close vote might lead one to think that opposition to removal was widespread. Such was not the case. Even those who were deeply sympathetic to the Indians believed it was in their best interests to be separated from white expansion. Opposition came either to the cost of removal or to the methods it was feared would be employed. People in areas of the country that had no Indian problem were reluctant to pay for a bill that benefitted another section of the nation. Many people were also familiar with Jackson's methods and feared for the welfare of those who would be displaced.[37]

William Ellsworth of Connecticut argued against the cost of removal, then against the methods he feared would be used: "I have no belief that the bill will bring along with it the proposed and desirable effect; and while I am ready to go as far as any gentleman to assist in an honorable removal of the Indians, I cannot do it under circumstances which admonish me that this bill is but a part of a united effort virtually to expel the Indians from their ancient possessions. . . . I feel that power is arrayed against right; and that the voluntary, unbiased expression of the Indians, as to their removal, is not likely to be had."[38] In agreement, a Mr. Evans argued that the "uniform language of all the petitions was that the Indians might not be coerced and compelled to remove. . . . The only opposition is to a forced, constrained, [and] compulsory removal."[39]

It was an ambitious piece of legislation. It called for all Indian tribes east of the Mississippi to be relocated to new lands west of the great river. More specifically, the five major Indian nations of the Southeast (Seminole, Creek, Cherokee, Choctaw, and Chickasaw) were to occupy land in what is today the State of Oklahoma. At that time, the land was in the western portion of the territory of Arkansas. The two territories were not separated until Arkansas became a state in 1836, after which it was officially known as the Indian Territory.[40]

On paper, the law seemed somewhat fair and humane. Most everyone felt that as long as white men and Indians lived together, warfare was unavoidable. The only solution seemed to be separation. White expansion was unstoppable, and Indian resistance to white encroachment was often violent. If peace was to be maintained, *and the Indians were to survive,* the two groups would have to be separated. The United States possessed large amounts of land west of the Mississippi that, to most whites, seemed an ideal place for the natives to live. Why was it ideal? Because the government considered it unsuitable for the type of agriculture white farmers practiced.

Throughout the South and West, negotiators and commissioners spread out, making new treaties with each individual tribe. If the Indians were reluctant, pressures were brought to bear. Bribes were paid, threats were made. If the majority of a tribe was adamant in their refusal to sell their homelands, treaties were made with more agreeable chiefs. The Indian Removal Act had called for the "voluntary" acquisition of Indian lands; in theory, no Indian was to be forcibly evicted from his or her home. In reality, they all were.

The law made some provision for the loss and expenses of the emigrants, and provided funds for transport and the setting up of new homes. For those who felt the law was the most humane solution to the problem, disappointment was in store. Many of the Indians were not peacefully guided to their new lands but herded at bayonet point. This was the time of the infamous Trail of Tears. Whatever the intent of the lawmakers, many of those whose job it was to carry out those laws saw their mission as nothing more serious than herding cattle.

Each affected tribe resisted in its own way, though none met with any real success. The Creeks and Cherokees, being the most familiar with white customs, put up the strongest legal resistance, but it was a losing cause. Today, American Indians are also American citizens. In 1830, their exact legal status had yet to be defined. Pressures from the State of Georgia and the passage of the Indian Removal Act forced the Cherokees to appeal to the Supreme Court for aid. To the Cherokees' minds, their tribe was a sovereign nation and the laws of the federal or state governments did not apply to them. Realizing that neither Jackson nor the southern states would accept such a status, Chief Justice John Marshall attempted to find some sort of middle ground. In a ruling that would come to define the exact status of the Indian nations, Marshall determined that the Indians were *Domestic Dependent Nations* under the protection of the United States. This ruling, and another the following year, effectively put the welfare of the Indians in Jackson's hands. By law, it was the administration's responsibility to protect the native tribes from outside pressures, either by a foreign power or one of the states of the Union. Jackson's approach to protection was to move the Indians west, away from white pressure. Marshall had declared that the relationship between the United States and the Indians was like "that of a ward to his guardian." Jackson proved to be a stern and authoritative guardian.[41]

More than eight years had passed since the signing of the Treaty of Moultrie Creek, and the animosity between the Seminoles and white Americans in Florida continued to grow. For the most part, the Indians dwelt within the boundaries of their reservation, but if they saw a need, they felt little restraint to leaving it. Sadly, because of crop failures and a shortage of game, they had been feeling the need to leave the reservation more often. The Seminoles were starving, and the procurement of food took precedence over keeping out of the way of whites. All too often, the most available source of food turned out to be the cattle of white settlers. Because Florida was open, unfenced range land, cattle roamed freely throughout the territory. Very often, cattle theft involved less the premeditated *taking* of an animal but more the convenient *finding* of one. Due to the fact that cattle were just as likely to wander off the reservation as on to it, accusations of cattle theft were common on either side of the boundary.

After the dismissal of Gad Humphreys, the position passed to John Phagan, who had been sub-agent in charge of the Apalachicola bands. Whether he acted out of compassion for the Indians or simply under orders, Phagan was determined to see the Seminoles moved west. To bring about the removal, the War Department appointed James Gadsden, the driving force behind the Treaty of Moultrie Creek, to negotiate a new agreement that would send the Seminoles west. By late spring 1832, Gadsden had gotten word out to the Indians to gather for a parley. The meeting was held at Payne's Landing, on the banks of the Oklawaha River, northeast of present-day Ocala.

The circumstances of the negotiations were different from those held nine years earlier at Moultrie Creek. The first instance was a very public affair, being held near the most populous settlement in the territory, and with three white negotiators. Hundreds of Indians and white spectators had shown up to watch the proceedings. Minutes were kept, and a large number of Seminole chiefs signed the document.

In contrast, the negotiations at Payne's Landing seem to have been almost secret. Although accompanied by a few soldiers and an interpreter, Gadsden worked alone. Payne's Landing, though accessible to both parties and convenient to the Indians, was a remote location, far from a large number of curious eyes. No minutes of the meetings were submitted, nor were there any detailed accounts of what had been said by either party. When the eventual disputes arose, this lack of open publicity only served to widen the chasm of distrust.

The Seminoles had seen little reason to negotiate for removal. True, the whites were constantly pressuring the Seminoles, but not as intensely as to the north. As far as rumors had it, the promised land in Arkansas was no heaven. It was hot and dry in the summer, and snow might fall in winter. Life in Florida was relatively easy. The Seminoles, having recently been forced onto one new reservation, were in no mood to move to another. There were other factors that were unacceptable to the Seminoles that Gadsden did not seem to understand. First, there was the demand that the Seminoles would once again become part of the Creek Nation. Second, there was the matter of the black Seminoles. It became obvious that many of the blacks would lose their hard-won freedom in the move. Black pressure, as much as anything, helped convince the Seminoles to resist emigration.

The stipulations of the treaty were simple, yet provided ample opportunity for future disagreement and conflict. If the land in the West was found suitable, the Seminoles would agree to emigrate there. The land would be part of the Creek reservation, and the Seminoles would once again become part of the Creek Confederation. In exchange for their land, the government would pay the Seminoles $15,400. In addition, the Indians would receive one blanket and a homespun frock each, the annuities agreed upon at Moultrie Creek would be extended for ten years, and an additional annuity of $3,000 a year would be paid for fifteen years. The Seminole's cattle would be purchased by the government, or be replaced upon the Indians' arrival in Arkansas. Moving expenses would, of course, be paid by Washington.

Events did not move swiftly. In Washington, the Office of Indian Affairs was being reorganized, and it was not until July that three white commissioners were dispatched to inspect the proposed Seminole territory and meet with the Indian delegation that was to come from Florida. The Indian delegation, in no hurry to make any sort of move, did not leave Florida until October 10, 1832.[42]

In the meantime, Gadsden was busy with some other Seminoles, those bands that lived along the Apalachicola River. During the summer of 1832, Gadsden met with the four head chiefs, offering them a separate deal from the rest of the tribe. Two of the chiefs, John Blunt and Davy, were quick to accept the offer, while two others, Econchatemico and Mulatto King, were hesitant. All in all, it was not until the spring of 1834 that the Apalachicolas began to make their way west.[43]

Initially, matters appeared to be on track with the main body of Seminoles. The delegation of seven chiefs arrived in Arkansas in the middle of winter, accompanied by Agent Phagan and Abraham, the black Seminole interpreter. For several months the group toured the territory, inspecting the land and talking with the Creeks who resided there. On March 28, 1833, at Fort Gibson, Arkansas, the seven chiefs signed a paper stating that they were satisfied with the proposed territory and agreeable to the emigration of their people. Now, at least as far as the government was concerned, the Seminoles had irrevocably signed away all rights to remain in Florida.

Washington's optimism was shattered almost immediately upon the delegation's return to Florida. Most of the delegation either denied signing the agreement at Fort Gibson or insisted they had been forced to sign. More important, the delegation claimed that they did not have the power to make the decision to emigrate for the whole Seminole Nation. As far as the Indians were concerned, the delegation was to report back to a council of chiefs who would then decide the matter. The dispute seemed to center on the word "they" as used in the preamble of the Treaty of Payne's Landing. In the abbreviated version given here, we have italicized the troublesome pronoun: "The Seminole Indians . . . are willing that their confidential chiefs . . . should be sent . . . to examine the country . . . and should *they* be satisfied . . . the articles of the compact and agreement . . . shall be binding on the respective parties." Who does "they" refer to? Is it the Seminole Nation as a whole, or the chiefs? Each side read the sentence differently. To the Indians, the word "they" meant the Seminole Nation. To the government, "they" meant the delegation.[44]

The questions surrounding the treaty are endless, and will never be adequately answered. The relative secrecy of the talks, both at Payne's Landing and at Fort Gibson, did not help resolve matters. At Payne's Landing, we have no idea what threats or promises, either implied or direct, Gadsden voiced to the Seminoles. At Fort Gibson, we must remember that the delegation was virtually alone in a strange land and very much at the mercy of Agent Phagan. With no record of what was said at the negotiations, it was one nation's word against another's.

The problem runs deeper than just a dispute over the muddy meaning of one pronoun. During the proceedings the treaty was read and an interpreter translated those words into the Seminole tongues. The whole process left ample room for misunderstanding, both accidental and intentional. Although there were government interpreters, the Seminoles would have relied upon their own interpreters, Abraham and Cudjo. Both were illiterate blacks who spoke the dialect of the plantation. Both would have been unfamiliar with the formal language used in legal documents. What they heard and what they understood may have been completely different. How they related that understanding to their chiefs may have been something different again.

If the Seminoles were more obstinate about resettlement than the other Indian nations of the Southeast, it was because they had more to lose. For the Cherokees, Creeks, and the others, they were giving up land that they were soon to lose anyway. Settlers were surrounding them and closing in from all sides. It was only a matter of time until they were forced from their homelands. The Seminoles did not feel the same. Florida was virtually unpopulated, with vast amounts of land that seemed unsuitable for white occupation.

FIGURE 7.
Abraham. Slave,
interpreter, and
advisor to Chief
Micanopy.
By permission of the
Florida State Archives.
Image #RC08709,
DBCN#AAM-7836.

The Seminoles were also being asked to give up more than just land: They, with some right, feared the loss of fellow tribesman. More subtle but no less powerful than the demand for Indian land was the demand that blacks be returned to slavery. Many of those blacks were close friends and, through intermarriage, relations to the Indians. Seminoles of mixed blood had the potential of causing the greatest conflict. To the Indians, a person of mixed parentage was an "Indian," whether a portion of that blood was black or white. To a slaver, any amount of black blood made a person eligible for slavery. To the more unscrupulous slavers, even a full blooded Indian was fair game. Moving west would not alleviate the problem. Through their long association with southern whites, the Creeks had learned the fine art of using and dealing in slaves. The Seminoles rightly feared that once in the West their black tribesmen would somehow be taken from them.

The year 1834 brought several important personnel changes to Florida. Of greatest importance to the Seminoles was the appointment of Wiley Thompson as their new agent. John Phagan had been removed when it was discovered that he had altered several vouchers and pocketed the difference. Farther up the administrative ladder, Governor DuVal had, after almost a dozen exasperating years, finally retired from office. His replacement, appointed by President Jackson, was John Eaton, the former secretary of war. Eaton's replacement in the War Department was Lewis Cass, a man well experienced in Indian affairs.[45]

There were also military changes affecting Florida. Duncan Clinch was still in charge of the army's forces in Florida but had since been promoted to the rank of brigadier general. Above Clinch, Maj. Gen. Winfield Scott had returned to the Eastern Department of the army while his rival, Edmund Gaines, had resumed his position as head of the Western Department, which included much of Florida. Owing to growing tensions, Fort King had been reopened, but both it and Fort Brooke were chronically understaffed.

The Seminoles, too, had undergone some political change. The Apalachicola bands, because of their distance from the more centrally located group and a growing acceptance of white ways, were much less powerful than they once had been. After the death of John Hicks, hereditary leadership of the Seminoles fell to his nephew Micanopy of the Alachua bands. Showing few leadership qualities, Micanopy was strongly influenced by his brother-in-law Jumper and by Abraham the interpreter and most powerful of the black Seminoles. Still considered separate, but closely allied with the Alachua Seminoles, were the Mikasukis. Foremost among that tribe were King Philip and the aging medicine man Abiaca, better known as Sam Jones.

Although the Treaty of Payne's Landing was signed in May 1832, the Senate did not get around to ratifying it until April 1834. The treaty had given the Indians three years in which to remove. The fact that the Senate had dragged its feet did not seem to bother the War Department. In their eyes, the clock had been running since 1832, so final removal was still expected in 1835. So confident was Washington in the pending success of the Seminole removal that the office of Seminole agent was set to be abolished in December of that year. By then, it was supposed, most of the Indians would be on their way west.

The new Seminole agent, Wiley Thompson, seems not to have realized the incompatibility of his two missions. On one hand, he appears to have been committed to seeing the Seminoles treated fairly, but he also appears to have been committed to their removal. Fifty-two at the time of his appointment, Thompson had made a career of public service. Born in

FIGURE 8.
Mick-e-no-pah (Micanopy), Chief of the Tribe, by George Catlin.
By permission of the Smithsonian American Art Museum;
gift of Mrs. Joseph Harrison Jr. #1985.66.300.

Virginia but raised in Georgia, he served with distinction in the War of
1812, and was elected to the rank of major general in the Georgia Militia
in 1817. After a few years in state politics, Thompson ran for Congress
and served for twelve years. After his stint in Washington, Thompson
returned to state politics, serving as a delegate to the convention that was
rewriting Georgia's state constitution. It was during this convention that
he showed himself to be in strong support of Indian removal and states'
rights concerning Indian land.[46]

In late October 1834, Thompson ordered the Seminoles to gather at
Fort King for a "talk." The Seminoles listened to the agent, quietly argued

among themselves and with Thompson, then calmly stated that they had no intentions of moving. They did not feel bound by the Treaties of Payne's Landing and Fort Gibson and argued that the Treaty of Moultrie Creek had guaranteed them an uncontested reservation for a period of twenty years. Concerned by the Seminoles' tone, Thompson asked Washington for more troops, writing: "I feel it an imperious duty to urge the necessity of a strong reinforcement of this Post, and the location of a strong force at Tampa Bay." He had reason to be worried: "The Indians after they had received the Annuity, purchased an unusually large quantity of Powder & Lead." The plea was largely ignored. Having been mostly successful in removing the other eastern tribes, the government did not realize just how intransigent the Seminoles were.[47]

It was during this period that the name of Osceola first began to draw the attention of whites. He was not, as is commonly believed, the head chief of the Seminole Nation. Rather, he was an angry young man who spoke his mind and gathered followers because of what he said and did. Articulate and forceful, he became the "war spirit" of the Seminoles, the one man who best defined their struggle.[48]

An uneasy stalemate continued for several months. Impatient to secure runaway slaves, a movement was underway in the Florida Legislature to put the Indians under territorial jurisdiction. In late January 1835, General Clinch warned Washington that the Seminoles had no intention of removing and that if the government was intent on using force, more troops would be needed: "If a sufficient military force, to overawe them, is not sent into the Nation, they will not be removed & the whole frontier may be laid waste by a combination of the Indians, Indian negroes, and the Negroes on the plantations—It is useless to mince this question." Knowing the War Department's preoccupation with economy, he also requested that the troops be fully prepared for battle, "& not with 13 rounds of cartridges pr. man."[49]

Clinch was not the only one getting nervous. Agent Thompson reported that the Indians "laugh at the idea of the little handful of men at this post (Fort King) being able to compel them to remove." Governor Eaton, who had been secretary of war during the negotiations at Payne's Landing, began to question the validity of the treaty and asked the attorney general for an opinion. He also warned that the "employing of a military force is an act of war, and the Indians will embody and fight in their defence."[50]

By February the administration had made up its mind. In a letter to Clinch, Secretary Cass stated that "it is impossible to yield to any wishes they may express on the subject of emigration. I fully appreciate the consequences which you predict. . . . It is the ultimate decision . . . of the president, that they shall be removed. . . . Let them be reasoned with, and if possible convinced. Let every measure short of actual force be first used . . . then, if necessary, let actual force be employed, and their removal effected." Meanwhile, Congress debated whether or not to allow the new Indian Territory to have a delegate in Congress. Fearing that such an act would open the door to a black representative, the idea was quickly killed.[51]

Thompson kept pushing the Indians to prepare to emigrate, while the Seminoles kept ignoring him. Finally, in late March 1835, Thompson again called the chiefs to a meeting. On this occasion, he read to them a letter from the Great Father in Washington, their old enemy, President Andrew Jackson. In the letter, Jackson informed the Indians that the time for discussion was over. "Should you . . . refuse to remove, I have then directed the Commanding officer to remove you by force," he wrote. The Seminoles, realizing the seriousness of the government's tone of voice, asked for thirty days in which to respond. A month later, the Seminoles informed Agent Thompson that they would not emigrate. Angry words erupted between the agent and the chiefs. Before violence could ensue, Clinch stepped in and restored order. In the end, eight chiefs agreed to emigrate but asked to be allowed to remain until the first of the year. Hoping to mollify the Indians, Clinch and Thompson agreed.[52]

It was at this time that Thompson made the first of several large blunders. Although eight chiefs had agreed to emigrate, five of the most powerful chiefs, including head chief Micanopy, adamantly refused. Angered, Thompson declared them to be removed from office. Such an intrusion into the internal affairs of the Seminole Nation could only serve to embitter the Indians. Later, as the threat of hostilities increased, Thompson forbid the sale of arms and ammunition to the Seminoles. While to us it might seem a wise precaution, the act only served to anger the Seminoles even more. Osceola was particularly incensed. Only slaves were denied the right to purchase gunpowder, he said. "The white man shall not make me black. I will make the white man red with blood; and then blacken him in the sun and rain . . . and the buzzard [shall] live upon his flesh."[53]

As the summer passed, tensions remained high. Oddly, the Indians came and went from the Agency at Fort King on a routine basis. Thompson even began to consider Osceola his friend and presented him with the gift of a fine rifle. Still, the agent saw a need to impose his authority. Early in June, during a visit to Fort King, Osceola became abusive and Thompson had him put in irons and confined. For the entire night, the Indian chieftain raged like a madman. The following day, however, he became more reasonable. To gain his freedom, he agreed to honor the Treaty of Payne's Landing and bring his followers in. Knowing that the cooperation of Osceola might very well be the key to getting the rest of the Seminoles to emigrate, Thompson was willing to free him. Colonel Fanning, knowing that confinement was an insult that an Indian would not forget, urged Thompson to keep Osceola under guard. The agent ignored the advice.

Shortly thereafter, animosity led to bloodshed. In Alachua County, seven whites assaulted five Indians who had been gathered around a campfire. While the attack was taking place, two other Indians arrived and opened fire. Three of the whites were wounded, while one Indian was killed and another wounded. Although few whites realized it, war was now inevitable. An Indian life had been taken; revenge was called for. An escalation of the conflict would soon take place.

The time for revenge arrived in August. Private Kinsley Dalton was carrying mail from Fort Brooke to Fort King. While en route he was waylaid and killed by a group of Seminoles. The Indians saw it as an act of justice. The whites saw it as a sign that the Seminoles were taking to the warpath. The killing of Dalton did not go unnoticed by Americans. In Georgia, the newly organized town of Dalton was named in his honor. Little could people expect that within a few years the number of soldiers to die in Florida would far exceed the number of new towns to name after them.[54]

To those who had been charged with protecting the frontier, the situation in Florida was a familiar one. Once again, the Indians were being pushed to the point of violent reaction. Once again, officials in Washington failed to understand the gravity of the situation. On October 8, 1835, General Clinch wrote to the secretary of war, stating that his present force was "entirely inadequate" to protect the frontier from "the Indians & from *another species of population* [slaves]" and that he needed permission to call out 150 mounted volunteers. Nine days later, he again wrote, apologizing that he "may have rather under estimated the means necessary to carry into effect the views and plans of the Government." With that, he asked for three additional companies of regulars. Four companies of regulars were, with no great haste, ordered to Florida, but the volunteers were not called out "because there is no appropriation authorizing it."[55]

The signal that a war had actually begun came in late November 1835. Ironically, the first act of hostility was committed by one Indian against another. Some Seminoles, wanting no part of war or sensing the futility of such an action, elected to emigrate. Foremost among these people was Charley Emathla, a well-respected chief. In late November, he sold his cattle to the government agents at Fort King and headed for Fort Brooke, where a ship was waiting to take him and his followers to their new homes in the Indian territory. For the Indians who had decided to stay and fight, maintaining solidarity was of extreme importance. To go against the expressed wishes of the entire tribe was considered treason. On the path to Fort Brooke, Osceola met Charley Emathla and carried out the death sentence. The time for discussion and friendly differences of opinion had passed.

To the residents of Florida and the military men on the scene, the meaning of Charley Emathla's execution was clear. Colonel Fanning, in command at Fort King, wrote an urgent letter to General Clinch at St. Augustine, requesting that he return to the interior of the territory immediately. Fanning understood the situation well: "There appears to be a general disaffection of the Indians, and, no doubt, War is determined. . . . We have fallen into the error committed at the Commencement of every Indian War: The display of too little force—The attempt to do too much with inadequate means."[56]

6 Shock and Aftershock

▲▲▲▲ ▲▲▲▲ ▲▲▲▲ ▲▲▲▲ ▲

For nearly a month following the death of Charley Emathla, the territory held its breath, awaiting the outbreak of Indian hostilities. The Seminoles, on the offensive in defense of their homes, had the luxury of knowing when serious fighting would commence. White Floridians could do little but wait.

Those Americans charged with the defense of the territory did their best to prepare for the coming war but were hampered by a lack of men and material. Brig. Gen. Joseph Hernandez of the St. Augustine Militia expressed an eagerness to defend the city but was forced to ask the War Department for a loan of 500 muskets. He would certainly need them: General Clinch had informed Hernandez that until reinforcements arrived, St. Augustine and the surrounding territory would have to defend itself.[1]

In the absence of Governor Eaton, Acting Governor George Walker called out 500 volunteers from Middle Florida and placed them under the command of Brig. Gen. Richard Keith Call. Walker also asked the Pensacola Navy Yard if it could dispatch a vessel to patrol the western coast of the peninsula, where it was reported that numerous Indian canoes were moving about. In response to such threats, the customs collector at St. Marks first asked for a revenue cutter to patrol the approaches to his post, then decided to move his family and office to Tallahassee.[2]

Despite all the preparation, officials were not in a state of panic. Past experience had led them to believe that bellicose Indians were easily awed. Acting Governor Walker had little doubt that the show of force would bring the Seminoles to their senses. Indeed, the militia enlistments were only for one month. In a letter to Secretary of War Lewis Cass, Walker stated that "the enemy are determined on resistance to the last extremity. But I do not doubt that the energetic measures taken will in a few weeks cause their compliance with the treaty."[3]

Officials may not have been living in a state of panic, but much of the population certainly was. As General Clinch traveled across Florida, he noted the condition of the population: "It is truly distressing to witness the panic and sufferings of the white frontier inhabitants. Men, women, and children are seen flying in every direction, and leaving everything behind them save a few articles of clothing. Many families that were comfortable . . . are now reduced to want; their houses . . . having been plundered and burned by small bands of Indians." Clinch also found it difficult to organize the settlers into defensive units. Men would not volunteer for military service until their families had been removed to a place of relative safety.[4]

Throughout the final weeks of 1835, scattered Indian war parties raided isolated settlements, but no major actions took place. The most serious fighting occurred on December 18, when Osceola and between fifty and sixty warriors attacked and captured a Florida Militia wagon train guarded by thirty mounted militiamen. The surprised white men were quickly routed with a loss of eight dead and six wounded. The Indian victory was lessened several days later when a portion of the raiding party was discovered and surrounded near a wooded pond. Outnumbered and taking casualties, the Indians fled, leaving behind much of what they had taken.[5]

It was during the final week of 1835 that major events began to take place. On the eastern coast a large force of Mikasukis, led by King Philip, attacked and destroyed most of the prosperous sugar plantations south of St. Augustine. The ruined remains of one of these sugar mills can be seen today at Bulow Plantation State Historic Site. Rightfully terrorized, white inhabitants fled to the safety of the walled city. By the middle of January, Florida's prosperous sugar industry was in ruins, and many of the slaves who had worked those plantations had joined the Seminoles. Not only were white Floridians living in fear of Indian depredations, they now began to fret over the possibility of a slave uprising. Throughout the northern part of the territory, whites deserted their homes and crowded into nearby fortifications or simply abandoned Florida altogether.[6]

What General Clinch had most feared was now becoming a reality. At his disposal were little more than 500 men, most of them split between Fort Brooke at Tampa and Fort Drane, about twenty miles northwest of

Fort King. Most vulnerable was the Indian Agency at Fort King, manned by only one small company. Fresh troops were on their way to Tampa by sea, but even after their arrival there would be 100 miles of hostile Indian territory between the reinforcements and Fort King. Until those men arrived at Fort King, the post would be in some danger of attack. Clinch, with too few men and short on supplies, could plan an attack but could not carry it out. For that, he would need the help of General Call's militia.

At Fort Brooke, the urgency of relief for Fort King was well understood. Since the killing of Charley Emathla, communications between the two forts had been severed, and the officers and men at Tampa Bay could only imagine what was happening to their friends and comrades in the center of the territory. They feared that if aid did not quickly reach Fort King, the Indians would take it, butchering all within. On the twenty-first of December it was decided to send the two companies that were available. Another two companies were expected any day and would quickly follow.[7]

Command of the detachment fell to Capt. George Washington Gardiner, but Gardiner was faced with a serious personal problem. His wife, who was with him at Fort Brooke, was extremely ill and in need of his care. Maj. Francis Langhorne Dade gallantly volunteered to lead the expedition so that Gardiner could remain with his wife. On the morning of the twenty-third, hours after Dade's command had headed out, Gardiner's plans again changed. A ship was about to depart for Key West, where medical facilities were superior and his wife's father was living. Feeling she would be better cared for in Key West, Gardiner put his wife aboard ship and hurried to catch up with his fellows.

Meanwhile, at Fort King, Agent Wiley Thompson did not seem overly concerned with the depleted condition of the fort's garrison. The Indians had threatened but had yet to take any serious action. Thompson was confident that once the army arrived in strength, the Seminoles would realize that resistance was futile and emigration would reluctantly take place. The agent should have been more wary. Outside Fort King, Osceola and a small band of followers were watching. The Indian leader had sworn to gain revenge for the time Thompson had confined him in irons.

Less than 100 miles to the south, other Indians were also watching and waiting. Major Dade's command was slowly marching north, fully aware that the Seminoles were shadowing them. Each night as they camped, they could hear the shouts and war whoops of the warriors. The

Indians had decided that the time for talk was past. These soldiers would only be the first of many who would come to drive them from their homes. If the white man was to be stopped, it would have to be now.

The Seminoles waited. The soldiers had been marching for four days through the heart of Indian territory. Numerous times Dade's men had been vulnerable, especially at the river crossings. Still, the Indians had not attacked, waiting for the return of Osceola, who had gone to Fort King to settle matters with Wiley Thompson. After five days, they believed they could wait no longer. Dade's men were soon to enter more open territory, where a surprise attack might not be possible. Micanopy, chief of the Seminoles, was, as always, hesitant. Jumper, his brother-in-law and one of the senior chiefs, issued the ultimatum: was Micanopy with them or not? Micanopy sensed that to back down might mean his own death.

On the morning of December 28, 1835, a party of 180 Seminole warriors hid themselves in the tall grass alongside the Fort King road. A line of about 100 soldiers, wrapped in their sky-blue greatcoats, marched toward them, some shivering in the cold morning air. Feeling confident because they had passed through the most dangerous part of Indian territory, Dade and his men began to relax. Cartridge boxes were buttoned under the coats. Flankers were not deployed. In two or three day's time, they felt, they would be safely within the walls of Fort King. As a seasoned military man, Dade should have known better. Never underestimate your enemy.

As the advance guard of Dade's command passed the hidden warriors, a single shot from Micanopy's rifle rang out and the major fell from his mount, a bullet through his heart. The rest of the Seminole war party rose and fired at close range into the stunned soldiers. Nearly half the command fell in that first volley. Terrified white hands clutched at wounds or frantically tore open greatcoats in a rush to load weapons and return the fire. Disciplined soldiers, the men did not panic and run but instead took up positions behind the pine trees or palmettos that afforded the only cover available. Captain Gardiner, again in command, rallied the men and began to consolidate the remaining forces. Their single cannon was unlimbered and prepared for firing. The Seminoles, safely covered behind tall pines, continued to pick off the exposed soldiers.

As the cannon fired, the Indians fell back. Gardiner brought his command together and assessed his losses. Over half his men were dead or gravely wounded. The enemy had been chased off but had not gone away; they were sure to return sooner or later. A triangular breastwork was hastily erected, about sixty feet on each side and three logs high. By late morning the Indians returned, slowly advancing, killing the soldiers one by one. By midafternoon, not a white man was left standing. With the exception of three badly wounded soldiers, Dade's entire command had been wiped out.

The day following the battle, two of the survivors, Ransom Clarke and Edwin DeCourcy, were spotted by a lone Seminole horseman. Hoping to elude the pursuer, the pair split, but DeCourcy was discovered and killed. Clarke, suffering from a broken arm, broken collarbone, a wounded leg and a bullet in the lung, managed to evade the warrior and continued crawling back to Fort Brooke, miraculously reaching safety on New Year's Eve. The other survivor, Joseph Sprague, arrived the following day.

To white America, Dade's defeat was seen as a "massacre." To the Seminoles, it was viewed as a great victory. The assault had been well planned and executed to perfection. Up until the moment Micanopy squeezed his trigger there was still some slim hope for peace. The deaths of Dade and his men had erased even that.[8]

On the same day, Osceola and his band waited outside of Fort King, hidden by the dense underbrush. It was midafternoon, close to the time when Dade's last soldier was dying. The gates of the fort opened and Agent Thompson appeared. With him was a young lieutenant, Constantine Smith, both of them out for an after-dinner stroll. As the two men walked toward the sutler's cabin, the loud crack of rifle fire broke the stillness. Thompson fell, shot fourteen times. His companion was also cut down. The Indians then turned on the sutler's cabin, killing most of the occupants and taking whatever valuables they could carry.

While the Seminoles were making war on the twenty-eighth of December, the army was making plans for an offensive of its own. Unaware of what had happened to Dade's command, General Clinch left Fort Drane on the twenty-ninth with about 750 men. As he left, he sent a letter to Secretary Cass, informing him of the death of Wiley Thompson. For Clinch, time was of the essence. About two-thirds of his force was made up of Florida volunteers whose terms of service were to end with the coming of the new year, two days away.[9]

The objective of the expedition was an area of numerous Indian settlements on the southwest side of the Withlacoochee River. This area, known as "the Cove," was considered the Seminole stronghold. Today called Lake Tsala Apopka, it is made up of a string of large lakes punctuated by numerous islands and peninsulas. It continues to be a watery maze to this day. It was believed that by rounding up the Indian families in the Cove, a prolonged war might be averted. If nothing else, attacking the Seminole settlements would cause the Indian warriors to concentrate on defending their own homes and not destroying those of the whites.

The army reached the Withlacoochee on New Year's Eve but could not get across. Due to an imperfect knowledge of the area, they had arrived not at the ford but at a point where the river was deep and swift flowing. General Clinch was now faced with a dilemma. The volunteers were scheduled to leave the next day. If they were not used that day, any chance of success would be lost. Not wishing to waste time trying to locate the ford, Clinch decided to ferry the troops across in a leaky canoe they happened upon.

The wisdom of dividing his force with nothing more than a failing dugout as an attachment was no doubt questioned, but the general's orders were carried out. In truth, there was good reason for Clinch to feel the move was safe. Unaware of what had befallen Major Dade, Clinch did not know that total warfare had commenced. In addition, history told him that Indians rarely attacked a large white force. The Seminoles were a relatively small tribe, often split into antagonistic factions. The very idea that they could mount a coordinated offensive may not have been seriously considered by the whites. There was also no reason to believe that the Indians knew he was at the river, and even if they had, the river was narrow and the crossing could be well covered.

Had he been given the choice, Clinch would gladly have been somewhere else. Tired of the military life and sensing opportunities in the civilian sector, Clinch had offered his resignation in 1834. The administration, aware of his knowledge of Florida and the Seminoles, had talked him into staying in Florida until the Seminoles were removed. Sadly, his wife of sixteen years had died in April 1835, leaving eight children between the ages of two and fifteen without a mother. The children were sent to live with their maternal grandparents, but the general was no doubt anxious to end his military service and return to his family.[10]

In groups of five or six, the soldiers were ferried across the river. It took some time, but eventually all the regulars were on the southern shore, waiting for the volunteers to cross. Seeing no hostiles, the soldiers moved a few hundred yards inland to a clearing surrounded by a dense hammock, where they stacked their arms, regrouped, and relaxed.

Suddenly, there were warning shouts and rifle shots. The surrounding hammock erupted with war whoops and gunfire. Surprised soldiers fell wounded or dying, while others lunged for their muskets. After some moments of initial confusion, the officers formed their men into ranks and began to return fire. It soon became obvious that if the well-concealed Indians were not forced from their hiding places, a massacre would result. The militia, unable or unwilling to come to the regulars' rescue, would be of no help. Colonel Fanning, a one-armed veteran of the war with Britain, urged General Clinch to order a bayonet charge. The general was at first reluctant, then agreed. Fanning's men fixed bayonets and ran toward the waiting Seminole rifles. Approximately a third of them were wounded in the assault, but the objective was achieved: the Indians were forced back, and the army was saved from annihilation.[11]

Clinch's men were not, however, out of danger. Seminole snipers continued to fire at the soldiers. It was obvious that the army needed to come back together, but should the militia cross the river or should the regulars retreat? If the entire force were to come across, the Seminoles might be engaged and decisively defeated, putting an end to the war. On the other hand, there were many wounded to be evacuated, and supplies and militia enlistments were running out. Clinch called for a retreat.

While the regulars had been under attack, General Call, leader of the Florida Militia, had managed to get some of his men across, while others had hurriedly built a makeshift bridge across the river. With the territorial troops forming two lines of protection, the wounded army made its way back across the river. Once safely across the Withlacoochee, Clinch and his men marched slowly back to Fort Drane.

Clinch had lost four men in the battle and suffered another fifty-nine wounded, many of them seriously. Miraculously, all but one survived. Hospital orderly John Bemrose later told how General Clinch comforted the mortally wounded man: "Frequently I saw him sitting on the dirty floor so as to bring himself near the dying soldier, conversing with him and throwing in sweet consolation as he only knew how."[12]

As often happens, both sides viewed the outcome of the battle differently. In the view of the army, Clinch and his men had fought bravely against a larger force and had, through their gallantry and courage, managed to avoid what could have been total annihilation. As far as the Semi-noles were concerned, the enemy had threatened their homeland and had been repulsed. In the end, the Seminoles had accomplished their objective—the protection of their homes—while Clinch had not.

As the year 1835 drew to a close, it was apparent to the people of Flor-ida that they had become embroiled in a full-scale Indian war. The Semi-nole Nation had scored two major victories against the forces of the United States and had suffered few casualties of their own. Osceola had told his people that they should fight for their homeland, and he had shown that it was not a hopeless cause. It would take almost seven years, thousands of lives, and tens of millions of dollars to prove him wrong.

The new year did not bring much hope to white Floridians. On January 17, a large band of Seminoles came upon a group of volunteers at Anderson's Plantation near St. Augustine. In what became known as the Battle of Dunlawton, the whites suffered four killed and thirteen wounded. Soon the entire eastern coast of Florida south of St. Augustine was abandoned. Throughout Florida, whites were fleeing to the safety of government fortifications, leaving the countryside in the hands of the Indians. The army, critically short of men and supplies, could do nothing but stand watch from inside the walls of their fortresses.[13]

Clinch's battle at the Withlacoochee had served to highlight several of the problems faced by the army. First of all was the lack of geographic knowledge of the territory they would be fighting in. No one within the white force had known exactly where to ford the river. The only guides were members of the enemy tribe. Maps were vague at best, and often wrong. White men were generally familiar only with the northernmost portions of the territory. The rest of the peninsula belonged to alligators, mosquitoes, and the Seminoles.

The army itself was part of the problem. At a total strength of less than 7,000 men, it was simply too small for the task at hand. Because of low pay and harsh discipline, recruits were often from the more desperate classes of society. Almost half of the American army was made up of recent immigrants. The revolution had fostered a strong dislike for the idea of a large standing army, something viewed as the tool of a potential tyrant. It was widely believed that if need be, a quickly organized army of citizen-soldiers could adequately defend the nation.[14]

It was, however, a large nation to defend. The border with Canada was not the peaceful boundary we know today. The exact position of the northern border was still a point of contention between the United States and Great Britain, and during the period of the Seminole War, the army would be called out to help settle a dispute over who owned what in northern Maine. In the opposite corner of the nation, problems with America's southern neighbors were multiplying. Fighting was underway in Texas; in less than a decade, it would draw the United States into a war with Mexico.

The nation's coasts were no less vulnerable. Invasion from across the sea was not unthinkable. Many of the leaders of 1836 had gained their reputations fighting the British about twenty years earlier. There was no reason to believe it could not happen again. Even America's old ally France was proving difficult. An argument had erupted over the payment of claims owed by France to U.S. citizens, giving Andrew Jackson more than enough opportunity to rattle the American saber. In response to such foreign pressures, the nation had long maintained a series of fortifications along the coast. Although habitually understaffed, these installations were a considerable drain on the army's resources.[15]

Dealing with foreign adversaries, however, was not the army's main occupation. In 1830, it had become the law of the land that all Indian nations east of the Mississippi would be moved west. Few of the natives had moved of their own accord. Many had to be led from their homelands under armed guard. Some, like the Seminoles, chose to remain and fight, but most, unlike the Seminoles, did not have a vast uncharted territory to seek refuge in. Resistance was usually short lived but nonetheless required the presence of a considerable number of U.S. soldiers.

Moving the Indians to the West did not make them any less ill-disposed toward their white brethren. Resentments and frictions were only shifted to another arena. The pressures of resettlement also increased conflict between the incoming Indian tribes and those who already lived there. Conflict often spilled over into the white settlements bordering Indian Territory. To protect the frontier, a string of forts grew up on the western border that rivaled those of the eastern seaboard. The minuscule U.S. Army was too thinly spread to fight a major war anywhere, especially in the swamps and hammocks of Florida.

To counter the chronic shortage of troops, the government relied on two types of citizen-soldiers. The first were the conscripted state militias. Their roots were the famed Minutemen of the Revolution, and today's National Guard is the direct descendant of those forces. In theory, they were already organized and trained, ready at a moment's notice to come to their country's defense. In practice, the militia tended to be lacking in discipline and equipment. Their senior officers were generally appointed by the state governor, and that was where their allegiance tended to gravitate. Periodic training was often seen as a good reason to get drunk around the campfire.

The other type of citizen-soldier was the volunteer. If discipline and cooperation were questionable in the militias, it was almost nonexistent with the volunteers. Their officers were the men who organized the companies, and their ranks were filled by men who felt little obligation to the professional soldiers they fought alongside. As volunteers, they often felt privileged to fight on their own terms or to not fight at all. Both civilian forces, whether conscripted militia or volunteer, tended to view their terms of service as an enjoyable adventure, a chance to go camping with the boys while making some fast cash off the government. The harsh and dangerous conditions of service in Florida were not what they had envisioned.

One Tennessee volunteer, Henry Hollingsworth, arrived in Florida with glorious expectations. What he found was something altogether different. His first disappointment came upon his arrival at Tallahassee:

> We being the first Tennessee troops that arrived there expected a pretty warm reception and at least a *treat* from the citizens. Under this impression every man who had a clean shirt ... put it on ... and arranged ourselves in the march to the very best advantage. ... In this order of procession ... we made our entrance into Tallahassee ... big with expectation of being met by the Governor and staff and hailed with exclamations of joy by a crowded populace and in the end receive an invitation to partake of some kind and generous hospitalities offered us on the altar of gratitude by the over-thankful and delightful inhabitants. ... What was our disappointment on penetrating the town and finding ourselves unnoticed! ... No Governor came out to meet us. ... No crowded populace thronged to salute us. No beautiful females from windows, porticoes and balconies with their fairy hands waved their white handkerchiefs to bid us welcome.[16]

It was, as much as anything, the cost of the civilian forces that made their use controversial. It could cost the government almost twice as much to field a temporary state force as it could to deploy a similar force of regulars. Yet whenever the government attempted to cut back on the number of militiamen it used, howls of protest rose from insulted state officers and militiamen who had gotten used to living on federal funds. Despite all the shortcomings of the civilian soldiers, they did perform useful service in the war. As the war progressed, discipline was imposed and the malcontents were weeded out. From the time of Clinch's battle on the Withlacoochee until long after the conclusion of the war, the army and the state forces continued to argue over who had been most responsible for failing to bring the war to a swift conclusion. It was more convenient to blame each other than to admit that they had been beaten by the Seminoles.[17]

News of the Indian offensive spread throughout the nation as rapidly as any news could at the time. America was shocked. Major Dade would become the Custer of his day, leader of a doomed force whose annihilation captured the nation's imagination. The destruction of the Florida sugar industry and the rout of the settlers made the Seminoles appear to be stronger than they actually were. Indeed, Clinch's defeat at the Withlacoochee was blamed not upon any miscalculations by the army but upon a supposed superiority in the numbers of the enemy. Somehow, Clinch's retreat was turned into a victory, and years later he would use the nickname of "Old Withlacoochee" when running for governor of Georgia.[18]

Newspaper accounts slowly filtered north, the facts changing slightly as they moved from city to city. Most of the reporting consisted of nothing more than the reprinting of letters, both official and unofficial, or of accounts from other newspapers. Errors were easy to make, depending on how one read those letters. The editor of the *New York Observer* stated that 139 men had been killed along with Major Dade. He had evidently missed that fact that the 39 men of Dade's own company had not joined the approximately 100 men of the other two companies. The source of other errors are more difficult to track down. The *New York Herald* stated the Indian strength at about 3,000 men, made up of "2000 Indians, 1000 negroes, and 600 vagabonds of all descriptions, commanded by young chiefs educated at the Military Academy at West Point." One editor admitted that the facts were obscure and that it appeared as if Dade's men had retreated four miles before being wiped out. Many reports were nothing more than wild rumors. The *Mobile Chronicle* of January 27 listed "various rumors," such as "Tallahassee has been surprised and sacked . . . Fort King had been stormed and taken, with 400 troops, who were all massacred . . . Apalachicola is in possession of the savage enemy."[19]

As might be expected, news of war in Florida caused more concern among southerners than among those living elsewhere in the nation. Word that blacks had committed atrocities on the fallen soldiers served to excite the emotions of the citizenry of the slaveholding states. Volunteer companies from South Carolina, Georgia, and Alabama began to organize, eager to avenge the deaths of their gallant brothers. Almost to a man, they envisioned a swift and glorious campaign that would quickly drive the Seminoles into the sea.

By the end of January help was on the way to the beleaguered peninsula. News had finally gotten to Washington of the events of the last week of December. Brig. Gen. Abraham Eustis was dispatched from Charleston to St. Augustine with whatever men and supplies he could gather. Congress immediately took action, and a total of $620,000 was appropriated for fighting the Seminoles. There was, of course, no need to declare war. That was a nicety reserved for "civilized" enemies.[20]

The War Department was also on the move. President Jackson and Secretary of War Cass called upon their most distinguished officer to direct the campaign. Maj. Gen. Winfield Scott was given the authority to requisition all the men and material he deemed necessary. It would take a month or two to bring it all together, but once the forces were in place, the might of the United States Army would surely bring the hostilities to a rapid close. Nothing but total victory was expected. Scott's orders also showed how closely the Seminole situation was tied to the issue of slavery. There was to be no peace with the Seminoles until all fugitive slaves were returned to their masters.[21]

Scott was not the only major general heading for Florida. In New Orleans, General Gaines, the commanding officer of the army's Western Department, also heard the news of Dade's demise. Because the dividing line between the Eastern and Western Departments ran down the length of Florida, Gaines felt obligated to take action in what he considered his jurisdiction. Due to the fact that communications between New Orleans and Washington could take many weeks, he felt no need to consult with his superiors, nor had he any way of knowing that Scott had been given command of the Florida theater. Gathering as many regulars as he could muster, Gaines also called upon the governor of Louisiana for volunteers. By February 4, Gaines and his force of 1,100 men were aboard ship, headed for Tampa Bay.[22]

At Gaines's first stop a wrench was thrown into his plans. When the ship docked at Pensacola he was shown a letter telling him of Scott's appointment to lead the Florida campaign. Because official orders had not been included, Gaines chose to ignore the news. His men were needed in Florida, and he was not about to take them back to New Orleans. Upon his February 9 arrival at Fort Brooke, he was handed official orders to proceed to the Mexican frontier. Now the decision was more difficult. He was in the theater of war with a large body of men who were desperately needed. Gaines was not the sort of man to use orders as an excuse to avoid combat.[23]

As the commander of forces on the remote frontier, Gaines knew that orders from Washington had to be taken in the proper context. Because of the time it took for news to travel through the wilderness, he was usually given the latitude needed to respond to any situation that presented itself. Very often, there was simply no time to check with his superiors back East. In the days before instant communications, the links in the chain of command were frequently disconnected. Gaines and the rest of the officers of the army were expected to make command decisions when necessity arose.

Necessity had certainly arisen in Florida. Fort Brooke, undermanned, vulnerable, and in fear of attack, had gotten cannon from Key West and men from the U.S. Navy. Of more concern to Gaines was the situation at Fort King. No word had been received from the fortification since before Dade's battle. For all he knew, the installation might be under siege at that very moment. The decision to proceed to Fort King was also made on a more practical level. Supplies at Fort Brooke were almost depleted. According to the word he had received, provisions for Scott's coming offensive were being sent to Fort King, so it seemed sensible to take his men there to meet them. One could argue, however, that if supplies had reached Fort King, reinforcements would have gotten there too.[24]

The force left Fort Brooke on the thirteenth of February, following the Fort King Road, the same military road that Major Dade had taken. This time, however, the Seminoles wisely kept their distance. For five days, the trek was peaceful, with little or no sign of conflict. On the sixth day, the column came upon the remains of Dade and his men: "A short distance in the rear of the little field work lay a few broken cartridge boxes, fragments of clothing, here and there a shoe or an old straw hat . . . then a cart partly burnt, with the oxen still yoked lying dead near it; a horse had fallen a little to the right, and here also a few bones of the hapless beings lay bleaching in the sun; while the scene within, and beyond the triangular enclosure, baffles all description. One would involuntarily turn aside from the horrible picture to shed a tear of sorrow."[25]

With haste, three burial pits were dug. Two were within the triangular breastwork that Dade's desperate soldiers had erected for their futile defense. Into this grave went the bodies of the enlisted men. Into a smaller grave a little to the north the officers were interred. The band played a dirge and marched three times around the graves. The cannon with which Dade's men had defended themselves was pulled from a nearby pond and placed, muzzle down, over the officer's graves. Gaines's column marched on. The place where Dade's doomed men fought their last battle has been preserved as a state historic park.[26]

Nine days after leaving Tampa Bay, the force arrived at Fort King. Gaines and his men, their rations depleted, had expected to find the fort well supplied, as sufficient time had passed for General Scott's provisions to have reached their destination, well in advance of the men who were going to need them. Inexplicably, none had arrived. Months later, fingers in Washington were still pointing back and forth, trying to lay blame for the lapse in transport.[27]

Gaines now faced a serious dilemma. Under his command were a thousand men who had exhausted their provisions, and none were to be had at Fort King. The fort barely had enough food for the small garrison that manned it. Scott and his supplies were not expected for some time, too much time for Gaines to wait. In desperation, he requested provisions from General Clinch, who had returned to Fort Drane. Clinch, unfortunately, had little to spare. All he could send was seven days' worth, just enough for Gaines to get his men back to Tampa Bay.[28]

Having nowhere else to go, Gaines and his men left Fort King on February 26, heading back to Fort Brooke. Determined to make something of the thus-far wasted trip, Gaines decided to follow a different route back to Tampa Bay. This path was similar to the one Clinch had taken on his abortive invasion of the Cove on New Year's Eve. Gaines no doubt hoped the Seminoles could again be drawn out in force.

As it turned out, Gaines's guides were no better than Clinch's, leading the army to the exact same spot Clinch had arrived at. The force divided into three columns, each in search of the crossing place. Once again, the

Seminoles were watching and waiting from the southern shore. Occasionally they would fire upon the soldiers, seeming to warn them that a river crossing would not be allowed. On the following morning the ford was located and a small group of soldiers entered the water. A shot rang out from the opposite shore and Lt. James Izard fell mortally wounded. Unable to cross and unable to go back, Gaines gathered his forces together and erected a small fortification, which he designated Camp Izard, in honor of the dying lieutenant.[29]

Gaines now sensed an opportunity. He seemed to be up against the entire Seminole Nation, a force totaling about 1,500 men. If he were to hold his position at Camp Izard, the Seminoles might remain concentrated around him. Then, if General Clinch could bring his forces from Fort Drane and attack the Indians on their flank, the war might be swiftly ended. Gaines dug in, sent orders to Clinch, and waited.[30]

For Osceola and the other Seminoles, this was a new type of military situation. Indians were not accustomed to waging siege warfare. Still, they kept up the pressure and allowed the soldiers no respite. An attempt was made to burn the soldiers out by setting fire to the dry grass that surrounded the fortification, but a shift in the wind foiled the plan.

Inside Camp Izard, the situation quickly deteriorated. The soldiers, short on rations when they had left Fort King, were virtually without sustenance within a few days. Horses and mules were slaughtered and fed to the troops. By the eighth day of the siege, the men were too weak to have mounted an offensive if they had wanted to mount one. Where was Clinch?

Duncan Clinch was a man in the middle, caught between two bitter rivals, Edmund Gaines and Winfield Scott, men of equal rank and position in the army. Both were equally superior to Clinch. Gaines was in command of the Western Department, of which Clinch was a part. Scott had been placed in charge of the Florida War, of which Clinch was also a part. Gaines had ordered Clinch to take the field. Scott ordered Clinch to stay put at Fort Drane.

Gaines and Scott occupied two poles at the opposite end of the military spectrum. Both men had earned their reputations during the War of 1812, showing themselves to be exceptional leaders, both having received nearly fatal wounds at the hands of the British. At that point, however, the similarity ended. Gaines was a sparse man, casual in appearance, active and decisive. His quick response to the troubles in Florida was true to character. Being in charge of the Western Department perfectly suited the old Indian fighter. Winfield Scott, on the other hand, was a tall, muscular man who enjoyed the pageantry associated with high rank. Being in charge of the Eastern Department, which normally dealt with foreign adversaries, also suited him well. A thoughtful, careful planner, his response to the Florida War was much more deliberate. He would not take the field until all preparations were ready for his grand strategy.

Scott, who had arrived in Florida about the same time as Gaines, was near St. Augustine, making preparations for the coming campaign. News that Gaines was in Florida did not please him in the least. Scott felt that his rival's actions would thoroughly upset his own carefully laid plans and therefore ordered Clinch not to cooperate with Gaines.[31]

One can only imagine Duncan Clinch's exasperation. He was no doubt inclined to go to the aid of Gaines, but that general would soon be leaving the theater of war, while Clinch would have to get along with Scott indefinitely. To be caught between two such powerful and envious men was a thankless position. He sent word to Scott, asking him to reconsider, and impatiently waited for a response.

Before the response could arrive, Clinch's patience ran out. A thousand good men were under siege and in need of relief. He could not, in good conscience, let them starve or be slaughtered. On March 5, Clinch gathered his troops and headed out for the Withlacoochee. Scott's permission to take the field arrived the next day.[32]

Gaines, in the meantime, was in a desperate situation. Living on small portions of horse meat and the occasional dog, the men were becoming emaciated and would be too weak to fight their way back to safety. The army had now been holed-up at Camp Izard for eight days. If the Indians mounted a full-scale attack, Gaines might not be able to hold them off. On the night of March 5, a voice called out of the darkness. The Seminoles wanted a parley. Having few options, Gaines agreed to let a senior officer meet with the Seminole leaders in the morning.[33]

In reality, John Caesar, a black Seminole, was the one who wanted to parley. He appears to have worked on his own initiative, as the Seminole camp was by no means in agreement on this move and some of the chiefs even threatened Caesar's life. Osceola, however, reportedly stood by the man. Word had probably been received that Clinch was on the way. There was a need to take some sort of action, but not all parties were of the same mind. Some may have favored an immediate assault on the encampment, while others may have wanted to simply melt away, taking their families to safety, no doubt fearing a white offensive once the siege was lifted. Still others may have felt that they had scored enough victories to force the whites to make a concession. Another group may have felt that a parley might be used as a ruse to make the whites lower their guard long enough for an assault to take place.

On the morning of the sixth, warriors and officers met outside of Camp Izard. The Indians offered an olive branch: they would cease hostilities if the whites allowed them to remain unmolested south of the Withlacoochee. Gaines, through an aide, replied that he did not have the authority to make such an agreement, but said that he would recommend it to his superiors. Gaines, on record as being opposed to Indian Removal, probably felt such an arrangement to be fair. He should also have known that Andrew Jackson would never agree to it.[34]

As the negotiations were taking place, the advance party from Clinch's column arrived on the scene. Seeing Indians, they opened fire. The Seminoles, naturally cautious, fled. Gaines, more interested in the health of his men than in a futile chase, did not order a pursuit. Indeed, he still held out hope that negotiations could end the war. For whatever their reasons, the Seminoles did not return to Camp Izard. Gaines waited three days, then turned command over to Clinch. For Gaines, the Florida War was over. Camp Izard, reclaimed by nature, has recently been relocated and partially excavated by the Seminole Wars Historic Foundation. The site has been preserved and will eventually be open to the public.[35]

The force, with many wounded and weakened men, made its way back to Fort Drane, arriving on March 11. On the thirteenth, Winfield Scott made his grand entrance into the fortification. For the remainder of that day, both major generals did their best to ignore each other. One can only imagine the awkwardness felt by Duncan Clinch and the rest of the men under his command. It must have been a great relief when Gaines departed the following day.[36]

As far as Edmund Gaines was concerned, the campaign had been a success. In Tallahassee and in Mobile it was announced that the war was probably over, and Gaines was treated like a conquering hero. The most unfortunate aspect of Gaines's campaign was the missed opportunity to end the war. The Seminoles might well have settled for some sort of reservation in the southern part of the territory, even if it meant abandoning the prize lands in the Cove of the Withlacoochee and the Alachua Prairie. The Indians knew they had been victorious so far, but they were certainly smart enough to know that they could not hold out forever.

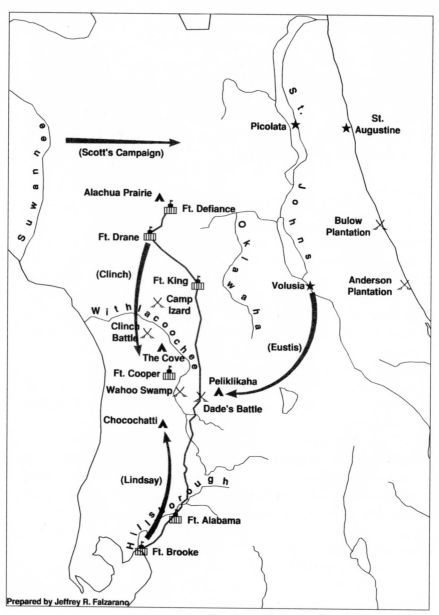

MAP 4. Florida War, 1836.

The administration, however, was in no mood to talk. The army had been severely bloodied and embarrassed. No one was yet ready to question the finality of the policy of Indian Removal. As more slaves fled from the plantations of the South, more Florida settlers fled to the safety of the forts. The United States stood firm. There would be no negotiations with the Seminoles. They would be crushed, defeated, and the survivors would be shipped west. Winfield Scott and thousands of young white men had been given their orders.

It was, of course, easy to understand the Seminoles' reasons for commencing hostilities. They were defending their homes and their way of life. The motives of whites in responding to those hostilities were much more complex. In one sense, their response was habitual. Since Jamestown, the newcomers had pushed and the Indians had fought back. "Dade's Massacre" was quite another thing. In an army that was so small, it seems every officer and enlisted man had lost a friend on December 28. Revenge was called for. The murder of Wiley Thompson seemed especially treacherous. In the southern states, the very idea that blacks were running around with guns in their hands raised the ever-present fear of a slave uprising. Others feared that the Seminoles were somehow being aided by or working with either British Bahamians or Spanish Cubans. The two unsuccessful attempts to cross the Withlacoochee were also a shock. To many, it appeared that the Seminoles were much stronger and better organized than other native adversaries had been. All in all, the threat seemed to call for a massive response.

Men and supplies were pouring into Florida. General Scott, careful and precise, had devised a grand strategy that would surely bring the war to a swift conclusion. It might have been expensive and complex, but it was in keeping with the finest tactics then practiced in Europe. On paper, the plan looked sound. Scott's forces would be divided into three wings, which would converge upon and entrap the hapless Seminoles. Once surrounded, there would be no escape for the Indian warriors and they would have to capitulate. This time, the army was large enough and well equipped enough to survive any attack the Indians could mount against them. Even Napoleon would have been impressed.[37]

Scott himself would be traveling with the right wing, which would be commanded by Duncan Clinch. They would be departing from Fort Drane, which had been erected on Clinch's plantation before the war had begun. This group was to head south, enter the Cove of the Withlacoo-

FIGURE 9.
Maj. Gen. Winfield
Scott. Engraving by
Henry S. Sadd.
By permission of the
National Portrait Gallery,
Smithsonian Institution.
#77.102.

GEN. WINFIELD SCOTT.

chee, then drive the Seminoles into the other two wings. The left wing, under General Eustis, would be coming from Volusia, far to the east. The center wing, commanded by Col. William Lindsay, would be coming from Fort Brooke on Tampa Bay.

It was imperative, of course, that both Eustis's and Lindsay's wings be in place when Clinch's right wing made its push. The deadline given the two commanders was March 25. On the twenty-sixth, Scott and Clinch would leave Fort Drane and head for the Cove. Timing had to be exact, but Winfield Scott was an experienced and precise man.

Colonel Lindsay departed Fort Brooke on the twenty-second of March, making his way north toward the Cove. On the twenty-sixth, right on schedule, Clinch and Scott exited Fort Drane, taking a southerly route toward the Cove. Unfortunately, General Eustis was nowhere near the Cove. He was, in fact, not far from Volusia, having left there on the twenty-fifth. Eustis had attempted to depart on the twenty-third, but an attack by the Seminoles had forced him to delay the departure for two days. Unknown to General Scott, the precise timing had already broken down.[38]

Still, all might not be lost. The timing might be tardy, but as long as it remained synchronized, Scott might still have his victory. On the twenty-eighth, Lindsay and his center wing finally reached Chocachatti, south of the Cove, the place they were supposed to have been three days earlier. Equally as tardy, Clinch and the right wing, coming from the north, finally reached Camp Izard on the Withlacoochee. Eustis, moving through unknown territory, made the unfortunate discovery that there were un-mapped hills in the center of Florida. Blazing trails through the dense woods and around the numerous small lakes added to the delay.[39]

The following morning, Clinch and his men began the real offensive, crossing the Withlacoochee and entering the Cove. The plan had been to drive the Indians toward Lindsay's force, waiting to the south. Unfortunately, there were no Indians. The only thing Clinch and Scott found were deserted fields and villages. Some of the Seminoles had gone slightly east and were fighting a small skirmish with General Eustis, delaying him even more. The others had simply fled, taking refuge to the south. On the thirtieth of March, five days late, Eustis at last reached his appointed station, Peliklikaha.[40]

Supplies were running low, and very few Indians had been captured or killed. On the thirty-first, Lindsay and his center wing decided to return to Fort Brooke. At the same time Eustis, to the east, also decided to head for Fort Brooke. Clinch, coming from the north, simply kept moving south, in the direction of Fort Brooke. Within a week all three forces were united on the shores of Tampa Bay. Scott's elaborate plan had failed miserably. The Seminoles may have been driven out of the Cove, but they were still in Florida, and no less belligerent.[41]

Through letters and newspaper accounts, America had followed the preparations for Scott's campaign with high anticipation. It would no doubt be a glorious event. Five thousand men were involved, from seasoned regulars to idealistic volunteers. Not since the War of 1812 had such a large force of America's finest been called to battle. The man in charge was nothing short of a legend. On the Niagara frontier of 1814, Scott had taken a defeated, undisciplined medley of citizen and regular soldiers and had molded them into a fighting force that had stood against hardened British veterans, many of them fresh from the Napoleonic Wars.

Scott was not, however, an Indian fighter. Those familiar with Florida and the Indian mode of warfare had doubted that Scott's complex plan could work, but none were in a position, or brave enough, to tell the general otherwise. To the nation as a whole, the failure of Scott's campaign was tantamount to a costly defeat. In the end, blame for the fiasco in Florida was laid to a lack of proper time for preparation and the inhospitable climate. For the army, it was the most expedient solution to a public relations nightmare.[42]

If Scott's tactics were faulty, the Seminoles' were exactly what they should have been. Having a limited number of warriors and with no hope of reinforcements, the Indians could not afford to take on the army in open battle. By necessity, they would have to limit themselves to defensive actions and surprise attacks. Their only hope was to wear the white men down. Retreating into the trackless swamps was a matter of survival.

We must, of course, put the war into its proper perspective. It was certainly not the only thing going on at the time. What is surprising, however, is how much it commanded the public's attention. A perusal of the major national newspapers quickly shows that the Florida War was *the* big news item of 1836. The statistic becomes even more impressive when we look at competing stories. There was, if nothing else, a presidential election taking place. There was also heated debate over a national bank and Treasury policy. The abolitionist movement had come alive, creating a stir throughout the nation. Above all else, there was the war for Texan independence. Remember the Alamo?

Yet if we count the number of articles devoted to these subjects in *Niles' Register,* a leading national newspaper, we find that more space was given to the Seminole conflict (sixty-four articles) than to the election and the Texas stories combined (fifty-two). Indeed, once the news of Dade's destruction reached Washington in late January, news from Florida rarely left the front page for the rest of the year. The headline on most of these articles simply said "Latest from Florida." No preface was needed; people knew what was going on.[43]

If the Seminoles had been intimidated by Winfield Scott, it did not show. Throughout April 1836, there was heavy traffic on the warpath. The Indians surrounded and besieged Camp Cooper in the Cove and attempted to overpower Fort Alabama, north of Fort Brooke. Farther east, a group of warriors attacked a burial party near Fort Barnwell, an army encampment outside Volusia.[44]

The Seminoles even had the temerity to attack Fort Drane, one of the stronger fortifications in the territory, on the twentieth of April. The fort, manned by a small contingent of mostly sick and wounded soldiers, held off the attackers and were relieved four days later by the arrival of Duncan Clinch and the remainder of his left wing. For Clinch, the war was over. Disgusted, he resigned his commission, took his retirement, and headed north.[45]

Farther south, the army had decided that Fort Alabama was not worth defending and abandoned it near the end of April. Before leaving, the soldiers booby-trapped the powder magazine, and soon after departing, a loud explosion was heard. It was later discovered that at least five Indians were killed. In retaliation, the Seminoles later attacked the departing soldiers, but were repulsed by a determined bayonet charge.[46]

As many northerners were soon to learn, there were only two seasons in Florida. Winters were mild, dry, cool, and conducive to the outdoor life that a soldier was forced to live. This was the time of year known as the "healthy season." Summer, on the other hand, was almost universally referred to as the "sickly season." It rained almost daily, and much of the land became flooded, making overland transport almost impossible. The intense heat and humidity sapped a man's strength while providing ideal conditions for the swarming of large numbers of biting and stinging insects, many of which carried infectious diseases. During the summer, the Seminoles did not have to wage war upon the whites; the unhealthy Florida environment killed more soldiers than Indian rifles ever could.

Faced with disease, death, and desertion, the army was forced to spend the summer of 1836 in a protracted retreat from the ravages of the climate. In late May, Fort King was abandoned. In early June, the garrison of a blockhouse on the Withlacoochee River that had somehow been forgotten about since April was finally rescued after being under siege for many weeks.[47]

The Seminoles, sensing the soldiers' reluctance to fight, became emboldened. If Clinch had hoped the presence of Fort Drane would protect his plantation, he was sadly mistaken. In late April the Seminoles destroyed the plantation's sugar works. On the ninth of June Osceola and about 250 warriors attacked Fort Defiance. Feeling up to the challenge,

FIGURE 10.
Governor Richard
Keith Call.
By permission of the
Florida State Archives.
Image #RK0598,
DBCN#AAH-6262.

Major Heileman brought his men out of the fort and met the enemy, driving them off "after an hour and twenty minutes' hard fighting under a broiling sun."[48]

In mid-July, Fort Drane was ordered to close down because of illness. Five of the 7 officers were on the sick list, along with 140 of their men. Although the move would no doubt save many a sickened soldier, such moves were dangerous. While transferring baggage from Fort Drane to Fort Defiance, a wagon train escorted by about 80 soldiers was attacked by approximately 200 Indians. The Seminoles were driven off, but not before inflicting several mortal wounds upon the defenders.[49]

Much farther south, the Indians attacked the lighthouse at Key Biscayne, near what would someday be the city of Miami. The lighthouse keeper and a black companion took refuge in the lighthouse, where they managed to keep the Indians at bay for the rest of the day. Thwarted, the Seminoles set fire to the building, forcing the keeper and the slave to flee to the top of the structure. As the flames began to reach the lantern room, the two men were forced into a desperate dilemma; staying inside meant being roasted alive. Venturing out onto the platform put them in range of the Seminole rifles. As the keeper later related, "My flesh was roasting and to put an end to my horrible suffering, I got up, threw the keg of gunpowder down the scuttle, instantly it exploded and shook the tower from the top to the bottom." Miraculously, the structure did not collapse. Still, the fire continued to rage, forcing the men out onto the platform. From the ground, the Indians began to shoot at the two men and succeeded in killing the slave. The Seminoles, deciding the white man was either dead or soon to die, finally left. Fortunately for the keeper, the crew of the navy ship *Motto* had heard the explosion and rescued him the following day. The lighthouse was soon rebuilt and remains to this day, the centerpiece of a state park.[50]

By early August, the evacuation of Fort Drane was complete. Soon after, a force was dispatched under Maj. B. K. Pierce to shut down Fort Defiance. While in the area, Pierce took the opportunity to attack Osceola and his men, who had taken over the abandoned Fort Drane. An inconclusive battle was fought, and the Indians once again melted into the swamps. By the end of the month, Fort Defiance was empty, leaving all of central Florida in the hands of the Seminoles. To the Seminoles, it may well have seemed as if they might actually be winning the war.[51]

After the Scott embarrassment, the War Department appeared to be in a state of confusion. No one was sure who should be in charge of what had become the Florida War. The army's two top generals, Gaines and Scott, had both been on the scene and had accomplished nothing. A lot of time, money, and lives had been wasted, and the press was beginning to ask embarrassing questions. Clinch, the officer most familiar with the territory, had resigned. A letter was sent offering him command of the forces in Florida if he would reconsider. The general politely declined.[52]

To make matters worse, another Indian War had broken out. Just to the north of Florida, the Creeks were being forced from their last remaining ancestral lands in Alabama. Perhaps encouraged by the example of the Seminoles, many Creeks resisted. Faced with another major Indian war, the army's focus temporarily shifted away from Florida. Considering the season, it may well have been a healthy diversion.

The only person who seemed anxious to pursue the Florida War was Jackson's old friend Richard Keith Call, who had been appointed governor of Florida on March 16. Believing that the state militias and volunteers could fight longer and better than the regular army, he proposed a summer campaign. The War Department agreed to Call's plan, but with a few qualifications. Foremost among these was the climate. Secretary of War Cass warned Call that "opinions upon the subject of carrying on a campaign during the summer have been variant. You must exercise a sound discretion upon the whole matter." Technically, command of the force was given to General Eustis, the ranking officer in the area, but he was given no orders to pursue the war, and was told to cooperate with Call as much as he saw fit.[53]

Congress, meanwhile, showed resolve in the matter, appropriating $1.5 million of the taxpayer's money for the suppression of Indian hostilities and allowing volunteers to be signed up for a year at a time. It was already evident that the Florida War was going to be a long and expensive affair. Supportive as they might have been, congressmen did not let the opportunity pass to air their views on the matter. Representative Thompson of South Carolina took time to praise the fighting qualities of westerners. "A thousand such men as could be raised in the West would have put an end to the war in Florida in one month." One senator pointed a finger at the administration, blaming it for the mismanagement of Indian affairs: "There are no people on earth so easy to deal with as our half civilized Indians. It only required ordinary justice, a mild but firm course of conduct, with a strict adherence to truth in all transactions with them, and it was the easiest thing in the world to keep them quiet."[54]

Governor Call may have envisioned a summer campaign, but the nature of the climate and the nature of the army conspired against him. Due to inevitable delays, it took the whole summer for him to get ready. While the army was busy abandoning posts, Call was attempting to gather supplies. Everything was slow in coming, including the troops. It was a day and age when people traveled slowly, usually by sailing ship, horse-drawn wagon, or on foot, none of which were very rapid. The great age of railroads was in its infancy, and the iron horse would play no significant part in the Florida War. Important messages or goods could be sent by steamboat or express rider, but even these methods could take weeks to reach a destination in another part of the country. Understandably, it took quite a bit of time for companies of volunteers and militias to be organized, provisioned, and sent on their way to the southern territory.

Keeping his troops fed was one of Call's biggest problems. The government could authorize all the men and material it wanted to, but if those men were not fed they would not fight. Florida was too sparsely populated to feed and equip the large number of troops that would be required to scour the territory in search of the slippery Seminoles. Ships and wagons had to be bought or hired, often from adjoining states. It was not until the end of summer that Call felt ready to take the field.

On September 29, 1836, Call was on the east side of the Suwannee River, which effectively put him in Indian territory. At this point, he divided his forces. Part of the force went with Gen. Leigh Read down the Suwannee and south along the coast, with the intent of heading up the Withlacoochee to set up a supply depot. The rest of the men, with ten day's rations, hurried to the abandoned Fort Drane. On the eighth of October, they were joined by a number of reinforcements and a limited amount of supplies. Now in full readiness, Call and his men headed for the Cove of the Withlacoochee.[55]

On the thirteenth, the army reached the Withlacoochee and immediately discovered a major hitch in their plans. Being near the end of the rainy season, they found the river too swollen and swift to be forded. They might have cut down trees to make rafts, but someone had neglected to bring axes. In addition, numerous Indians were on the south side of the river, always quick to take aim at anyone who ventured too close to the water. Call was stymied. Unable to cross the river, he headed west, hoping to meet Read at the supply depot.

There was no supply depot, at least not where it was supposed to be. While traveling up river, Read's steamer *Izard* had run aground, broken in two, and sunk. The young naval officer in command of the steamer, Raphael Semmes, would later earn fame as a captain in the Confederate navy, but in 1836 the only thing he earned was the wrath of Governor Call. Left with two barges full of supplies, Read was forced to establish his supply depot much closer to the Gulf than had been planned. Call, unaware of the problem, searched in vain for Read and his much-needed provisions. Out of food and facing starvation, Call was forced to return to Fort Drane. Andrew Jackson was not impressed.[56]

Disgruntled soldiers were quick to complain of the lack of provisions, and they placed the blame on Governor Call. While certainly somewhat at fault, Call also fell prey to some extraordinary bad luck. One shipment was delayed at sea by unfavorable winds, while another large ship sprung a leak and nearly sank, ruining the supplies in its hold. Another large quantity of provisions was stored in a waterfront warehouse at St. Marks, which collapsed under the weight, dumping its entire contents into the river.[57]

By mid-November, Call was ready to try again. This time he was able to cross the Withlacoochee, but when he entered the Cove, he found it abandoned. The governor did not know exactly where the Indians were, but it was a safe bet that they were somewhere to the south and not very far ahead of him. Sending part of his force back across the river, he began to move both columns south, one on each side of the Withlacoochee. Sooner or later, one of the columns was bound to run into hostiles.

On November 17, a large Seminole camp was discovered and the defenders routed. The whites gave chase and on the following day a short battle was fought near a hammock outside the Cove. Call knew where the Seminoles were fleeing. Just to the east was the Wahoo Swamp, a favorite Indian haunt. Call waited a day until the column on the west side of the river was able to cross and join him, then headed for the swamp.

On the twenty-first of November, the white forces entered the Wahoo Swamp. The Seminoles, with their women and children just ahead of them, had no choice but to make a stand. It was a sharp fight, and when the army charged, the Indians were forced to retreat to the opposite side of a small stream. Call now faced a dilemma. His men were exhausted and extremely low on rations. Fording a deep stream while under fire would take time and would cost many lives. In order to ascertain how deep the water was, Maj. David Moniac, a full-blooded Creek who had been the first of his race to graduate from West Point, waded in. It was a fatal move. The Seminoles opened fire, and the slain Moniac slipped beneath the dark water. No one could tell that he had fallen in only three feet of water. To the white officers, the stream looked much deeper. Call held a staff meeting. If they attempted to cross, the loss of life would be heavy and the pursuit of the Indians might take days or even weeks. The troops, already short on supplies, might not have enough food to make it to a place where they could reprovision. Reluctantly, the governor decided to let the Indians be.[58]

By the first week of December, Call and his men were resting at the supply depot at Volusia. The Seminoles had finally been engaged and had been forced from the Cove of the Withlacoochee, but they had not been captured or defeated. The War Department had let the governor have his try at the war, and nothing had come of it. Jackson, deeply disappointed, expressed his displeasure. Governor Call, a longtime friend of the president, was alienated and would eventually become a political opponent.

On the ninth of December, Call was relieved of command and was succeeded by Maj. Gen. Thomas Sidney Jesup. Three days later, Jesup and his army headed west from Volusia for Fort Brooke, where many of the volunteers, their enlistments finished, would depart for home. All in all, 1836 had not been a very good year for the U.S. Army.

1 The Destruction of Trust

▲▲▲▲▲▲▲▲▲▲▲▲▲▲▲▲▲▲▲

America's little army had almost run out of generals with a rank high enough to run the Florida War. Indeed, there were only four men who held the exalted rank of major general, and two of them, Gaines and Scott, had already tried their hands without success. Alexander Macomb was the commanding general, superior to all the others, but his was a desk job, not a battlefield position. That left only Thomas Sidney Jesup, who held the supposedly noncombatant position of quartermaster general.

Superior rank was an important factor in deciding who should be in charge of the Florida War. Because about half of the regular army and thousands of State troops would be serving in Florida, a major general was needed to outrank any brigadier generals who would be on the scene. There was already considerable friction between the enlisted men of the regular army and the state militias. The War Department needed the commander to be someone who possessed sufficient rank to settle all the petty squabbles that would arise between his junior officers.

Thomas Jesup held the post of quartermaster general for a longer period than any other man in the army, either before or after. Appointed to the position in 1818, he would occupy it until the eve of the Civil War. Decisive and efficient, he was extremely well suited to the job. He had fought with distinction in the War of 1812, having served under Winfield Scott at the battles of Chippewa and Lundy's Lane. In the latter contest, he had led his men brilliantly, getting the better of a superior British force in extremely close fighting. Despite the fact that his position as quartermaster general required him to reside and work in Washington, Jesup spent as much time as possible in the field, examining facilities and meeting with junior officers.[1]

The duties of the Quartermaster's Department might, at first, seem trivial. The all-important tasks of purchasing provisions and weaponry were not Jesup's responsibility but belonged to the Commissary and Ordinance Departments. Having men, weaponry, and provisions was one thing; getting them where they needed to be was another. It was the duty of the quartermasters to hire or purchase both land and water transportation for the army's needs. The other major responsibility of the department was, as the name suggests, the quartering of the troops. This involved everything from the purchase of tents to the construction of forts. In addition, the quartermasters were in charge of obtaining forage for the army's numerous horses and distributing uniforms to the men. When things were not where they were supposed to be, as often happened early in the Florida War, it was the quartermaster general who, rightly or wrongly, was pointed to as the villain.[2]

Jesup arrived in Florida fresh from another Indian war. In the summer of 1836, trouble had broken out among the Creek Indians of eastern Alabama and western Georgia, who, like the Seminoles, were resisting forced removal to the west. Jesup had been dispatched by President Jackson to take command in the area pending the arrival of Winfield Scott from Florida. Both generals happened to arrive in Georgia at the same time, and Jesup immediately put himself under Scott's command. Scott's plan was similar to the one he had employed in Florida. Jesup was sent to lead the Alabama wing, while Scott would lead the Georgia wing. As in Florida, the plan was to crush the Indians between the converging wings. As usual, Scott moved slowly and carefully, refusing to take action until everything was in proper order. Jesup, faced with open hostilities close to his position in Alabama, went on the offensive. By the time Scott was ready to move, Jesup had nearly ended the war.[3]

Jesup's initiative not only defeated the Creeks but also ended his close friendship with Scott. Feeling upstaged by Jesup, Scott expressed his frustration in a letter. Jesup responded in a like manner. As angry letters continued to be exchanged, one of Jesup's found its way to the president's desk. In it were the words "We have the Florida scenes enacted over again. The war ought to have been ended a week ago." Jackson had heard enough. Fed up with the procrastinating Scott, he recalled the general to Washington. Jesup, on the other hand, had earned Jackson's respect. Decisive action was what Old Hickory appreciated. In the aging president's eyes, Jesup was just the sort of man to put an end to the embarrassing Seminole situation.[4]

FIGURE II.

Maj. Gen. Thomas Sidney Jesup.

By permission of the Florida State Archives. Image #PRO9829, DBCN#AAI-7345.

Jesup arrived in Tampa early in November but did not take immediate command in deference to Governor Call, who was about to launch his second offensive. Unlike many of his fellow officers, Jesup was not a glory-seeker. After Call's failure at Wahoo Swamp, Jesup set out for Volusia, where the majority of the governor's army was encamped. As his small force headed east, Jesup kept an eye open for Seminole villages or war parties. Few were discovered, and only one Indian was taken prisoner. The biggest prize was the capture of thirty to forty blacks, along with the intelligence that there were about 300 other escaped slaves in the vicinity.

Upon relieving Call, Jesup immediately began a march back to Tampa Bay, where many of the volunteers, their enlistments soon to expire, would depart for home. Eager to make the most of the limited time the volunteers would be available, Jesup sent detachments off to hunt for Indians as the column moved across the territory. As had happened earlier, few were found. In a letter to the War Department, Jesup warned his superiors not to expect too much: "You shall not be disappointed in my efforts, though you may be in their results. The country is so extensive, and contains so many hiding places for large as well as small parties, that the enemy may escape from me."[5]

It was a new type of war, one that would require a new set of tactics. The tried-and-true method of simply sending a large force into the enemy's homeland would not work in Florida: The territory was too large and too little explored. The Seminoles were also less firmly settled. Unlike their counterparts in the remainder of the eastern United States, the Seminoles were relatively mobile and operated within a territory with which they alone were familiar. It would become the nation's first large-scale guerrilla war, and the army was not prepared for it. Jesup soon came to the conclusion that the only way he could hope to conquer these Indians was to wear them down. By continually pressuring the Seminoles, Jesup sought to force the Indians into giving up their hopeless cause. The only way to keep that sort of pressure on was to have a massive presence in Florida. Jesup would eventually need a force of more than 9,000 men, more soldiers than Winfield Scott used to conquer Mexico City less than a decade later. It would be a tall order for an army that numbered little more than 7,000.[6]

It was not, however, an impossible request to fill. About half the force would be volunteers and militia. Knowing it would be a long, hard campaign, Jesup had the volunteers signed up for one-year enlistments, instead of the usual three months. Congress, with extreme reluctance, allowed for a slight increase in the size of the army. Jesup was also able to call upon the navy for help. For once, the seagoing service was able to participate in an Indian War. Florida has a long, porous coastline ideal (even today) for smuggling. It was widely believed that the Seminoles were being supplied by traders from Cuba and the Bahamas, so it was deemed necessary to send a small naval squadron to the peninsula in order to patrol the coast. Naval officers patrolling the Florida coastline were also able to send many of their sailors ashore to man forts and to patrol the many lakes and rivers that covered the territory.

Jesup also received further help from the navy in the form of a brigade of marines under the command of the commandant of the corps, Col.

Archibald Henderson. The conflict was drawing men and material from all corners of the nation and remained front page news in all the major papers. It may have been called the Florida War, but it was becoming national in scope.

It was an almost imperceptible change, but the luck of the Seminoles began to turn. No longer were they facing a disorganized army, one that had been rushed to the scene for the purpose of handling an emergency situation. The army had learned some of the lessons of the previous year and was prepared to carry the war to its bitter conclusion. The difficulty of keeping the troops supplied, though ever-present, was not as severe as in the early days of the war. As quartermaster general, Jesup knew where to get necessary supplies, how to ship them, and where to put them. While waiting for a fresh supply of fighting men, Jesup put his available forces to work. The results appeared minor but proved telling.

On January 10, 1837, after capturing about fifteen blacks, Jesup learned that Osceola was ill and in the company of only a few followers. On January 15, a boat was destroyed on the Withlacoochee, killing ten Indians and wounding another twenty. Two days later, the local militia from St. Augustine caught up with a band of Seminoles that had been ravaging plantations on the peninsula's eastern coast. During the fight, John Caesar, the same black Seminole who had opened negotiations with Gaines, was killed.[7]

The fact that blacks were involved in many of the depredations had the white population of St. Augustine concerned. On January 23, two free blacks were charged with supplying ammunition to the hostile Indians. When it was realized that some of the supplies captured with the Seminoles had come from within the city walls, the white residents began to look with understandable suspicion upon the black refugees who dwelt among them. Fears of a slave uprising were ever-present in the South. General Jesup played upon that fear when writing to the governors of neighboring states, requesting volunteers. Whether he believed it or not, Jesup told the governor of Georgia, "This . . . is a negro, not an Indian war." The volunteers were soon forthcoming.[8]

Late in January, near Lake Apopka, Osuchee (Cooper) and a band of followers were surprised by a company of regulars. The chief and three other men were killed and many of his followers captured. Not far away, Colonel Henderson and his Marines were seeing action. On the twenty-seventh of January, the whites came upon a Seminole camp and launched an attack. The ensuing Battle of Hatchee-Lustee was furious but accomplished less than hoped for. The Indian warriors fought from the nearby swamp, then made their usual escape. Still, they had not gotten away without loss. Thirty to forty Indians and blacks were taken prisoner, most of them being women and children. The army knew how important it was to capture the women and children. With his family shipped west, there would be little incentive for a Seminole warrior to keep up the fight. About 100 ponies were also seized, many of them loaded with packs, in addition to about 1,400 head of cattle. Such losses were bound to have a demoralizing effect upon the Indians.[9]

The futility of the struggle must have been becoming apparent to many a Seminole warrior and his family. Up until January the Indians had done well against the whites but had gained nothing. The white men were unwilling to yield on the matter of emigration and showed no signs of leaving Indian land. The Indians knew they could continue the war for years, but to what end? The Seminoles were finite in number and could expect little or no help, such as the United States had gotten from France during the Revolution. The whites, on the other hand, seemed to have an endless supply of soldiers and equipment. Sooner or later, the Seminoles would be reduced to a few wandering bands, forever on the run, forever hiding in the most inhospitable places, prisoners of their own quest for freedom.

Following the successes of mid-January, Jesup had reason to believe that a breakthrough was possible. Prisoners were telling him that the Indians were tired of fighting and might be willing to surrender. One such captive was sent as a messenger on January 28 and returned the following day "with pacific messages from Alligator and Abraham." Two days later the black chief Abraham came to the American camp and spoke with Jesup. The conversation went well, and on February 3, Abraham returned with a delegation of chiefs that included Alligator, Jumper, and a nephew of Micanopy. A truce was called, and a formal meeting was scheduled for the eighteenth.[10]

The truce was slow to take effect. On February 8, a large force under King Philip and his son Coacoochee attacked the camp of Colonel Fanning on the shore of Lake Monroe, near today's town of Sanford. The battle started before dawn and lasted for about four hours, ending in disappointment for the Indians. The element of surprise, so critical in the victories over Dade and Clinch, was no longer available to the Seminole warriors. Soldiers slept with their loaded muskets by their sides behind a protective breastwork, with sentries posted. At the commencement of the battle, a gun crew was dispatched to a small steamer anchored offshore, which was able to put its cannon to effective use. Under such heavy pressure, the Indians were forced to retreat, having killed but one white man, Captain Mellon.[11]

February 18, the appointed day for the talks, came and went without the appearance of Indians at Fort Dade, where the talks were to take place. Some did show up in a day or two, but these were low-ranking chiefs. Jesup wanted to talk with Micanopy and would settle for no one else. Finally, in early March, Jumper and a few other high chiefs came in to talk and convinced Jesup they had the authority to speak for Micanopy.

On March 6, 1837, a "Capitulation" was signed by Jesup and the chiefs who were present. Micanopy came in twelve days later and also signed the pact. The most controversial aspect of the agreement concerned the fate of the black Seminoles. With the exception of recent runaways, Jesup seemed content to let the blacks go west with their Indian friends. Yet no matter how definite the wording of the treaty, it soon became a matter of interpretation as to which blacks would be allowed to travel west with the Indians. The treaty read, "The Seminoles and their allies." Did this mean free blacks or did it simply refer to the Mikasukis, Yuchis, and other tribes that were associated with the Seminoles? In his 1858 book *The Exiles of Florida*, Joshua Giddings, an abolitionist congressman from Ohio, stated emphatically that "allies" meant black Seminoles. Unfortunately, Giddings work was extremely one-sided. The treaty also mentioned "their negroes, their *bona fide* property, shall accompany them to the west." But how did an Indian, who possessed no written bill of sale, prove that he was the bona fide owner of a certain slave? As with the word "they" in the Treaty of Payne's Landing, the exact meaning could be interpreted in whatever way was most convenient to the reader.[12]

The problem with slave catchers was serious enough to cause Jesup to issue an order banning all whites from the southern half of the peninsula. There was also a problem with whites attempting to have Indians arrested for crimes or unpaid debts. Bad faith was building on both sides, even as the Indians began to turn themselves in. The unscrupulous actions of slave catchers must have caused many a Seminole to doubt the sincerity of the general's word. At the same time, white officers noticed that many of the warriors who entered the camps arrived without families and seemed more interested in gathering supplies and liquor. The outbreak of disease slowed the influx of emigrants, but still, the numbers waiting for deportation increased. By the end of May, many senior chiefs, including Micanopy and Jumper, had surrendered. Although things were not going as smoothly as Jesup would have liked, it appeared as if the war might actually be ending.[13]

Reports coming out of Florida varied from week to week. Readers of the *National Intelligencer* had every right to be confused and concerned. March 3: "Nothing could be more certain" than that the war was over. March 8: "The war not ended yet!" March 13: "It is the general opinion that the war is drawing to a close." March 19: "The prospect of peace . . . is growing dim and indistinct." April 7: "General Jesup believes the war to be at an end." April 26: "Interference of unprincipled white men . . . will . . . lead to a renewal of the war." May 10: "Indians are coming in as fast as can be expected." June 5: "Indians did not intend to emigrate." June 6: "The delay of the Indians . . . is very suspicious." June 9: "The close of the war as yet far distant."[14]

The two Seminole leaders Jesup worried about most were Osceola and Sam Jones. Both were violently opposed to emigration. In their eyes, Micanopy had no authority to order them to surrender. Osceola, young and determined, was the "war spirit," the man who best defined the Seminole attitude. Sam Jones (also known as Abiaca) was a different sort. An old man when the war began, he was just as defiant, in his own way, as any of the younger warriors. The combination of Osceola and Sam Jones was a powerful one, and it soon made itself felt.

On the night of June 2, the two chiefs, with about 200 warriors, slipped into the detention camp outside Fort Brooke on Tampa Bay. Either by force or by plan, they were able to lead the entire group of potential emigrants, about 700 people, away. Exactly how this happened remains a bit of a mystery. Jesup had been warned such an occurrence might take place and had taken precautions. Creek spies had been sent into the camp, and sentries were posted. It was not, however, a secure camp. There were no walls and no fences to contain the natives. They had supposedly come in voluntarily and were not considered prisoners in need of confinement. On June 21, the readers of the *National Intelligencer* received the unwelcome news: "Our hopes are all blasted. We have war again."[15]

The peace treaty had fallen apart; the war was not over. Blame was immediately pointed in Jesup's direction, and he offered to relinquish command. Several weeks later, stung by criticism, he withdrew the offer.

He would not leave Florida a defeated man. The entire incident seems to have deeply embittered a man who held personal honor in high esteem. As far as General Jesup was concerned, the word of an Indian was never to be trusted again. He also came to believe that because the Indians had been treacherous toward him, he could be just as deceitful toward them. It was a change in policy that would make martyrs of the Seminoles and a villain of Thomas Jesup.[16]

While the shooting war was going on in Florida, a war of words was taking place in Frederick, Maryland. Standing before a Military Court of Inquiry was Maj. Gen. Winfield Scott. Upon receipt of the letter from General Jesup complaining of Scott's foot dragging against the Creeks, President Jackson had ordered Scott back to Washington to explain the failure of his Florida campaign. Also brought before the court was the matter of Gaines's conduct and the contents of various letters published by or on behalf of all three major generals. The three highest field officers in the United States Army were on trial, and the public anxiously awaited the show.

They were not disappointed. First came a letter from Gaines, defending his own actions then placing blame upon Scott for Gaines's embarrassments at Camp Izard on the Withlacoochee. Gaines's tone was personal and to the point: Scott held a personal grudge against Gaines and had sought to do more damage to his personal enemy than to the Indian enemy. In one letter, Gaines went as far as to equate Scott with Benedict Arnold.[17]

Gaines's letter had been long, but Scott's verbal response overwhelmed it. No one escaped Scott's wrath. He started with President Jackson, switched to Jesup, then zeroed in on Gaines. His attitude was best shown in his opening statement to the court: "When the Doge of Genoa, for some imaginary offence imputed by Louis XIV, was torn from his government and compelled to visit France to debase himself before that inflated monarch, he was asked, in the palace, what struck him with the greatest wonder amid the blaze of magnificence in his view? 'To find *myself* here!' was the reply of the indignant Lescaro."[18]

Scott went on for days. His defense, delivered by himself, not by any advocate, filled about thirty pages of fine print in the *Army and Navy Chronicle* and extended for three issues. The whole piece is a masterwork of logic and rhetoric. One can feel envy for those present in the courtroom for having the good fortune to witness such a display. One can also feel sympathy for their having to sit through it all. In the end, Scott managed to vindicate himself before the court and had the satisfaction of seeing both Gaines and Jesup get their wrists slapped for comments made in the press. All in all, it seemed nothing more than a grand opportunity for proud men to air their differences in public.[19]

Next to enter the public relations fray was the retired General Clinch and the former secretary of war, Lewis Cass. In testimony given to the Court of Inquiry, Clinch had accused Cass of not providing the necessary support Clinch had requested prior to the outbreak of hostilities. Cass leapt to his own defense, attacking Clinch in the press. For many Americans, it seemed the army was spending more time in battle with itself than in battle with the Seminoles.[20]

In some ways, that was true. For the most part, the war had been put on hold. The sickly season was commencing, and the army was in no condition to take the field. Because Jesup had felt the war to be ending, he had not made preparations for a massive campaign. As it stood, several companies of regulars had already been ordered to posts in other parts of the nation and would have to be reassigned to Florida. In addition, many of the state forces had been sent home. Jesup was determined to defeat the Seminoles, but the task would have to wait until the Florida environment allowed it.

The Seminoles, as they did for every year of the war, took advantage of the white reluctance to fight during the summer. Crops were planted and supplies were gathered. Skins and fish were caught and traded to Cubans and Bahamians who had slipped past the navy's thin blockade or to whites who were making a profit selling war materiel and whiskey to both sides. This ability to recuperate during the summer was one of the primary reasons the war lasted as long as it did.

The situation may not have changed in Florida, but it had in Washington. Andrew Jackson had left office, replaced by his chosen successor, Martin Van Buren. With a new president came a new secretary of war, Joel Roberts Poinsett. The changes were subtle, not dramatic. Because the Jacksonian Democrats were still in power, national policy had not been altered, even if the faces had. Still, the overpowering presence of Andrew Jackson was no longer a daily factor in the lives of those who had to deal with the national government or were a part of it. Jackson had been a national hero and practically unassailable. Martin Van Buren was a professional politician and vulnerable. His political opponents would no doubt make good use of an unpopular war on the southern frontier.

Politics were somewhat different in the early nineteenth century than they are in the early twenty-first. Two distinct political parties had just evolved, the Whigs (conservative) and the Democrats (liberal). Great orators, such as Henry Clay and Daniel Webster, were prominent, and their speeches could last for hours and draw a great crowd. Fistfights and the occasional duel between congressmen were not uncommon. Like the army in Florida, Congress took the summer off. Indeed, it was the habit of Congress to adjourn on the day the president took office, March 4. Normally, they would not reconvene until December.

Another event had taken place that proved far more serious than the administrative changes in Washington. The Panic of 1837 had struck, and the national economy was hurting. For several years the sale of government owned land had served to wipe out the national debt. Most of that land had been purchased on credit, much of it questionable. As was inevitable, the speculative bubble had burst. When the Florida War had commenced, the government had been faced with the enviable problem of what to do with millions of dollars of surplus revenues. As a result of the panic, the cost of the war soon became a matter for serious debate.

For the most part, the financial woes seem to have generated a lot of debate but little action concerning the war. When the secretary of war asked Congress for $1.6 million to fight the war, the request was quickly granted. Ironically, this large appropriation was passed during a special session of Congress that had been called to deal with the financial crisis. As usual, it was the little fellow that bore the weight of economic hardship: On August 3, 1837, the army was ordered to quit supplying government rations to the settlers who had fled to the safety of the military fortifications.[21]

General Jesup, unable to mount a summer offensive, turned to other strategies. Keeping small detachments in the field and on the move helped maintain a pressure on the Seminoles. Jesup hoped such pressure would force the Indians into surrendering or, at the least, to head south, away from white settlements. More important, the general began to notice a significant number of blacks turning themselves in. Apparently they had grown tired of life on the run and of living in inhospitable hammocks and swamps. For many, returning to slavery may not have been as difficult a decision as we might believe. Some had been taken by force, either by Seminole raiders intent on destroying white wealth or by peer pressure from other slaves more intent on obtaining freedom. Others wished to rejoin loved ones who had not escaped. Still others longed for a life where food, shelter, and security were readily available, even if it meant returning to bondage. An existence where you had to live off the land while in fear of being slain would not appeal to everyone. Jesup, along with most other whites, felt that if the blacks were removed from the equation, the Indians might be more agreeable to emigration.

In order to speed the taking of blacks, Jesup allowed that any captured blacks could be considered plunder, and their value divided among the captors. The policy tended to backfire. Runaways had been coming in with the hope of being returned to familiar plantations but now found themselves the property of soldiers or Creek warriors who would quickly sell them to the highest bidder.[22]

Later, noticing that the number of incoming blacks was slowing down, Jesup changed his policy and ordered that all blacks be held until the secretary of war decided their fate. The number of surrendering blacks now increased again, but the policy created legal problems. The government now found itself the owner of a large number of slaves, a situation it had never been in before. Jesup, perhaps hoping to quickly remove both a large group of combatants and a possible legal problem, changed his policy again and shipped most of the blacks west to join the Seminoles who had already been settled in the Indian Territory. The policy of offering a safe haven for blacks proved fruitful, if controversial. By the summer of the next year, few blacks remained among the Seminole forces.[23]

Unfortunately for General Jesup, the removal of the black Seminoles did not end the war. True, the Indian ranks had been thinned considerably, but their resolve was stronger, and they would continue to hold on for a number of years to come. Above and beyond everything else, the Seminoles were determined to stay in Florida, with or without their black allies.

Jesup now began to make plans for the winter campaign of 1837. Equipment and supplies better suited to the Florida environment were requisitioned and delivered. Still smarting from the escape of June 2, his policy regarding the Indians hardened. No longer would he hold peace negotiations with the Seminoles. If the Indians wanted to talk, the only subject he would discuss would be the details of their immediate surrender for emigration. Jesup could be compassionate and understanding, but he was not going to be toyed with again.[24]

In September 1837, things finally began to go right for the general. South of St. Augustine, a detachment of regulars and Florida Militia under Brig. Gen. Joseph Hernandez were guided by a former slave of King Philip to an Indian encampment. Creeping up at night and surrounding the camp, they were able to completely surprise the Indians, capturing all but one of them. Included in the haul was none other than King Philip himself. One of the most powerful chiefs of the Seminole Nation had been captured, along with a large number of his followers.[25]

General Hernandez's luck continued the next night. One of the captured Indians agreed to lead the white men to another camp nearby, this one populated by Yuchi Indians. Once again, the whites were able to encircle the camp and capture nearly the entire band. The Yuchis were able to mount a short, desperate defense, and one man on each side was killed. Captured this time was another important chief, Yuchi Billy.[26]

Seeing an opportunity to end the war, Jesup now embarked upon a policy that was to bring him lasting infamy. A runner was sent out from the captured King Philip, requesting that his son Coacoochee (also known as Wildcat), come in to hold a parley with the whites. Arriving under a flag of truce, Coacoochee and his companion, Blue Snake, were taken prisoner. Coacoochee was later released in order to bring in his followers, but threats upon the life of his father served to ensure the young chief's return.[27]

Late in October, the biggest prize of all was captured. Osceola and another influential chief, Coa Hadjo, called for a parley. A site south of St. Augustine was agreed upon, and General Hernandez, under orders from Jesup, set out to meet them. A white flag was flying when Osceola and Coa Hadjo came forward. After a short talk with the Indians, Hernandez gave a prearranged signal and a circle of soldiers quickly surrounded the two Seminole leaders. Jesup had once again violated the most sacred custom of warfare.[28]

For Osceola, the war was over. Taken to the fortress at St. Augustine, he was later transferred to Fort Moultrie at Charleston. Three months after his capture, Osceola was dead. The official cause of death was quinsy (severe sore throat) and complications from malaria. There was little reason to doubt the doctor's word. Surgeon Jarvis had reported that

FIGURE 12.
Ee-mat-lá, King Philip, Second Chief, by George Catlin.
By permission of the Smithsonian American Art Museum;
gift of Mrs. Joseph Harrison Jr. #1985.66.302.

Osceola did not look well when captured, and rumors had been circulating for some time that the Indian leader was ill.[29]

If news of the Florida War had slipped from the front pages of the papers, it now reappeared with a vengeance. The legend of Osceola, already commenced before his capture, only intensified with his death. In a nation with no mythic heroes from some long gone golden age, the tale of Osceola filled a certain need. His passion, and those of the Seminoles who fought beside him, was something that any person could understand. No matter how much exaggerated, the basic facts caught the American people's romantic imagination. A simple man had fought des-

FIGURE 13.

Seminole chief Osceola, by George Catlin. Painted shortly before his death.
By permission of the Florida State Archives. Image #RC02428, DBCN#AAM-1872.

perately to defend his homeland against impossible odds, had been captured by treachery, and had died a prisoner. Totally accurate or not, it was
the kind of tragic tale Americans could easily embrace.

A writer in the *Knickerbocker* magazine pointed out that Osceola's "life
was engaged in a nobler cause than that which incites the actions of
many whom the world calls great. If those who have devastated the earth
to gratify their selfish ambition or thirst for conquest have historians to
record their deeds and poets to sing their praises, let us not withhold a
token of applause to one who committed fewer wrongs, and during his
life was a brave defender of his country."[30]

In many ways, Osceola was an enigma. The name itself is a corruption
of the Creek name Asi-Yoholo. This most famous of Seminoles may not

have been a full-blooded Indian. His mother had, at one time, been married to a white trader named William Powell, and throughout the war Osceola was often called Powell. He was also not a Seminole by birth, though he certainly died one. Instead, he was a Red Stick Creek who had been driven to Florida by Andrew Jackson's victory in the Creek War of 1814. He was not, as popularly believed, head chief of the Seminoles. Indeed, many of the hereditary Seminole chiefs did not care for Osceola. In the final analysis, Osceola was simply a very gifted leader who could inspire with his words and deeds. As the writer of a *Niles' Register* article remarked, "Such was Osceola, who will long be remembered as the man that with the feeblest means produced the most terrible effects."[31]

It is difficult for us to realize just how famous Osceola became. Today, his image looks less like an Indian warrior and more like a costumed dandy. We have seen so many western movies that we forget the fact that the attire of the Plains Indians was not suitable to subtropical Florida. Yet for almost forty years Osceola was *the* symbol of the Indian resistance to the inexorable onslaught of the white man. Almost half the states of the union have a town or some other public area named after the man. Oddly enough, Oklahoma, where the emigrating Seminoles were shipped to, seems to have no public place named in honor of the tribe's most famous warrior. It was not until the time of Sitting Bull and Chief Joseph that another Indian was able to eclipse the fame of Osceola.[32]

If Osceola was the hero of these newly created folk tales, Thomas Jesup was the villain. There is no doubt that Jesup was the one who gave the order to take Osceola and the others prisoner; he never denied it. The question remains: What were his justifications for doing it? After the escape of June 2, he may well have felt that the rules of polite warfare no longer applied. Yet if no one honored a flag of truce, how could a conflict be ended other than by the complete annihilation of one side by the other? In his own defense, Jesup held that the capitulation of March 6 was still in effect, and that a white flag was honored only for surrender, not for new negotiations. In Jesup's eyes, Osceola and the others had come in to surrender; their capture was intended to prevent any Indian treachery. In the end, the practical considerations meant nothing to those steeped in the romantic tradition. The cult of Osceola had begun, and there was no stopping it.

General Jesup now had some reason to feel confident. A good many of the Indian leaders had been captured, and others were less than optimistic about their chances for holding off the whites. The leadership and manpower of the Seminole Nation had been severely damaged and there was every reason to believe that a strong offensive would bring in the remainder of the Seminole bands. Throughout the summer of 1837, men and supplies had been pouring into Florida. Indeed, the call for volunteers had been so successful that Jesup found he had more men than he could feed. Companies of volunteers had come from as far west as Missouri and as far north as Pennsylvania. By the time the campaign commenced, the total force was about 9,000 men, an unprecedented number for an Indian war.[33]

Such a grand army called for a grand strategy. Jesup's plan was simple in principal but complex in organization. He divided his force into several columns, each one moving independently, but all going in the same general direction. The easternmost force was commanded by General Hernandez, whom Jesup appears to have held in high regard. Hernandez's force was itself divided into several columns of both regular and volunteer troops that scoured the area between the St. Johns River and the Atlantic coast, continually heading south toward the area northeast of Lake Okeechobee. Traveling down the St. Johns by boat was General Eustis's column, accompanied by General Jesup. At Volusia, this force was joined by two other columns, which had been cleaning out north-central Florida. Colonel Twiggs had covered the area between the St. Johns and the Oklawaha, while Colonel Mills had come from the Suwannee, then through the area bordered by the Withlacoochee and the Oklawaha. Col. Zachary Taylor had left Tampa with a large force and was moving down the center of the territory, between the Peace and Kissimmee Rivers. Taylor was also responsible for securing the western half of the peninsula between Tampa Bay and the Caloosahatchee River. Sooner or later, if need be, all these forces would unite to capture or crush the Seminoles.[34]

As large as Jesup's force was, it was only a portion of the total military force employed in Florida. A combined unit from the army and navy was operating on the bays and rivers of the East Coast under the command of Lt. Levin Powell of the navy. A large number of Louisiana volunteers under Col. Persifor Smith were penetrating the southwest portion of the peninsula via the Caloosahatchee River. To the north, troops under General Nelson were patrolling the northwest portion of the territory, while Colonel Snodgrass worked the northeast. In the center of Florida, Lieutenant Colonel Coffee was attempting to keep the warriors and their

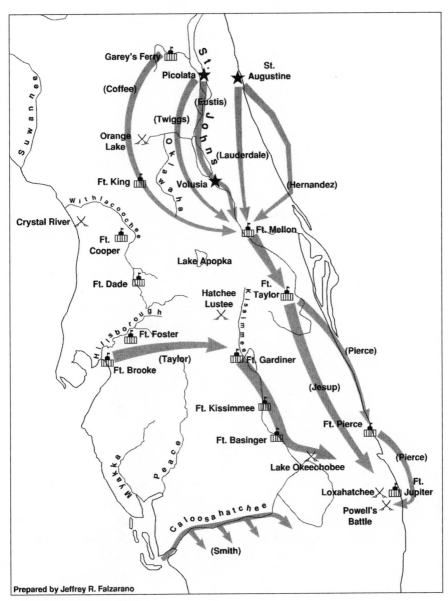

MAP 5. Florida War, 1837.

families on the run. For the harried Seminoles, it must have seemed as if there was a soldier lurking behind every stand of trees.[35]

While the plan certainly had more facets than that of Winfield Scott, Jesup was careful not to make the same mistakes. Most important, Jesup's moves were not so perfectly timed. Well aware of the fact that his men were moving through unexplored territory, he held them to no specific timetable. If the Seminoles chose to stand and fight, he would be glad to accommodate. If the Indians chose to flee, he would be happy to pursue. As the columns moved, they would build roads and open supply depots, allowing the army to maintain a presence in the field, keeping a relentless pressure on the natives. Sooner or later, the Indians would be forced to surrender or stand their ground.

In the meantime, some of the Indians that had already been taken out of action were making plans of their own. Most of the Seminoles that had been captured under the flags of truce were being kept at Fort Marion in St. Augustine. It was an imposing stone fortress originally built by the Spanish and is still standing. Today it is a national monument that has reverted to its original name of Castillo de San Marcos and remains the centerpiece of the nation's oldest city. In late 1837, it was part of a system of coastal defense, a garrison protecting a frontier town surrounded by hostile Indians, and a prison where the most important of the captured Seminoles were kept.

There was little doubt in anyone's mind that Fort Marion was the most secure structure in all of Florida. There was little chance of Indian invaders getting in, nor was it likely that any of the captives would get out. There was, however, at least one Indian who felt otherwise. Coacoochee was a natural leader and was determined to carry on the war. It was going to be a difficult thing to do, however, from inside a cell at Fort Marion.

The cell was a large room with a high, curved ceiling that had originally been a storeroom. In all, it held about twenty-five people. Imprisoned with Coacoochee were Osceola, King Philip, and John Cavallo, a well-known black Seminole leader. Courage, cunning, and desperation led to a plan of escape. High on the wall was a narrow opening that let in a small amount of light and ventilation. The opening was about three feet high but only eight inches wide. In addition, two bars ran across it, preventing even a child from crawling through. For weeks, the Indians ate as little as possible, losing weight so that they could fit through the opening. Placing the blade of a knife between the rocks, the Indians were able to stand upon the handle to reach the window. From that position a warrior would slowly work at the mortar that held the bars in place. Eventually, one of the bars came free.

The time for a decision had been reached. King Philip was too old and declined to accompany his son. Osceola also chose to remain behind. One can only assume that the flaming spirit of Osceola had been quenched by sickness. Perhaps he sensed that his end was near. Perhaps he felt too weak to travel. Perhaps he had simply been defeated. We can only mourn the fact that no one recorded the conversations that took place that night between Coacoochee, his father, and the failing spirit of Osceola.

Coacoochee, John Cavallo, sixteen men, and two women decided to take their chances on the night of November 29, 1837. Frustrated by a guard who wanted to socialize with the captives, they ignored him until he went outside and fell asleep. They then climbed up to the small ledge just below the window and, one by one, slipped through. It could not have been easy. The coquina rock that makes up the walls of the fortress is composed of sharp fossilized shells, which cut and scraped their skin as they inched through. Once outside, a rope of knotted blankets was used to lower the escapees to the ground, some twenty-five feet below. Free of their captivity, the warriors and their two women made their way south. The Seminoles now had a new leader and a war spirit who would continue the struggle that Osceola and King Philip had started.[36]

In the fall of 1837, the government sent a delegation of Cherokees to Florida in an effort to persuade the Seminoles to move west. On December 5, the Cherokees met with General Jesup, who was less than enthusiastic about the help they offered. Jesup was in the process of beginning his winter campaign and saw the Cherokee delegation's effort as a useless delay. In no mood to be deceived again, Jesup insisted the Seminoles fulfill the unconditional terms of the March 6 capitulation. Sensing what he felt to be Seminole stalling tactics, Jesup ordered Micanopy and his followers, who had come to the meeting under a white flag, seized. Outraged, Cherokee leader John Ross protested to the secretary of war, declaring the action an "unprecedented violation of that sacred rule which has ever been recognized by every nation, civilized or uncivilized, of treating with all due respect those who had ever presented themselves under a flag of truce before the enemy." Jesup responded that he had informed the Cherokees that any Seminole who came in would not be permitted to return to their homes. He also felt that many of the Seminoles had used the Cherokee negotiations as a means to buy time. The general seems to have discovered that the only way to catch a Seminole chief was to give him a white flag.[37]

Finished with the Cherokees, Jesup began his winter offensive. Making its way south through the peninsula was the largest army the United States had assembled since the war with Britain. The importance of the Seminole War was evident. Over half of the regular army and thousands of state troops from across the country had been dispatched in an effort to suppress a disorganized force that could not gather more than 500 warriors in any one place. The pride of the American people had been wounded, their dreams had been tarnished, and a portion of their economy had been assailed. Few people doubted that the Seminoles had to be crushed.

Of the various columns that made up Jesup's army, the one commanded by Zachary Taylor was making the most progress. Already known as "Old Rough and Ready," Taylor was ready to handle the rough terrain he encountered. After taking on supplies from the depot at Fort Gardiner, Taylor and about 1,000 men headed south along the Kissimmee River on December 19.

It did not take them long to find the fleeing Seminoles. On the first day out, Jumper and sixty-three followers turned themselves in. The next day another twenty-six gave up. On the third day, Fort Basinger was built to house the heavy artillery, the baggage, and the sick. The following day, the army was again on the move, somewhat reduced in size due to sickness and the need to leave troops behind to guard captives and supplies.

Taylor found the fleeing Seminoles on Christmas Day 1837. On wetlands along the north shore of Lake Okeechobee, Taylor captured a lone Indian who pointed to the place where the warriors were waiting. The Seminoles had taken up positions in a dense hammock surrounded by a waterlogged field of sawgrass. To get to them, the soldiers would have to wade through thick mud and lacerating vegetation. They would then face withering fire from the Seminoles who were perched in the trees, practically hidden from view. The troops at the front of the American line would no doubt suffer the severest casualties.

For this dubious honor Taylor chose the Missouri volunteers, the only nonregulars in the force. Opposed to Taylor's force of around 800 men was less than half that number of Indians, led by Sam Jones, Alligator, and Coacoochee, newly arrived from St. Augustine. The whites advanced at 12:30. As expected, the Missourians and the regulars behind them suffered greatly. The Indians targeted the officers, and many companies were soon without leaders. Col. Richard Gentry, at the head of the Missouri Volunteers, was one of the first to die. Three junior officers and more than twenty enlisted men fell before the remaining volunteers pulled back.

The departure of the volunteers brought the approximately 200 men of the Sixth Infantry to the front of the line. Their commander, Lt. Col. Alexander Thompson, was hit three times. One ball entered his abdomen, another his chest, and, finally and fatally, a shot tore through his chin and neck. His adjutant, Lt. J. P. Center, was shot through the head, while Capt. J. Van Swearingen died from a severe neck wound. Another young officer, Lt. Francis Brooke, was killed by a ball through the heart. Almost leaderless, the men of the Sixth Infantry pressed on, suffering nearly 40 percent casualties in close fighting with the Seminoles.[38]

Their ranks decimated, the Sixth fell back and was replaced by about 160 men of the Fourth Infantry. This force, under Lt. Col. William S. Foster and aided by the remnants of the Sixth and a few volunteers, were able to gain the hammock and began to drive the Indians toward the lake. Taylor then sent his reserves against the Indian's right side. Faced with a fresh, superior force, Sam Jones began a retreat. Alligator and Coacoochee soon followed suit. Their mission had been to slow the Americans down enough to allow the women and children to escape. The mission accomplished, it was time to go. After two and a half hours of desperate fighting, the entire Seminole force disappeared across Lake Okeechobee. Having a large number of wounded and possessing no boats, Taylor could not give chase. The largest battle of the Second Seminole War was over.

Eager for some good news, the army hailed it as a victory and Zachary Taylor became an instant hero, earning a promotion to brigadier general and lasting national fame. Calling it a victory was stretching the truth, though technically correct. At the end of the day, the United States Army held the disputed ground. The fact that the Americans had suffered horrendous casualties and had killed little more than a dozen Indians seemed unimportant. Taylor had charged the enemy and routed them. The fact that the Seminoles had escaped was also overlooked. Americans expected a war filled with great battles and heroic charges, and Zachary Taylor had given them just what they wanted.[39]

It has been argued that the Battle of Lake Okeechobee was the beginning of the road that eventually led Zachary Taylor to the White House.

Although many events are needed to bring anyone to such a prominent position, there is some truth in the statement. Before the battle, Taylor was just another colonel in the army. His victory gave him the rank and fame he would need to gain further renown in the Mexican War. He would probably have gained the rank in the intervening years, but not necessarily the fame. His victory in Florida gave him a reputation as a winner. That reputation made him the logical choice to be given command in the early stages of the Mexican War. His victories in that war were what made him president. It is one of those strange and interesting twists of fate that allowed the Seminoles to make a very unintentional mark on American history.

As the year 1838 opened, it began to appear as if the Florida War might be headed toward a conclusion. As Jesup's huge army swept through the territory, it seemed to leave no refuge unchecked. Before long, the Indians would surely have their backs to the sea. Granted, the war had taken somewhat longer than anticipated, but Jesup could feel as if he were making some real progress.

Jesup's forces kept on the move, sweeping toward the southeast coast. The columns of Eustis, Hernandez, Warren, and Taylor had come together and were making their way down the eastern side of Lake Okeechobee, now under the direct command of General Jesup. Colonel Smith's column was patrolling the Caloosahatchee, preventing any Seminole escape around the west side of the Lake. Lieutenant Powell of the navy and his motley crew of sailors and soldiers were working their way down the East Coast and would soon converge with Jesup's column.

Lieutenant Powell had chased off several small bands of Seminoles while on his journey, but on January 15 it was his turn to run. After capturing an Indian woman, the lieutenant forced her to lead him to a Seminole encampment. With a force of about eighty men, Powell was making his way along a well-traveled path when he was nearly surrounded by a superior Seminole force. The naval officer ordered a charge but was repulsed, suffering heavy casualties. Nearly every officer was taken out of action, along with about a fourth of the men. Beating a hasty retreat back to their boats, the Americans suffered four dead and twenty-two wounded. Among those killed was the party's surgeon, Frederick Leitner. The party's retreat was skillfully covered by Lt. Joseph Johnston, who would later earn fame as a Confederate general.[40]

Near the end of January, as the army labored its way painfully through the deep swamps east of Lake Okeechobee, word was received that a large force of Indians was awaiting battle within a hammock just ahead. Jesup immediately ordered an attack. As rockets and cannon fire tore through the hammock, the Seminoles retreated to a position on the opposite side of a wide stream. From there, they seemed to be able to hold the whites off. Sensing a loss of momentum, Jesup rode forward to rally his men. As the general stopped to survey the progress of battle, an Indian bullet smashed his spectacles and severely cut his cheek. Calmly picking up the remains of his glasses, Jesup moved to a safer position.[41]

The fight, which became known as the Battle of Loxahatchee, continued for a short while longer. The white force was simply too large for the Seminoles to stop. The best the warriors could do was hope to inflict more casualties than they received. Perhaps they were buying time, diverting Jesup's attention from families that were fleeing from the advancing troops. At any rate, the fighting slowly ceased and the Indians, once again, disappeared into the endless swamp. Though no one knew it at the time, the last major battle of the war had been fought.

The Florida War was not all that America's little army had to worry about. Indeed, forces were spread so thin that there was a severe shortage of senior officers. To counter this problem, the War Department was forced to rely on officers whose duties entailed more than leading men into battle. Quartermaster General Jesup was a primary example, although he was not the only staff officer pressed into battlefield service. Inspector General Wool was in New England and upper New York taking care of delicate problems along the Canadian border. To his west, on the volatile Niagara frontier, Colonel Worth of the Ordinance Department was filling in for Winfield Scott, who had been forced to take care of Indian problems in Michigan. Even Surgeon General Lawson was serving in Florida, as commander of Fort Poinsett at Cape Sable in the Everglades. Fortunately, most of these staff officers were also experienced line officers, having seen battle in the War of 1812. Still, it all served to show how much of a drain the Florida War was having on the nation's defense establishment.[42]

By the end of January 1838, Jesup had accomplished much of what he had set out to do. The Seminoles were considerably weakened and the majority were either on their way west or already there. Most of the others were on the run and scattered throughout the Everglades. For many Seminoles, the time for fighting had passed. It had become evident that the army would pursue them until every last Indian was either dead or in the Indian Territory. Osceola, the war spirit, was dying in a white prison. Micanopy, King Philip, and Jumper, the senior leaders of their nation, had all been captured. Countless families had been split between the wilds of Florida and the strange land in the West. Perhaps it was time to make peace. In early February, two important chiefs, Tuskegee and Halleck Hadjo, met with Jesup. The talks went well. The Seminoles agreed to stop fighting if they might be allowed to remain south of Lake Okeechobee.

Clearly, it was time for a change in tactics. Recognizing the futility of attempting to capture the remnants, General Eustis, Colonel Twiggs, and other officers urged Jesup to terminate the war by making a temporary arrangement with the Indians, allowing them to remain in southern Florida until the land was needed by the whites. Jesup had already been considering such a course of action and decided to make the attempt.[43]

On February 11, Jesup forwarded his recommendation to Secretary of War Poinsett: "In regard to the Seminoles, we have committed the error of attempting to remove them when their lands were not required for agricultural purposes; when they were not in the way of white inhabitants; and when the greater portion of their country was an unexplored wilderness. . . . My decided opinion is, that unless *immediate* emigration be abandoned, the war will continue for years to come, and at constantly accumulating expense."[44]

To show good faith, the Seminoles agreed to encamp near the army. While waiting for word to travel to and from Washington, the two camps settled into a routine. The Seminoles, in what finery they still held onto, attended a ceremonial council at the white camp, while white officers, bringing plenty of whiskey, attended a dance at the Indian camp. It had been a hard war on both sides; everyone was no doubt looking forward to peace.[45]

The letter took two weeks to reach Washington. A few days after its arrival, Poinsett responded to Jesup, rejecting the suggestion. Referring to the Indian Removal Act, Poinsett wrote, "It is useless to recur to the principles and motives which induced the government to determine their removal to the west. The acts of the executive and the laws of congress evince a determination to carry out measures, and it is to be regarded as the settled policy of the country. . . . Whether the government ought not to have waited until the Seminoles were pressed upon by the white population . . . is not a question for the executive now to consider."[46]

Trusting the war would end with Jesup's campaign, Poinsett instructed him to continue the offensive: "It is hoped, however, that you will be able to put it out of the power of these Indians to do any further mischief. They ought to be captured, or destroyed."[47]

Prior to receiving Poinsett's answer, Jesup wrote a second letter to the secretary clarifying the basis for his recommendation. Warning of the consequences of not rethinking the policy, Jesup argued, "To persevere in the course we have been pursuing for three years past would be a reckless waste of blood and treasure."[48]

It must be kept in mind that Jesup was not, in any way, asking Poinsett to abandon the removal policy. He was asking for nothing more than a slight modification to it. Indeed, he saw his proposal as the best way to *speed* the Indian's removal. He felt that capturing the many small groups scattered over the peninsula would take years to accomplish. It did. He knew that in the meantime, the Indians would continue their desperate attacks on homesteaders. They did. By allowing the Indians to live peacefully in remote regions, he hoped the killings would stop, and, when the time for removal arrived, the government would know where the Indians were and could easily round them up. It was a sound recommendation that appears to have been rejected with little or no thought.

In a war full of bad decisions, Poinsett's rejection of Jesup's proposal stands out as one of the worst. The officers most knowledgeable in the subject had recommended a plan of action which could terminate an unpopular and expensive war, yet the government had ignored their advice. In the end, it was a political decision, not a military one. To leave even a few hundred Seminoles in Florida was politically unacceptable.

The decision to carry on with the war seems to have rested solely with the secretary of war. Son of a wealthy physician, Poinsett was well educated and had traveled extensively in Europe as a youth. As did many Americans of the age, Poinsett shared in a belief of American greatness and in a republican form of government. Energetic and intensely interested in military matters, the young Poinsett became a diplomat, serving first in South America, then as his country's first ambassador to the newly independent Mexico. Whenever possible, he sang the praises of

FIGURE 14.
Secretary of War Joel Roberts Poinsett, by Charles Fenderich.
By permission of the National Portrait Gallery, Smithsonian Institution. #66.89.

republicanism and democracy, sometimes earning the enmity of monarchists and dictators.

Interested in the sciences, he was responsible for bringing the poinsettia to the United States and helped found the National Institution for the Promotion of Science, which was soon superseded by the Smithsonian, an institution he also helped promote. Part of that interest in science extended to ethnography, especially where it applied to the Indians. He understood the Indians to be a "degraded" race, and that the degradation had been brought on by the coming of the white man. He therefore felt it was the responsibility of the white man to care for the Indian and to help them reach some state of civilization. When it came to Indian Removal, Poinsett was convinced that it was best for both races.[49]

Poinsett did not reject Jesup's proposal because he felt it would not work. At no time did he argue with the general's reasoning. An intelligent and thoughtful man, Poinsett understood the political realities. For many, it seemed an affront to national honor for America to acquiesce to the Seminoles on any point and to any degree. Allowing one Seminole to remain meant that America had given up, that the glorious United States had been defeated by a group of "savages." As the *St. Augustine Herald* reported, "The people of Florida will not submit to it. . . . The national honor and dignity are too deeply concerned for it to listen for one moment to the proposed arrangement."[50]

Most of the opposition to any "dishonorable" compromise with the Seminoles came from two quarters. First were the residents of Florida, who understandably lived in fear of the Indians. Next were southern slaveholders. Although the flow of runaways to Florida had all but ceased and most of the blacks had been removed from the conflict, slave owners could not forget the fears they had lived with for so long. The idea of leaving the Seminoles in Florida still appeared as a threat to their economic and social well-being.

Another strong influence upon Poinsett's mind was former president Andrew Jackson. Jackson may have retired from office, but he was still the most influential man in America, even though his tide of domination was on the ebb. Both Poinsett and Van Buren owed their positions to Jackson, and both had helped formulate many of his policies. Contacted frequently by Poinsett regarding Indian Removal, Jackson responded with more than just advice and opinions. On August 14, 1837, Jackson informed Poinsett that Major Lauderdale, with five companies of volunteers, would be put in service for one year to "put an end to this punic war or die in the attempt."[51]

Recommending a method for ending the war, on October 1, 1837, Jackson told Poinsett to "find where their women are . . . and capture them—this done, they will at once surrender." Disappointed with the war, Jackson's December 13, 1837, letter might have impressed upon Poinsett the need for the administration to prove itself. "I am truly surprised at the force collected in Florida—half that force was sufficient to put a speedy end to the war. . . . It has been a disgraceful war to the American character, and its army."[52]

The most pressing reason for rejecting Jesup's proposal was the one Poinsett had alluded to: it threatened the whole policy of Indian Removal. Today, when Native Americans are seen (stereotypically) as spiritual icons or tourist attractions, we find it hard to imagine the threat they posed, rightly or wrongly, to white society. In the early nineteenth century, America was growing at an astounding rate, and the biggest threat to that growth was the presence of Native Americans. The United States had a large frontier that was forever moving, and everywhere along that frontier, white settlers lived in mortal fear of their Indian neighbors.

It was, of course, a two-sided coin. Indians also lived on that frontier and also lived in fear for their homes and families. The two groups existed side by side, engaged in a clash of cultures that seemed impossible to avoid. Even those who saw the evils of white expansionism believed that the only way to prevent Indian hostilities was to somehow separate the two groups.

Jackson and his followers had spent considerable "political capital" in getting the Indian Removal Act pushed through Congress and were not about to let the effort be weakened. Among those followers were Van Buren and Poinsett. To admit the policy to be in error, even in the smallest degree, seems to have been almost unthinkable to them. To renegotiate with the Seminoles might lead to renegotiation with the Cherokees, who were claiming fraud concerning the treaty that was forcing that tribe from its homeland. News of government flexibility might give heart to other Indian nations who were fighting to retain their homelands. The "domino theory" was as well understood in the 1830s as it was in the 1960s. In the end, the government lacked the courage to modify its policy, and the war continued, as Jesup had warned, with "a reckless waste of blood and treasure."

8 Wedded to War

▲▲▲ ▲▲▲▲ ▲▲▲▲ ▲▲▲▲ ▲

General Jesup's plan for ending the war had been rejected. A message was sent to the chiefs of the nearby Seminole camp to attend a conference at the general's quarters. The Indians politely declined but did not flee their camps. Jesup now faced a dilemma. Within the Indian encampment were more than 500 Seminoles who had come in peace and were not his prisoners. Could he simply let them melt away into the wilds? For Jesup, the opportunity was too great to be ignored. A force of Dragoons was dispatched to take the Seminoles captive. The Indians put up little resistance, perhaps having already come to the conclusion that for them the fighting was over.[1]

For many Seminoles, it must have seemed as if there was no further use to carry on the war. As loved ones either turned themselves in or were taken prisoner, family ties and friendships became stronger than the will to fight. In early April, a large group led by Alligator surrendered. Lured by a promise of freedom if they would emigrate, black Seminoles saw little reason to remain in Florida. Among those turning themselves in was John Cavallo, the last important black Seminole leader. Jesup should have felt a degree of satisfaction. It had been a distasteful campaign and he had been subject to harsh public criticism, but he had gotten the job done. Jesup had, in the best American tradition, done the soldier's duty.[2]

Still, we wonder if Jesup was satisfied with his performance or angrily frustrated with the outcome of the campaign. Overall, he could claim to have accomplished the task with which he had been charged. His men had faced the Seminoles several times and, with the exception of Lt. Powell's battle, had not been defeated. He had, in the course of his tenure, captured or otherwise removed most of the powerful leaders of the Seminole Nation and the majority of their followers. Thanks to his efforts, there would soon be more Seminoles in Arkansas than in Florida.

The enemy forces that remained were scattered, desperate, and destitute. From a tactical perspective, the Seminoles had been defeated. In this respect, the general could take pride in what he had accomplished.

Yet the war was not over. One can only imagine Jesup's frustration. He had won the war, but Washington would not let it end. Although scattered and on the run, the Seminoles were still on the warpath. The fact that many of the Indians had been captured in a less-than-honorable fashion stained the reputation of an honorable man. The general had, contrary to his own beliefs, turned the army into slave catchers. His orders had been to remove the Seminoles from Florida, and he had followed those orders as best he could. Jesup had not asked for the position and seems to have taken no joy in it. Distasteful as it might have been, he had done his duty. The nation did not thank him.

Jesup was tired of the Florida War and asked to be relieved. The time was right. The nature of the conflict had changed, and it was time for a fresh approach. With the approach of the sickly season, Jesup's peak force of around 9,000 men was reduced to about 2,300. There would be no more large scale offensives. There was no longer the need for a man of Jesup's high rank to be in command. On April 29, 1838, he received word that when all was in order, he could resume his position as quartermaster general. In a little more than two weeks, he was able to turn command over to Zachary Taylor.[3]

We now encounter a situation that poses a bit of a problem for any one who proposes to write a narrative of the Second Seminole War: most of the "action" of the war takes place in the first two years of the conflict, yet the war continued on for another four and a half years. The problem faced by the writer (and eventually the reader) is how to put it all in perspective. Few major events took place during the final four years of the war, but the killing and suffering did not cease. As humans, writers tend to devote numerous pages to the dramatic moments of life while they waste few words on the tedious, everyday happenings. It can be likened to the work of a soldier during the Seminole Wars. He might spend weeks trudging through the slashing blades of a sawgrass prairie or wading through the knee-deep water of a cypress swamp, afflicted by fevers and diarrhea, sleeping unprotected from the elements on the wet earth, plagued by innumerable hordes of biting and stinging insects, all to spend an hour or two engaged in mortal combat with an illusive foe. The whole patrol, from start to finish, could have been described as "pure hell," but when the soldiers returned to the relative comfort of their post, what aspect of the patrol did they spend the most time talking about? In their own memories, the only thing that "happened" was the fight.

Historical records are no different. Historians devote their time almost exclusively to the mileposts, not the road. We note the battles, not the endless miles of the march. We record the changes of command, not the countless hours of administration. We report the senseless dying, not the innumerable days of productive living. The Second Seminole War presents us with a classic example of this problem. We can devote two lengthy chapters to a span of slightly more than two years, yet we have a hard time filling a third chapter on the remaining four years. It is, quite simply, a combination of the nature of the human mind and the nature of the conflict itself.

In order to spend more time on the later years of the war, we will devote more time looking at how the war fit in to American history in general. The underlying causes of the war were national issues, and the progress of the war affected the nation as a whole. Occasionally we will venture back into the earlier years of the war when the subject calls for it. The men and women who endured those difficult times deserve to be understood. It is not enough to simply say *what* happened. We must attempt to discover *why*.

If the beginning of Jesup's command marked a turning point in the war, the end of his command brought with it a fundamental alteration in the manner in which the war was to be carried on. The United States was no longer waging a war against the Seminole Nation. With the exception of old Sam Jones and young Coacoochee, most of the important leaders of the tribe had been killed or transported. The "official" Seminole Nation was now in Arkansas. As Jesup had recommended, the administration should have declared the war over, with the acknowledgment that a sizable military presence would have to be maintained until the territory was completely pacified. No one did this; officially, the conflict raged on.

Did it really make a difference what the official position was? How did rhetoric in Washington affect deeds on the ground in Florida? It all seemed to revolve around the term "expectations." With the war unfinished, the army was expected to go on the offensive. They were also expected to remain on the offensive until every Seminole was gone from

Florida. Only then would the war be considered over. If, on the other hand, "peace" had been declared, the army could take up defensive positions, reacting only to aggressions by the Indians.

Going on the offensive led to its own set of expectations. The American people expected battles, and the army was expected to be victorious. The army expected to be well equipped, and suppliers expected to be paid. The militia, ever eager for a piece of the financial pie, expected to be called out. With some right, settlers expected to be safe within their homes while the army was out chasing hostile Indians. By contrast, a simple guarding of the frontier raised few such expectations, other than those of the lonely homesteader.

The weight of these expectations fell most heavily upon the shoulders of Brig. Gen. Zachary Taylor. His victory at the Battle of Lake Okeechobee had marked him a winner, had made him a general, and had made him Jesup's successor. It was Taylor who was expected to bring the war to a conclusion. In that, he failed.

The Seminoles, their numbers depleted and their former homes either occupied or under the careful watch of the army, had divided into small bands, living in whatever hideouts they could find. For them, the reasons for fighting had not changed. They still wished to remain in their homelands, free to live life in the manner to which they had become accustomed. The fact that most of their friends and relations had been expelled from Florida was sad and infuriating but somewhat immaterial. There was nothing they could do about it.

Like the army, the Seminoles' situation forced them to reevaluate their strategy, though not in any sort of official manner. They were, quite simply, reacting to the prevailing realities. Unable to mount a coordinated offensive, they concentrated on targets of opportunity. The isolated white settlements were the most vulnerable and suffered the worst. Lonely travelers were also at risk. When the occasion presented itself, warriors also attacked small parties of unwary soldiers and militiamen.

Most disturbing to the whites, the Seminoles refused to remain confined to the inhospitable Everglades. Near the end of May 1838, an inconclusive battle was fought between Florida militiamen and a group of Indians outside the Okefenokee Swamp in southern Georgia. By June, the Seminoles were back in the Cove of the Withlacoochee, busily burning bridges over the strategic river. Fighting was reported near the San Felasco Hammock late in June. Isolated murders and depredations were

FIGURE 15.
Zachary Taylor.
From a poster
commemorating
the Battle of Lake
Okeechobee.
By permission of the
Florida State Archives.
Image #PRI2505,
DBCN#AAJ-3804.

occurring throughout the territory. Everywhere in Florida, nervous whites kept a wary eye over their shoulders, never knowing when the wily Seminoles would appear.[4]

A good many people in the nation could not understand why it was taking so long to subdue the Florida Indians. Not willing to give the Seminoles the credit due them, people often suggested that the Bahamians or the Cubans were supplying the Seminoles with weapons and provisions. There was probably some truth to the allegations, but the support amounted to nothing more than the continuation of a long-established trade. If the Seminoles had *any* ally, it was the land of Florida itself.

Although the majority of Seminoles had not been residents of southern Florida before the war, they had been intimately familiar with the land. Since the eighteenth century, bands of Creek and Seminole hunters had traveled the peninsula in search of game on their annual hunting trips. They had found the best places to camp, the best sources of wild foodstuffs, and the best routes to travel. When war broke out, they already knew the best places to hide. White officers, on the other hand, possessed only crude maps of the interior, many of which were based solely on rumor and conjecture. As one officer put it, "Any Negro guide could make a better one in the sand." Obviously, there had been no Lewis and Clark for the Florida Territory.[5]

The Seminoles were not, however, mythical supermen who found the wilds of Florida to be a well-stocked supermarket. Surviving in untamed Florida was possible but not easy. Game was relatively abundant, but not just standing around waiting to be shot. Indeed, shooting game presented a problem in itself. The sound of a gunshot could alert white troops to an otherwise hidden Seminole presence. The staple diet of the Seminoles consisted of fruits and vegetables grown on small fields near their villages. Such villages required a certain amount of high, dry land, a scarce commodity in South Florida. During wartime, such locations also required a high degree of concealment.

The one foodstuff that was abundant was the root of the coontie plant, a form of arrowroot, but the root was toxic if not properly processed into flour. That required time and a small amount of simple equipment; it was not the sort of thing one could do on the run. Life for the refugee Seminoles was not easy. A determination to remain in their homeland was all that kept them going.[6]

For the Seminoles, fighting the war was secondary to keeping the family safe. The army did not have to defeat the warriors; it only had to locate the hiding places of the women and children. Andrew Jackson had been correct when he told Poinsett to capture the women and children and then the men would surrender. If nothing else, the average Seminole warrior was a devoted family man. Both the army and the Indians understood that knowledge of the Seminoles' hiding places was key to the outcome of the conflict. What Andrew Jackson never understood was that the army had no idea where those hiding places were.[7]

Fighting a guerrilla war was not something the U.S. Army was prepared for. The Second Seminole War stands out as the first time the United States was forced to fight a protracted guerrilla war. Unlike their Indian adversaries, white soldiers could not (or would not) live off the land. They required heavy wagons or packs to carry their supplies. They wore light blue uniforms with white cross-belts that formed an X right over the soldier's heart. The Indians could not have asked for a better target. It was not until late in the war that the army began to fight the Indians on their own terms.

Zachary Taylor's strategy was neither grand, nor outwardly impressive. It was, nonetheless, practical and flexible. Because most Floridians lived in the northern part of the territory, Taylor concentrated his efforts in keeping that portion of the peninsula relatively free of Seminole warriors. With too few men and too few roads, it would not be a quickly accomplished task. Knowing the topography of Florida and the tenacity of the Seminoles, Taylor felt that if he could drive the Indians from North Florida, settlers could once again populate the area and the Indian problem would be largely solved.[8]

There was no doubt in anyone's mind that the Indian problem in North Florida was a big one. In July, a family living along the Santa Fe River was murdered within a few miles of an army post. One of the soldiers on the scene described the condition in which he found the deceased mother: "She was not scalped, but was made the victim of a cruelty deeper and more refined. The wretches had dashed out the brains of her infant, and placed the mangled innocent in its mother's arms. *There she lay, the murdered mother, fondling with the icy embrace of death the murdered child.*"[9]

At about the same time, another family was killed near the capitol, Tallahassee. It was somehow ironic that the news was reported by James Gadsden, the very man who had negotiated the Treaties of Moultrie Creek and Payne's Landing. Far to the east, attacking from their hiding places in the Okefenokee Swamp, Seminole warriors murdered two families in Georgia. Once again, rescuers arrived too late and could only report the sad details:

> Three children of the six were alive when we reached the spot, one about 3 years old had been shot through the abdomen, and lay asleep on the dead mother. But, O, *horrid* to tell, I found a fine young lady of 18, shot in two places and dirked in another, with about 20 hogs around her, and she yet alive and had her senses perfectly. This was the most trying time I had ever seen. I gave her cold water which she wished much, and remained with her as long as I could, till obliged to go in search of the Indians. We left a guard to protect them and administer to them all that they could, but all *expired* in less than twenty minutes after we left.[10]

If there seemed to be no place in Florida where a white person could feel secure, the same might also be said for the majority of Indians.

While white families cowered around army posts and large towns, Indian families hid in dense hammocks, fearful of discovery by the occasional detachments of soldiers who continued to scour the countryside. The Seminoles, who had once lived in modest log cabins, now dwelt in hastily constructed chickees. Children learned to play in silence and campfires were used with care, so as not to send a "smoke signal" to the army. Everyone in Florida wanted to feel safe, but no one was willing to make peace.

As happened every summer, the war was temporarily put on hold. Unhealthy interior posts were closed and the soldiers moved to stations near the coast. As the heat and sickness increased, patrols were sent out less often. The Seminoles also cut back their efforts. For them, the summer was a time to tend their fields, heal their wounds, and gather supplies for the coming winter. It was a time for hunting and for tribal gatherings, a time for rest before resuming the fight.

With the approach of the autumn of 1838, Taylor felt obliged to put his army in the field. This time, there would be no grand strategy or protracted campaign. Washington had refused to end the war but was also somewhat reluctant to pursue it. Though no one cared to admit it, Jesup's message had gotten through. Chasing Seminoles in the swamp was not going to accomplish anything positive. Instead, Taylor would divide his forces into large groups that would search and defend specific areas, responding to threats and opportunities as they arose. His best hope was to slowly force the Indians south of a line that roughly corresponds to today's Interstate 4, which runs from Tampa to Daytona.

The plan would take time and effort. Posts and roads would have to be built, garrisons would have to be outfitted and provisioned, supply lines would have to be set up and maintained. All this would take a steady influx of money from a government that was becoming increasingly reluctant to appropriate funds for a war that seemed to be going nowhere. Feeling rather like a parent who remains in a marriage "for the sake of the children," Congress appropriated the necessary funds, and a force of approximately 3,500 men began to assemble in Florida.[11]

Though by no means a small army, Taylor now commanded less than half the number of men his predecessor had. The biggest difference was in the number of citizen soldiers. Almost half of Jesup's force had been volunteers from various states of the Union. Taylor commanded no volunteers and only about 350 conscripted militia, all of them coming from

Florida and southern Georgia. Congress and the War Department had finally come to the realization that citizen soldiers were simply too expensive to employ.[12]

Indeed, the Florida War was proving such a drain on the army's resources that Congress had been forced to increase the size of the army. Like it or not, troops were needed elsewhere. Although difficulties along the Texas frontier were temporarily on hold, that was only because the Mexicans were having to fight off French invaders. A victory by one side or the other might lead the United States into war, in defense of either the Monroe Doctrine or Texan independence. Far to the north, the question of the northern boundary of Maine appeared as if it might need to be settled militarily, which would bring America into direct conflict, once again, with the British. And, of course, there was always some other Indian tribe that Washington wanted to forcibly resettle. Never before, and never again, would an Indian war use up such a large percentage of the army's time and manpower as would the Florida War.

Taylor put his plans into operation and experienced mixed results. In October, the general took two companies of mounted men to the Panhandle to oversee the removal of the remaining Apalachicola tribes. Working his way back to Tampa, he met with his junior officers, assigning each an area to be covered. In December, a large Seminole camp was discovered but no Indians were captured. Col. David Twiggs, one of Taylor's most experienced officers, was sent to reopen Forts Pierce, Lauderdale, and Dallas (Miami) and to harass the Seminoles in that quarter.[13]

Taylor's plans to attack the Seminoles in South Florida were derailed by several murders in the Tallahassee area. Feeling it more important to protect citizens than to chase Seminoles, the general removed forces from South Florida and sent them north. Taylor knew that until the Indians were driven from their hiding places, northern Florida could not be considered a safe place for settlers to live. He also knew that the only way to accomplish such a thing was to keep the entire area under constant watch.[14]

On paper, Taylor's plan looked deceptively simple. His idea was to divide North Florida into twenty-mile squares, each square containing a small post garrisoned by twenty or thirty men. Roads would then be built around the perimeters of the squares, along with roads connecting the posts to each other and to any likely Seminole hiding places. In late January, Secretary of War Poinsett gave approval to the plan and Taylor began to carry it out.

As usual, the devil would reside in the details. Building so many posts would require a lot of manpower. Opening so many roads would require a lot of time. Many of the posts would have to be closed when the sickly season set in. Horses would have to be procured for each installation, and supply lines developed. Still, Taylor realized it was probably the best use he could make of his men. It had become apparent that the Seminoles were not going to come out and fight the army.

All in all, the winter campaign of 1838–39 seemed to entail more construction than warfare. Taylor's tally of Seminoles for the period seemed dismal: not many were killed and fewer than 200 were shipped west. On the bright side, only 2 officers and about 7 enlisted men had died at the hands of the native warriors. The army's foremost victories had been accomplished with axes and shovels. Taylor proudly reported that "it will be observed that fifty-three new posts have been established, eight hundred and forty-eight miles of wagon-road, and three thousand six hundred and forty-three feet of causeway and bridges opened and constructed." It was, indeed, a strange way to wage a war.[15]

While the amount of human blood that was flowing in Florida had lessened, the political blood being shed in Washington had increased. One of the wounded was President Martin Van Buren. His Democratic Party had lost a number of seats to the Whigs during the 1838 midterm congressional elections, a change in the attitude of Congress that would soon have a very profound effect upon the conduct of the war in Florida. An amendment providing $5,000 for an effort to negotiate a settlement with the Seminoles was added to the bill that funded the war. As the amendment's sponsor put it, "Dismiss one of the Seminole prisoners with a message that, if the Seminoles will not cross a designated line, you will not. Both sides are equally tired of the war; and that line, I have no doubt, would be respected." He then went on to remind his colleagues that "on those terms, you could have had peace a year ago."[16]

The change in the attitude in Congress reflected a similar change in the attitude of the nation. A sizable portion of the American public was willing to admit that the Seminoles had won the right to stay in Florida. For what may have been the first time in American history (and probably the last), the United States had been forced to sue for peace by a native people. Ironically, it was this very peace initiative that served to prolong

FIGURE 16.
Maj. Gen. Alexander Macomb Jr. at age forty-three. Head
from plaster bust, from life mask, taken September 1825 by
John Henri Isaac Browere.
By permission of the New York State Historical Association, Fenimore Art
Museum, Cooperstown, New York. Photo credit Richard Walker. #N-245-40.

the war for another three years and eventually led to the almost total expulsion of Seminoles from Florida.

This was obviously something the Whigs were shoving down Van Buren's throat. Yet maybe the administration was ready to take the medicine. Taylor's plan may have been sound, but it was not going to end the war anytime soon. The war was unpopular, and the longer it lasted, the worse Van Buren looked. Although a settlement that allowed any Seminoles to remain in Florida would not be popular among his southernmost constituents, he may have felt it was worth the risk. There was a presidential election coming up the following year, and Van Buren was vulnerable. Besides, it was of little political consequence if Floridians were upset: living in a territory, they could not vote in national elections.

While we do not know Van Buren's or Poinsett's true feelings in regard to the mandated negotiations, it must be admitted that they put forth a good effort to make peace a reality. Had they wished, they could have dispatched some junior officer to Florida with instructions to make a lot of noise but accomplish nothing. Instead, they sent someone with both the position and the authority to negotiate a real settlement—Maj. Gen. Alexander Macomb, the commanding general of the army.

Macomb was, in actuality, the only real major general in the army. The other three men who held that rank (Scott, Gaines, and Jesup) held it by brevet. Brevet rank was a troublesome tool used by Congress to reward the army's officers without spending any money. An officer might receive a brevet promotion for some conspicuous action, such as Taylor had received after the Battle of Lake Okeechobee. More often, brevet rank would be conferred for ten years' faithful service in any given rank, as had been the case with General Jesup. A breveted officer would have the title and privileges of his new rank but would not receive the extra pay. Brevet rank also held the stigma of not being "real," which caused considerable resentment within the officer corps. Breveted officers resented not receiving their proper due, while officers of actual rank resented junior officers receiving equal privilege.

Like his contemporaries, Macomb had been a hero of the War of 1812, holding off a superior British force at Plattsburgh, New York, in the fall of 1814. The action earned Macomb a brevet promotion to major general and, like Gaines, Scott, Jesup, and Jackson, lasting fame. Drastic cutbacks in the size of the army in 1821 forced Macomb to revert to the rank of colonel, but President Monroe personally promised Macomb that the drop in rank would not affect any future promotions.[17]

In 1828, Commanding General Jacob Brown died. The two men immediately below him, Gaines and Scott, both claimed the coveted position. At this point, one of the problems of brevet rank became apparent. Scott claimed seniority by his brevet rank, while Gaines claimed it by his actual rank. The two men had never liked each other, and the very public quarrel over the prestigious position only made their arguments more acrimonious.

In the midst of the bitter feud between Gaines and Scott, someone reminded President John Quincy Adams of the promise his predecessor had made to Macomb. Before taking the demotion to colonel, Macomb had been superior to both Gaines and Scott. Bypassing the feuding parties, Adams promoted Macomb to commanding general. Gaines and Scott were furious but could do nothing about it. Settling into his office, Macomb took up the army's top spot, answerable only to the president and the secretary of war.[18]

Exactly what Macomb was instructed to do in Florida remains unclear. His written orders were so ill-defined as to be useless. He was directed to "prosecute the war with vigor" yet "treat the Indians with kindness and attention." He could "call out the militia" if he felt the need, while at the same time he could "withdraw such portions of the regular troops . . . as he thought expedient." Finally, and most important, he was instructed to "make a treaty of peace with the Indians, based upon the treaty made at Payne's Landing." But the Treaty of Payne's Landing was what all the fighting was about. According to John Sprague, who was serving as one of Macomb's aides, the general more or less disregarded his orders and did as he saw fit. What we do not know is whether Macomb had been given any *verbal* orders by Van Buren or Poinsett.[19]

Whatever the situation, Macomb took his duty seriously. In early April, the general arrived in Florida to take command. Zachary Taylor was not, however, pushed aside. Macomb was not interested in the day-to-day operations of the war. In truth, the sickly season was underway and there was not much of a war to prosecute. Taylor, physically sick and sick of the war, asked to be relieved, but the request was denied. Macomb had been dispatched to negotiate with the Indians, and for the most part he confined himself to that task. He did order changes to Taylor's operations, but only in relation to matters that had some bearing on the negotiations.[20]

Throughout April and into May, Macomb talked to any chief that would listen. Few, however, were willing to give him an audience. The Seminoles had, quite rightly, found little reason to believe the word of any government officer. One chief was reported to have expressed the opinion that the "white man had two faces; that while a paper proposing a Treaty was circulating among them, the soldiers were hunting them down." Their experiences with past treaties and with General Jesup had made them very cynical.[21]

It appears that no one but Macomb held out much hope of success. A feeling of resignation had fallen over Florida. The editor of the *Pensacola Gazette* was ready to admit defeat. "The truth is that they [the Seminoles] consider the whites to have been badly whipped, and it is nearly time that we should take the same view of the matter." When Macomb arrived in Florida, almost every officer he ran into was quick to inform him of their feelings on the matter. According to Sprague, "The officers appear to be completely discouraged. The Indians are in every part of the country in parties of two and three, and there is no prospect or probability of capturing them nor of ending the war."[22]

While the negotiations were taking place, Taylor attempted to continue with his normal operations. For the most part, the junior general steered clear of the commanding general. Although professionally cordial, the two men were of differing temperaments. Taylor was "Old Rough and Ready" and, after a frustrating year and a half in Florida, pointedly pessimistic. Macomb was cheerily optimistic and eager to impress the Indians with the pageantry of his rank.

Slowly, Macomb began to make progress in his negotiations. Through the efforts of Lt. Col. William S. Harney, Macomb had managed to make contact with several important chiefs, notably the aged Sam Jones. Although Jones did not negotiate directly, he sent his chosen successor, Chitto Tustenuggee, to talk with Macomb at Fort King. Despite the fact that most of the hostile chiefs, including Coacoochee, were not party to the talks, Macomb probably felt that if Sam Jones agreed to an arrangement, the others would follow.[23]

On May 18, 1839, Macomb announced that negotiations were complete, and that hostilities would cease. In exchange for a secure reservation in southern Florida, the Seminoles would "bury the tomahawk and scalping knife." Inducements were given to those who wished to emigrate, and a few did. Although most whites hoped the war was truly going to end, few, including General Taylor, had any faith in the agreement. Macomb, knowing that written treaties meant little or nothing to the Indians, had not even bothered to have one penned and signed.[24]

For the most part, Indian depredations had indeed slowed. The occasional murder was attributed to undisciplined youths or warriors who had not yet received word of the truce. Other murders could be blamed on outlaw whites. The killing of a militiaman was deemed suspicious when a musket ball was found in his body and a bottle of whiskey was found near by. As every soldier knew, Indians *always* used rifles and *never* left an unfinished bottle of whiskey behind.[25]

As expected, Floridians were incensed at the agreement. A Tallahassee newspaper printed in bold type, "Shame!!! shame!!! shame!!!" above and below Macomb's announcement that hostilities had ceased. Reports circulated that the territorial government was going to continue the war on its own and was offering a bounty of $200 for each Indian brought in, dead or alive. More practical Floridians were not so quick to condemn. Two distinguished Florida Militia officers assured General Macomb that the criticisms came from city dwellers, not from the rural residents who had suffered most from the war. True, they wanted the Seminoles totally expelled, but they knew the impracticality of it. Foremost, they simply wanted the war to end.[26]

As June passed into July, General Macomb's agreement seemed to be working out as planned. True, there was an occasional incident, but on the whole the Indians seemed to be friendly and moving in the direction of their new homes. As part of the agreement, a trading post was estab-lished on the Caloosahatchee River, near what is now the city of Cape Coral. To keep an eye on things, a detachment of twenty-three soldiers under Colonel Harney was encamped nearby. The natives who fre-quented the post seemed pleased with the arrangement and friendly to-ward the whites. Soldiers and civilians in Florida began to relax; peace was finally at hand.

It did not last. In the predawn hours of July 23, a force of about 150 Indians attacked the Caloosahatchee trading post and its guard. The sur-prise was complete. Some of the soldiers, rudely awakened by the war whoop and the firing of guns, were killed in their beds. In the confusion, the survivors ran for the river, some being shot down as they fled. Several of the men were lured back to shore with promises that they would not be harmed, then savagely murdered. The remainder kept swimming until they located a boat and made their way down river to the safety of a small ship waiting to come up river. At least two men hid out for almost two weeks before being rescued.[27]

One of those fortunate enough to escape was Colonel Harney. Having returned from a hunting expedition late at night, he had fallen asleep some distance from the rest of the men. When the shooting started he, like the others, made for the river. He was soon joined by one of his men, and the two worked their way down river until they located a canoe and fled to the safety of the waiting ship.

Gathering what few men and guns remained, Harney quickly re-turned to the scene of the fight in hopes of finding survivors. Instead, he found only mutilated corpses. The sutler's trading post had been ran-sacked and several thousand dollars worth of goods taken. The sutler and his assistants, along with a river pilot and two interpreters, were either dead or taken prisoner. Also gone were a number of Colt repeating rifles, a new invention that Harney was trying out. General Macomb's longed-for peace had been violently shattered. The war was on again.[28]

We can, without much difficulty, understand the Seminoles' reasons for going to war in 1835. Pressed to their limits, they reacted the way most all of us would. Understanding the reasons for the Harney Massacre, as it came to be known, presents us with more of a problem. The Seminoles had, as much as they were likely to, gotten what they wanted. They had worn the patience of the white men down to the point where Washington was willing to negotiate on favorable terms. Had the Indians remained peaceably within the land allotted them, the war would have ended.

The brutal, unexpected attack on the trading post, however, forced the government to reopen the war. The national pride, already wounded from having to sue for peace in the first place, was dealt a shocking blow. Americans felt as if they had extended their hands in friendship only to be stabbed in the back at the first opportunity. There was, in reality, no choice but to continue the war until the Seminole threat was completely removed.

Wounded pride is not, of course, an emotion that is restricted to Caucasians. Indeed, almost every encounter between Indian and white resulted in the humiliation, to some degree, of the Indian. The lies, the treachery, and the arrogance of whites, both in and out of government, had brought on the war and had marked its most memorable moments. One could say, with some justification, that the Seminoles were due a measure of revenge. Their timing, however, could not have been worse. Having attained the prize they had fought so hard for, they appeared to have simply thrown it away.

The attack exposed the peace agreement's main weakness. Macomb had made his truce with Sam Jones, not the majority of Seminoles. Indeed, Jones was a leader of the Mikasukis, a group that took pride in being independent from the "mainstream" Seminoles. The Indians, divided into individual bands, each with its own chief, had no central authority. An agreement made by one group was not the least bit binding on the others. In light of that reality, it could be argued that those who attacked the trading post were not party to the agreement. Indeed, the leaders were identified as Hospetarke and Chakaika. Chakaika was chief of the "Spanish Indians," an amorphous group that had lived in southwestern Florida for quite some time and had enjoyed close relations with

Spanish Cuba. In a way, the Spanish Indians could be viewed as "out-laws," a collection of outsiders and outcasts who, for one reason or another, were unwelcome in the more established bands. If the Spanish Indians were indeed responsible for the attack, then the logic behind the event was simple thievery, as one contemporary writer maintained: "The temptation of plunder, alone, was too great for the virtue of savages."[29]

Another explanation for the attack on Colonel Harney and his men was that the Indians simply did not believe that the war was over. Past experience might well have led them to believe that Macomb's mission was simply a ploy to make them relax their guard and reveal their hiding places. If the Seminoles were to settle at a known location near the trading post, they might be more easily rounded up. Indeed, that is precisely what the government had in mind, although the idea seems to have been more wishful thinking than anything else. Getting the Seminoles to gather anywhere was hard enough, rounding them up had proven almost impossible.

In addition to their natural skepticism, the Seminoles may have been told by people they trusted that the whole affair was nothing more than a trap. Interpreters and other people making a living off the war were in no hurry for the conflict to end. The influence, both good and bad, of the interpreters was made evident in a letter published in the *St. Augustine Herald* on September 26. A correspondent from Fort Lauderdale reported on Sam Jones's reluctance to believe that the peace agreement with General Macomb was real: "Sam remarked that interpreters were generally liars, and he feared the news brought by Sandy was too good to be true." Sandy, the interpreter, replied, "All the promises and professions of the whites were a pack of lies; they were at war with *eight* foreign and frontier nations, and had been *beaten*." For this reason, the United States had decided to sue for peace, but "next year the whites would hold another council, and take new measures to drive the Indians out." This same interpreter was captured at Harney's Massacre and later burned to death by the Indians in a process that took five or six hours to complete. It is, indeed, hard to tell what the Indians really believed.[30]

Exactly *who* carried out the raid was also open for debate. While consensus blamed the Spanish Indians; others saw the hand of Sam Jones in the affair. The correspondent for the *St. Augustine Herald* gave his opinion: about half the warriors in Florida resided with Sam Jones, just west of Fort Lauderdale. "A part of them went over to Carloosa, and were parties in the massacre, but it suits their convenience to make scapegoats of the `Spanish Indians,' and to make the negro interpreters, who, in all probability, were privy to the whole, the *sole* instigators of the plot."[31]

The case against Sam Jones was strengthened in September 1839, about two months after the attack. In order to appease the angry Colonel Harney, Jones had volunteered to bring in the men responsible for the massacre, including the Spanish Indians, and had promised to return with them in thirty-three days. In the meantime, the Indians around Fort Lauderdale continued to exhibit the most friendly attitude toward the white soldiers. On the twenty-seventh, the officers were invited to a dance at the Seminole camp, and although they declined the invitation, they sent two soldiers and a black interpreter to the camp with a keg of whiskey. Upon arriving, the trio was fired upon by a large force of warriors. Both soldiers were killed, but the interpreter managed to dive into the river and escape. His tale, after being rescued, implicated both Sam Jones and Chitto Tustenuggee, the very man who had negotiated with General Macomb.[32]

In truth, it was more than the Harney Massacre that seemed to indicate Indian duplicity. Throughout the territory, the Seminoles had gone on the offensive, as if the action on the Caloosahatchee had been a cue to recommence hostilities. To many Americans, it was easy to believe that the Seminoles had never intended to abide by the agreement they had made with General Macomb. A letter in the *Army and Navy Chronicle* related news from the last week of August:

> On the 23rd . . . the Indians attacked Fort McClure, wounded one volunteer and killed 10 horses. On the 27th they attacked a party of volunteers on Orange Lake, killed and took prisoners the whole party, with the exception of one horse. On the 28th the steamer R. K. Call was . . . twice fired on by a party of Indians, about 20 in number. . . . Captain Miles adds that the Indians are very thick around Fort White. Lieut. Wood, commanding at Ft. Andrews, reports that 17 of his men had an engagement . . . with a party of Indians about 40 strong, in which two of his men were killed and five wounded.[33]

While it is certainly true that it was the Indians who broke the truce, we must be careful not to place too much blame on their shoulders. A large portion of the responsibility for the failure of the peace belongs to the general himself. Macomb's first mistake in the whole matter was his immediate departure for Washington after the conclusion of the talks. Had he remained in the peninsula, contacting other chiefs and reassuring those he had already made agreements with, Seminole misconceptions would have been greatly reduced. His second mistake was leaving Zachary Taylor in charge. The junior general had no faith in Macomb's agreement and did nothing to support its implementation. Indeed, Colonel Harney later placed partial blame for the massacre upon Taylor, pointing out that Taylor had denied his request for two full companies to guard the Caloosahatchee facility and implement the treaty. Finally, Macomb had been less than candid with the Indians. Finding it "impolitic," Macomb never mentioned that fact that the Seminoles were still expected to remove at some later date.[34]

Whatever the reason for the Harney Massacre, it effectively put an end to any talk of peace or to any hopes that the Seminoles might be allowed to remain in Florida. The Seminoles may have considered the attack a great victory, or they simply may have rejoiced at the amount of loot they had taken. It did not matter. From that point forward, their fate was sealed. As one officer put it, "The Government will be *compelled to continue* the war, on the ground that the Indians *no longer have any confidence* in the white race, and, *vice versa,* the *white race* in the Indians."[35]

Reaction to the Harney Massacre was predictable. An officer serving in Florida wrote, "Let the white flag be hung out at points where immediate transportation can be given them to their new homes; and in the field let there be nothing less than a war of extermination. Any thing short of this, at the present stage of the game, looks to me very like positive madness. . . . A few skeletons left to hang and bleach in the wild, would teach them too surely we were in earnest, and they would shortly be found suing for peace on any terms."[36]

The cry for new methods to bring the war to an end brought about the most politically controversial episode of the conflict. Surprisingly, it had nothing to do with false treaties, the inefficiency of the various forces, or the wasted millions of dollars. It many ways, the whole matter seems silly to us today. How could anyone get upset about a pack of dogs?

Frustrated and embarrassed by the Seminoles' success in thwarting the army's efforts, many Americans looked for some "magic bullet" to end the war. Others looked to history for an answer. Both found what they were looking for in Jamaica. From 1655 to 1737, the British had tried in vain to capture insurgent blacks who had escaped to the heavily for-

MAP 6. Florida War, 1838–1842.

ested mountains of the island. Although the English repeatedly attempted to discover the blacks' hideouts, they met with nothing but frustration. The situation reminded many Americans of their own frustrations in trying to locate the haunts of the Seminoles. It was not until the British introduced bloodhounds to the conflict that the so-called Maroon Wars ended. For eighty-two years, the former slaves had managed to elude their pursuers; soon after the dogs' arrival, they gave up. Bloodhounds seemed just the sort of salvation of which war-weary Floridians dreamed.[37]

The idea of using bloodhounds did not arise with the indignation over the Harney Massacre. A year before the event, General Taylor had written to Secretary Poinsett requesting permission to procure and employ the animals, and had received permission to do so. For whatever reasons, Taylor had never bothered to follow up on the matter. Poinsett believed that all types of dogs, not just bloodhounds, would be useful in the war effort. "I still think that every cabin, every military post, and every detachment, should be attended by dogs," he wrote. "That precaution might have saved Dade's command from massacre, and by giving timely warning, have prevented many of the cruel murders which have been committed by the Indians in Middle Florida."[38]

If the federal government was not in any hurry to procure the animals, the Territory of Florida was. A delegation was dispatched to Cuba to purchase a pack of the hounds and to hire the services of several handlers. On January 7, 1840, the delegation returned to Florida with thirty-three bloodhounds and five Cuban handlers. Early reports seemed to indicate that the dogs would perform as advertised. As one man related, "The means are now certainly discovered of ending the war in good earnest, and almost without bloodshed." Others, however, were not much impressed. One correspondent noted that in several trials with an Indian prisoner the hounds failed to take up the trail. Still, initial success encouraged most people to place considerable faith in the bloodhounds.[39]

So what was the *political* problem? Even if the dogs failed to track the Indians, there was little money wasted in the effort. Simply put, it was not so much the *tracking* that bothered people, it was the *catching*. Humanitarians seem to have possessed visions of the dogs tearing captured Indians, including women and children, to pieces. Memorials began to pour into Congress in protest of the employment of the bloodhounds. Secretary of War Poinsett was forced to issue an order specifying that the dogs be muzzled and leashed when in use.[40]

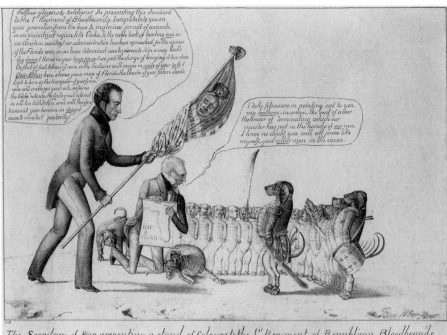

FIGURE 17.

"The Secretary of War presenting a stand of Colours to the 1st Regiment of Republican Bloodhounds." The kneeling figure is Francis P. Blair, publisher of the pro-Jackson newspaper *Washington Globe*. Lithograph by H. Bucholzer, 1840.
By permission of the Library of Congress. LC-USZ62–91404.

Were they really that ferocious? It depended on who you asked. A reporter for the *St. Augustine Herald* reported, "Such a set of ferocious beasts I never before saw." Another writer had a differing opinion: "As to their ferocity, it is all humbug—a child may fondle with them. They have been more grossly misrepresented than any set of animals in the world, the army not excepted."[41]

Like numerous issues of the time, the bloodhounds became a sectional concern. Many of those who were protesting the use of the dogs were also members of the antislavery movement. Indeed, abolitionists believed that the dogs were imported not to hunt Indians but to track down runaway slaves. Perhaps, but abolitionists tended to see *everything* in relation to the slavery issue. Slave catching aside, there can be little doubt that Floridians hoped the dogs would prove useful in locating the hiding places of the Seminoles. At any rate, the matter became a hot political issue, something for the opposition Whig party to use in convincing the American people of the moral bankruptcy of the Van Buren administration. It was, after all, an election year.[42]

Indeed, if anyone in America was morally bankrupt, it was the people who ran the nation's election campaigns. America had entered a period of smoke-filled rooms and ruthless electioneering, a no-holds-barred arena in which the army's use of bloodhounds proved a potent weapon. It is interesting to note that in the political cartoons that have survived from the 1840 election, the Seminole War does not seem to have been much of an issue. One would think the expense of the war or the embarrassing length of the conflict would have provided plenty of ammunition for the Whig forces. Perhaps because Whigs had supported the war effort almost as much as Democrats, the party shied away from the subject. Bloodhounds were another matter, and the cartoonists had a field day with the subject.

The critic's efforts were aided by the fact that the hounds were not very adept at tracking Indians. Congressman Joshua Giddings, an abolitionist from Ohio, claimed, "It was well known that these animals were trained to pursue *negroes,* and *only* negroes." An officer in Florida agreed, noting that the "companies were *ordered* to take some of these dogs and try them. In every case it was a failure; these dogs would no more trail an Indian, than a deer hound would point a partridge." Another factor that worked against the bloodhounds was the fact that Florida was one big wetland. Indians had long ago learned to take to the water when fleeing the whites. Once a trail entered the water, the nose of the bloodhound was of little value. In the end, General Taylor refused to reimburse the territory for the expense of the dogs.[43]

The matter of the bloodhounds serves to highlight the subject of sympathy for the Indian. The fate of Osceola provided the focal point for some much needed national soul searching. His capture under a flag of truce had struck deeply at many an American's sense of honor. His death as a prisoner of war in Charleston, reported in glowing terms and accompanied by George Catlin's flattering portrait, had served to create a martyr. There was an uneasiness about the nation's treatment of Native Americans. There were a large number of people in the nation who felt the war had been brought on by the government's unfair policies. Many, such as Quakers, were opposed to any sort of war. Others mourned the loss of the Indians' culture. Still others, who had business with the Indians, mourned the financial loss. For whatever reason, a significant number of people put pressure upon their elected representatives to deal more fairly with the Indians.

There had always been a certain amount of public sympathy for the Indians, but it had become more pronounced after the Jackson administration began its campaign of removing them to lands west of the Mississippi. During the infamous Trail of Tears, an estimated 4,000 out of 18,000 Cherokees had died during capture, detention, or removal. For those who had hoped removal would benefit the Indians, the whole affair was a shocking disappointment.[44]

Others felt sympathy for the Indians for less practical reasons. It was the romantic age, and the idea of the noble savage was fashionable. The Industrial Revolution had begun to complicate people's lives, making them long for so-called simpler times. Even letters sent home from army officers spoke wistfully of the "children of the forest." Perhaps the highly regimented military lifestyle made soldiers long for a world where a man's primary responsibility was to go hunting. It was an unrealistic vision, but one that we still employ today.

Some of the people who were most sympathetic to the plight of the Seminoles were the men charged with hunting them down. The Seminole's fierce determination to remain in Florida had earned the grudging respect of many an army officer. A sympathetic officer of the Fourth Artillery questioned the nation's morals in dealing with the Seminoles: "After much suffering, they have been driven into the swamps and unwholesome places of their country, and they are now clinging with the last efforts of desperation to their beloved home. Can any Christian in this republic know this and still pray for the continuance of blessings, when he is about to wrest from the unhappy Seminole all that the Great Spirit ever conferred upon him?"[45]

It was a sentiment echoed by many Americans. Had not their own Revolution been a long, sometimes hopeless, war against a much more powerful antagonist? Weren't the Seminoles simply defending their homes and families, one of the most basic of human instincts? It may well have been true, but the arguments often fell on deaf ears, and that deafness was often caused by the actions of the Seminoles themselves. Unable to stand up to the powerful U.S. Army, they waged a guerrilla war, attacking isolated homesteads and solitary travelers. Sympathy for the Indian was often negated by tales of cruel butchery. Politicians, as well as newspaper editors, seemed to delight in retelling tales of Indian cruelty. Governor Robert Reid, who had succeeded to the office after R. K. Call had fallen into disfavor with the White House, addressed the legislative council, reading portions of a letter relating the aftermath of an attack near the Apalachicola River:

> I found Mrs. H. lying prostrate on the ground . . . with her throat cut, a ball shot through her arm, one in her back, and a fatal shot in the head. . . . Her youngest son . . . lay near her side, with his skull fractured by a pine stick which lay near him. He exhibited signs of life . . . and faint hopes are now entertained of his recovery. Had you witnessed the heart-rending sight of Mr. H. embracing his little son, and calling him by his nick-name, 'Buddy!' 'Buddy!' 'Buddy!' with the solemn sound of parental affection, sunk to the lowest ebb of dejection; and then running to the corpse of his wife, throwing his arms around her, crying out, 'My wife!' 'My dear wife!' 'Oh! my dear wife!' I know your feelings would have given way as mine did; I had always felt a sympathy for these merciless savages, but my heart now assumed a stern fortitude, foreign to its nature, and I felt like not leaving an Indian foot to make a track in the ashes of the desolation they have made.[46]

Indeed, it was this barbarity that often doomed the Indians. Taking a scalp was understandable; soldiers had always collected trophies, and white soldiers often scalped slain Seminoles. Mutilating and abusing the dead was harder for many whites to accept. Had the Indians stuck to killing soldiers and male settlers, they would have garnered much more sympathy. If they had simply burnt homesteads instead of butchering the occupants, whites would have given the Indians their grudging respect. Osceola seems to have been one of the few who understood this, but even he could not alter a culture that had evolved over centuries. The Seminoles were simply practicing Indian warfare, unaware that they lived in the romantic age, a time when women and children, even those of the enemy, were not to be harmed. To have behaved any differently than they did, the Seminoles would have had to give up the very culture they were fighting to preserve.

The question will always remain as to the extent that whites committed atrocities upon Indian women and children. Human nature and the admittedly degenerate attitude of many civilians and soldiers would seem to make it probable. Militia officers tended to have little sympathy for the Indians and would have exercised minimal control over the rapacious tendencies of their men. In contrast, officers of the regular army often considered themselves to be the last bastions of chivalry. Still, we are not all that surprised when we read a report about Colonel Harney, "who had ravished Indian girls at night, and then strung them up to the limb of a live oak in the morning." All in all, it was not the sort of subject the papers would have gotten into or that a soldier would have written home about. For better or for worse, the standards of journalism have changed considerably in 160 years.[47]

Savage warfare, along with the perceived faithlessness of the Indians, forced many Americans to question their feelings for the natives. Perhaps, they thought, it *was* better to ship them west. Sympathy for the Indian could not, in the end, stop the war; the cry for their removal was too great. Indeed, the encouragement given the Indian cause may well have served to prolong the conflict.

Throughout the fall of 1839, General Taylor continued with his plan of squares for North Florida. Work progressed slowly, but as time passed, a web of new roads began to form. Little by little, the Seminoles were being pushed south. Florida was still very much an unexplored wilderness, however, and as the war entered its fifth year, much of the territory was either in the hands of the Seminoles or simply unoccupied.

The healthy winter had arrived, and along with it came the call for a new campaign. Taylor, somewhat limited in manpower, did not possess the number of troops necessary to mount a large scale offensive and, in truth, saw little need for one. The army, addicted to grand strategies and large columns of tightly formed men, was beginning to rethink its methods. The *Army and Navy Chronicle* reported that the "approaching campaign then will partake more of a defensive than offensive character, as it will be confined to driving the Indians from the settled portions of Florida, where they have committed depredations almost without check. It having been found impossible to force the Indians from their fastnesses, any further attempt to effect that object would only be attended with a needless sacrifice of life and money." Simply put, the army had run out of ideas.[48]

Opening any sort of a campaign before December was almost impossible. The army was simply too sick. As one officer reported, "We are all overwhelmed with grief and despondency. Disease and death are making fearful ravages over this devoted land. . . . Thus within a short month, the mysterious hand of death has snatched from our midst three gallant and generous spirits—three of the brightest ornaments of our little army. . . . No season since the beginning of the war has been so productive of disease and death. . . . Gloom and sorrow prevail."[49]

At the Naval Hospital in Pensacola, the mortality rate was no better. In a letter published in the *New York Gazette,* the writer reported the deaths of three officers and the hospitalization of seven or eight others, along with thirty sailors. Before mailing the letter, he was forced to reopen it to add the name of another deceased officer. He closed the letter with the line "God grant that I many close this, without having the pain to record another."[50]

From reading the papers, one might have gotten the impression that only *officers* were dying. In a republic that prided itself on its democratic philosophy, there was still a strong tendency to recognize class distinctions. Enlisted men were rarely named and seldom appreciated when they died. Almost invariably, the account of a battle would list the names of the officers killed or wounded but give only the *number* of enlisted men who had suffered just as much. One can easily assume that in a force in which enlisted men outnumbered officers by at least ten to one, fatalities were ten times higher than for officers. For many a widow, the words "'Til death us do part" had become a reality.

In sickness or in health, the war continued. In southern Florida, the navy was expanding its role. Taking to canoes, sailors and marines began to push up the Miami River to explore the Everglades, hoping to discover the hiding places of the enemy. In the northern part of the peninsula, General Taylor kept his men on the move, scouring the territory from east to west. Indian camps were discovered and the occupants forced to flee. A correspondent to the *New York Commercial Advertiser* put the whole effort into perspective: "Notwithstanding all these efforts, the savage, secret foe constantly carries on his work of blood and death. In the past year it is estimated that not less than eighty individuals have been killed by the Indians in Florida, while only perhaps a dozen of their number have shared a similar fate. Middle Florida, it was hoped, had been relieved of the enemy; but this hope is proved fallacious. Within ten miles of this place [Tallahassee] houses were burnt and families murdered last summer!"[51]

On the eastern coast, things were no better. On February 13, 1840, the mail stage from St. Augustine to Jacksonville was ambushed and the driver, a youth of sixteen or seventeen, slain. While searching for the boy's murderers, soldiers discovered the body of another mail carrier. The writer related the city's grief: "Garcias was a native of this city, and a young man about 22 years of age, of exemplary character and integrity. He was married about four months since, and when his mangled corpse was brought home, what were the feelings of his young wife may possibly be felt, but never described."[52]

The Florida War had degenerated to a fierce guerrilla war that the United States appeared to be losing. Detachments of troops scoured the countryside but found few Indians. Seminole war parties hid in the bushes alongside the territory's roads and ambushed travelers seemingly at will. Soldiers, stationed at posts only twenty miles apart, reacted as quickly as they could to the murders but were usually too late to catch the perpetrators. A feeling of helplessness and depression hung over Florida, and the army seemed powerless to end it.

By the time the summer of 1840 began to approach, Zachary Taylor was tired of Florida. He had served as commanding officer for two years, a longer period than any of his predecessors. A transfer was asked for and granted, and the man who would one day become president of the United States boarded ship for New Orleans. Upon his arrival in Pensacola, the *Gazette* reported that "Gen. T. is in very bad health." The victor of the Battle of Lake Okeechobee was already a man with a great reputation. The article concluded that, "There are few men, of any rank, who have devoted themselves to the great objects of the war, with an assiduity like that of the veteran Taylor, and the utter hopelessness of the war cannot be better illustrated than by reference to the fact, that even he, with all his energy and his eminent talents for command, has done nothing."[53]

9

"I Feel the Irons in My Heart"

▲▲▲ ▲▲▲ ▲▲▲ ▲▲▲ ▲

One aspect of the war that had changed considerably was the influence of the black Seminoles. By the time Zachary Taylor had taken command of the war, the majority of blacks were out of the conflict, due to death, capture, or voluntary surrender. Although many of those who had been captured were returned to slavery, a large number were allowed to go west as free men and women. Still others remained in Florida to serve as guides and interpreters for the army.

There were several reasons black Seminoles went to work for the army. First, the pay was good. Also, for many it was a matter of survival. They knew that in a slave society, a free black often needed a protector. Being valuable to the army was one way to keep from being sold or stolen. Building a personal relationship with a high-ranking officer might also prove useful at some future place and time. In 1844, John Cavallo, who had become the primary leader of the black Seminoles in Oklahoma, was able to call upon General Jesup for help in dealing with unfulfilled promises from the War Department.[1]

Many Seminoles held mixed views concerning this change of heart on the part of the blacks. Those Indians who had already emigrated could have cared less. Those who wished to remain in Florida usually, and with good cause, considered these blacks traitors. John Sprague gives an account of one battle in which John Cavallo, also known as Gopher John, was a primary target:

> The tall figure of the negro interpreter, Gopher John, his loud voice, and negro accent, the repeated discharge of his unerring rifle, well known to the Indians as he was, made him a conspicuous object of assault. The balls flew by him so thick, striking the trees around, that he suspected his courage was oozing out, when, pulling from

his pocket a well-filled flask: "God-e, massa," said he to an officer by his side, "I feel all over, mighty queer, de ingen fight so strong! I must take a big un"; and suiting the action to the word, he drained his bottle, reprimed his rifle, whooped, and was soon lost in the midst of foliage and smoke.[2]

Some Seminoles held a grudge for many years, while others were willing to accept the fact that most blacks had simply been acting out of self-preservation. In the late 1840s, an unsuccessful attempt was made on Cavallo's life. The black chief blamed members of Alligator's band, claiming they were still upset about his being a guide and interpreter during the war. On the other side of the coin, Cavallo and Coacoochee became close friends and later led a party of emigrants into Mexico, where slavery had been abolished.[3]

Throughout the course of the conflict, slave owners had two objectives. First, they wanted the Indians removed in order to eliminate the sanctuary to which many of their slaves hoped to flee. Second, they wanted more slaves, in the form of either their returned property or new slaves taken from the Seminoles. Oddly, the two objectives often conflicted. Forcing the Seminoles out meant that many of the blacks would be going west with them. Allowing the Seminoles to remain meant the continued hope of sanctuary for many plantation-bound slaves.

Pressure from slaveholders often drove national policy. In order to keep the Union together, concessions were often made to the slave states. In the Treaties of Moultrie Creek and Payne's Landing, specific provisions were made for the return of runaway slaves. Still, we must be careful not to overstate the influence of the proslavery lobby. For a negotiator or an officer who had to deal with the Seminoles the priority would be getting a treaty or ending the war. Pleasing the slavers might be important, but it would have to be a secondary consideration.

The link between slavery and the Florida War came to a focus in the House of Representatives. To avoid divisive debate on the slavery issue, the House had passed a "gag rule," which forbid discussion of the subject in House debate. Congressman Joshua Giddings of Ohio concentrated on the connection between slavery and the Seminole War, thereby giving him a justification to carry on about the evils of slavery. On one occasion, in response to the protest of a fellow congressman, Giddings informed the Chair, "I will, however, assure this gentleman from South Carolina that I shall only allude to the subject of slavery so far as it stands con-

FIGURE 18.
"Gopher John" Cavallo, black Seminole leader.
By permission of the Florida State Archives. Image #RC08718, DBCN#AAM-1623.

nected with the Florida war." He then continued on with his harangue, "alluding" to the subject of slavery no less than 267 times. Long after the war was over, Giddings continued with his crusade. His 1858 book *The Exiles of Florida* was a scathing indictment of government policy toward the Seminoles and their black allies.[4]

It is hard to pin down exactly how much influence the issue of slavery had upon the war. Would there have been a Second Seminole War without the presence of blacks? It all depends on how strongly the Seminoles wanted to stay in Florida. Were their minds changed by their black friends or was black support simply more weight on a balance already tipped in favor of war? The presence of runaways certainly made the Seminole Wars different from other Indians wars, but in the end it was still a conflict between the advancement of white culture and the Indian's wish to retain his land and his way of life. After all, the Seminoles were fighting for the freedom of their own people, not for the slaves of Georgia and South Carolina.

What Americans seem to have forgotten is how strongly another form of racism influenced nineteenth century America. For many early Americans, the fear, hatred, and ignorance concerning Native Americans was just as strong as it was toward African Americans. For reasons the nation should not take pride in, America no longer has an "Indian problem." Yes, the slavery question was an immense factor in the Seminole Wars. Yet we should be careful not to let our own perspective blind us to the knowledge that Indian Removal was just as powerful a force. In the minds of most Americans, the Seminoles had to be removed because they were Indians, not because blacks were living among them.

Upon the departure of Zachary Taylor in May 1840, command passed to Brig. Gen. Walker Keith Armistead. The new commander was already a veteran of Florida service, having been second in command to General Jesup. Of all the commanders of the Florida War, Armistead is the most shadowy. His date of birth seems to be unrecorded, though we find him entering West Point in May 1801. He graduated at the top of his class, but in a class of three, that is no great distinction. By the beginning of the War of 1812 he was a lieutenant colonel, but he did not advance to colonel until well after the war. His brevet promotion to brigadier general was for the usual "ten years of faithful service." Taylor had resented having to serve under Armistead earlier in the war, complaining that a portion of

FIGURE 19.
Brig. Gen. Walker Keith Armistead, by Thomas Sully.
By permission of the West Point Museum Art Collection,
United States Military Academy. #9049.

those ten years of faithful service had been "passed on his farm near Uppersville."[5]

Immediately upon assuming command in May 1840, Armistead ordered major changes to the manner in which the war was to be conducted. For all the praise that had been heaped upon the fighting abilities of Zachary Taylor, the departing general's strategy had been one of defense. The new commander, as much as he was able to, intended to go on the offensive.

One of Armistead's first orders was to concentrate 900 men at Fort King, then dispatch them in groups of 100 to search for the Seminoles and their hideouts. The general was aware of the fact that it was planting time for the Indians and also the time for them to gather for the annual Green Corn Dance, their most important social and ceremonial event. The new commanding officer realized what most of his predecessors had failed to understand: the summer hiatus gave the Seminoles time to rest and recuperate, time to gather supplies and put away stores of food. If Armistead could break this cycle, he might be able to bring the war to a close.[6]

Armistead was not the only one on the offensive. On the twenty-third of May, Coacoochee and a party of warriors attacked two wagonloads of thespians a little more than five miles from St. Augustine. Three of the actors were killed, along with another trio of travelers who happened upon the scene. If the Indians thought the wagons were loaded with gunpowder, lead, or some other store of valuable provisions, they were disappointed. Instead, the trunk loads of costumes provided the Seminoles with some highly interesting apparel.

Even armed parties were not safe from assault. In six separate attacks occurring in varying parts of the territory, two soldiers were killed each day on July 12, 13, 14, 16, 19, 20, and 26. On the same day Coacoochee was ruining the theatrical season at St. Augustine, the *Savannah Georgian* ran this "Extract from the Report":[7]

> Lieut. Martin, 2d infantry, left Micanopy on the morning of the 19th, with three men from his post, Wakahoota, after proceeding about four miles he was fired upon by Indians. He received three balls, one through the lower part of the abdomen, one through the arm, and one in his hand—one of his men and all the horses killed—the other two missing. Lieut. Sanderson, 7th infantry, with a party of seventeen men, was sent in pursuit; he fell in with the Indians, and *he* and five of his men were killed. . . . Lieut. Sanderson had his fingers cut off and stuck in his mouth.

Later reports showed that Lieutenant Martin survived his wounds, but the two missing men were never found.[8]

Although the Seminoles managed to score several small victories, they also suffered a number of defeats. Troops discovered several well-hidden villages where the women and children were taken prisoner and the buildings and crops destroyed. On one mission, the army came upon the natives during preparations for the Green Corn Dance. Surprised, the Indians fled into the forest, leaving behind most all their possessions

and even a sleeping infant. Another mission, led by Colonel Harney, succeeded in capturing the mother and daughter of Coacoochee.[9]

The Indian attacks continued into August. Most notable was a daring
raid on Indian Key, located in the middle of the Florida Keys. The attack,
which took place on August 7, 1840, was carried out by approximately
eighty-five of the Spanish Indians led by Chakaika, one of those believed
responsible for the Harney Massacre of the previous year. One of the
inhabitants of Indian Key was Dr. Henry Perrine, a noted botanist who
had come to South Florida to conduct experiments with tropical plants.

It was a most unusual Indian raid. Chakaika and his warriors crossed
Florida Bay in seventeen canoes and completely surprised the island's
residents in the middle of the night. Seven of those living on the island
were murdered, including Perrine and four nonrelated children. The
doctor's wife and children were able to make their escape by hiding under the burning house until forced to flee from the collapsing structure.
Taking to a small boat, they fled to a schooner anchored about a mile
offshore. Another resident of the island fled to nearby Tea Table Key,
where a small naval hospital was located. A number of invalids from the
hospital attempted a rescue mission but were driven off when the Indians fired a cannon at the approaching sailors.[10]

Armistead's job was to remove the Indians from Florida, and he was
willing to try various methods to accomplish that task. Believing that
some of the hostile bands could be persuaded to emigrate by friends and
family who had already been sent west, the general arranged for a delegation of chiefs to be brought from Arkansas to Florida. At first, the effort
seemed promising. Halleck Tustenuggee and Tiger Tail, two of the more
dangerous chiefs still at large, seemed willing to listen. In early November 1840, a truce was called, and a large number of Seminoles began to
gather at Fort King, where the talks were being held. Both Halleck and
Tiger Tail voiced a willingness to emigrate. As a further inducement, Armistead offered the chiefs sizable bribes if they would take their people
west. In agreement with the practice, Congress later allocated $100,000
for the effort.[11]

Then, on November 15, with no forewarning, the Indians fled their
camps, returning to the wilds. Not totally surprised, Armistead called off
the truce and ordered his men to once again take the field. Parts of the
order read: "The Indians having acted with their usual want of faith, the

armistice is at end; the commanding officers of Districts, Regiments, and Posts will therefore be prepared to act offensively on the promulgation of this order. . . . Should the enemy hereafter appear with the white flag, they are to be made prisoners, and diligently guarded until further orders." Armistead had tried to negotiate, been rebuffed, and was left with no other course of action.[12]

After the aborted peace talks of November, hostilities resumed and both sides inflicted occasional casualties on the other. In late December, exactly five years after Dade's command had been wiped out, another tragic loss occurred. Near Micanopy, a wagon was being escorted by a group of eleven soldiers under the command of Lt. Walter Sherwood. Along for the trip was Mrs. Montgomery, the young newlywed wife of another officer. From the roadside, shots rang out, wounding several of the soldiers and killing Mrs. Montgomery. Not willing to leave the lady's body to be mutilated by the Indians, the soldiers stood their ground, fighting off the attackers hand to hand. Alerted by the arrival of riderless horses, a rescue party, led by Lieutenant Montgomery, quickly left Micanopy. Arriving too late, Montgomery found the bodies of his wife, Lt. Sherwood, and his men. By the lady's side was a dying private who told the grieving officer, "I fought for your wife as long as I could." It was a sad and heroic tale that cried out for revenge.[13]

The whites were not the only ones suffering losses. In early December, Colonel Harney finally made amends for the attacks on the Caloosahatchee and at Indian Key. With an escaped slave as a guide, Harney and his men silently pushed their canoes into the Everglades, looking for the camp of Chakaika and the Spanish Indians. Seeing it in the distance, the soldiers changed into Indian garb and approached the camp. With complete surprise, Harney captured the village, and Chakaika was slain trying to escape. Harney then informed the Seminoles that the nature of the war had changed; no longer would he take the warriors as prisoners. Several of the captured warriors were immediately hanged, strung up beside the body of their dead leader.[14]

General Armistead's aggressive approach to the war and the accompanying successes of Harney and others signaled a turning point. No longer could the Seminoles rely upon the quiet months of the summer season to rest, gather their crops, and prepare for the winter's warfare. No longer were they able to live in security in the trackless Everglades. No longer was the army willing to play by the rules of civilized warfare. The Seminoles, long considered merciless hunters by many whites, found themselves being hunted by a merciless army. Though few could see it at the time, the war was beginning to end.

Taking the war to the Seminoles had required a drastic change in the mindset of the army and, for the first time in an Indian war, the inclusion of the navy. From the beginning of the conflict, the navy had played a role, but only a minor one. For the most part, they had supplied manpower when called upon in emergencies and had performed valuable service in patrolling the coastline and in ferrying supplies and soldiers.

Yet as early as 1837, at least one naval officer realized that the navy could play a much more important role in the fight against the Indians. Lt. Levin Powell proposed entering the Everglades in small boats to discover and attack the Seminoles' hideouts. In the fall of that year, he commenced several expeditions up the short rivers that emptied into the Atlantic Coast south of Lake Okeechobee. Powell soon discovered the shortcomings of his plan. Finding his way through the monotonous Everglades was almost impossible without competent guides, which he lacked, and the standard navy boats were not suited to the shallow, tangled, twisted streams of South Florida. More than anything else, he found that expeditions into the Everglades required specially trained men. His motley collection of sailors and volunteer soldiers were simply not up to the task.[15]

Powell's lessons were not forgotten. The following year, command of the Florida squadron was given to Lt. John T. McLaughlin, a young navy officer who was ready to take the war to the Seminoles. Like Powell, McLaughlin wanted to enter the Everglades and make life miserable for the Indians. He intended to traverse and explore the entire southern portion of the peninsula, from one coast to the other. Impressed with both his and Powell's plans, the administration gave them their support. Shallow-draft schooners, better suited to working the Florida coast, were added to the fleet. McLaughlin's flagship, the *Flirt*, was built expressly for Florida duty. Flat-bottom boats, barges, and a large number of canoes were built or purchased. The whole collection of vessels became known as the "Mosquito Fleet."

What was most impressive about McLaughlin's efforts was the amount of cooperation between the army and the navy. Though obviously a naval officer, McLaughlin was serving under General Armistead. A considerable portion of the men who were part of his expeditions were soldiers. It must have been a strange looking group. Sailors (many of them black), marines, and soldiers, all mixed together, paddling silently into the Everglades. Throughout the final years of the war, McLaughlin and his men, during several expeditions, explored and mapped the Everglades, a portion of the territory where few white men had ever visited. Hidden villages and fields were located and destroyed. By the time the war ended, the Seminoles were not the only people who knew their way around the "River of Grass."

For sailors used to life on the open sea or soldiers who spent every night sleeping on terra firma, it would prove the most unusual, grueling work they could imagine. The canoes would travel in large groups, in total silence, very often at night. To escape detection by the Indians, fires were rarely allowed. Because the Everglades were covered almost entirely by water and sawgrass, the crews often had to sleep in their boats. Even in winter, the mosquitos could be unbelievably thick. Although rations were packed, much of the food had to be captured or gathered along the way. The discovery of a Seminole garden must have been a welcome sight to the weary men. Well removed from any military installation, the sick made out as best they could, and those that died were consigned to a watery grave far from any ocean.

It was, all in all, a new experience for the navy. Working for the army was strange enough. Sailing up narrow streams in canoes was altogether revolutionary. It was, in short, not the way things were normally done. Credit must be given to the officers and administrators who realized that new tactics were called for and had the courage to carry them out. They knew that if the Seminole War was to be won, they would have to meet the Indians on the Indians' own terms, in the Indians' own territory.

Despite its initial success, Armistead's offensive began to slow just at the time when it should have been growing stronger. Maj. Ethan Allen Hitchcock complained that the general seemed to have lost his direction. The younger officer also blamed the collapse of the talks in November on Armistead's inept handling of negotiations and on the fact that while Armistead was attempting to talk the chiefs into emigrating, troops were out harassing the natives. In late January, the officer in charge of negotiations was complaining of the same problem. By early February, Armistead was being ordered to pursue the war more forcefully. Whatever the problem, during the early months of 1841, when the weather was conducive to campaigning, very little action took place.[16]

·   ·   ·

The economics of a conflict can often have as much of an effect on its conduct as military considerations. In Congress, debate arose whenever it came time to appropriate the monies needed to pursue the war. Congressman Henry Wise of Virginia complained that

> appropriations were extracted from this House, like teeth, without the proper investigation and inquiry. The officers of Government waited until appropriations were immediately wanted, and then they called upon the House to pass them, without investigation, without inquiry, and without discussion. It is in this manner that nine-tenths, if not all of the eight, nine or ten millions of dollars which had been appropriated for this fatal, disastrous, disgraceful Seminole campaign had been obtained. . . . Would any corporation or company take thirty millions of dollars to pay the expenditures of this disgraceful Indian war?[17]

After the initial setbacks of the war, opponents of either the administration or the war had questioned if the monies were being well spent. Such had not been the case at the beginning of the war, primarily because the nation had been experiencing a booming economy. The budget of 1836 called for revenues of about $35 million while expenditures were scheduled to be only $25 million. For the only time in the nation's history, the government was debt free and looking forward to a large surplus.[18]

The booming economy and huge surplus could be attributed in part to the policies of Andrew Jackson. In the 1830s, Jackson declared war on the National Bank, feeling it to be corrupt and operated in a manner contrary to the interests of the western states. His policy of closing the National Bank and depositing federal funds in selected state banks made more money available for land speculation. As the sale of public lands skyrocketed, revenues poured in.

The figures were astounding. Sale of public lands escalated between 1834 and 1836, rising from $4.9 million to $24.9 million. The number of banks increased from 330 to 788 between 1830 and 1836. Bank loans increased from $200.5 million to $525.1 million and bank notes from $61.3 million to $149.2 million during the same years. Credit from England also fueled the growing economy. The net trade balance rose from $7.9 million to $62.2 million and the aggregate debt increased from $74.9 million to $220.3 million from 1830 to 1836. Between 1834 and 1835, $37 million of Treasury surplus was deposited in state banks. An additional $35 million in specie flowed into the country, the bulk going into bank vaults for future notes. From 1834 to 1836, the supply of money rose from $172 million to $277 million.[19]

The success of his policies began to make Jackson nervous. Distrusting paper money, the president initiated the Specie Circular in mid-1836 that demanded payment for government land in gold or silver. Unfortunately, there was not enough specie in circulation. Unable to redeem notes in hard money, all but six of the 788 banks suspended payment of specie in May 1837. The resulting Panic of 1837, as it became known, created an economic contraction followed by a severe depression that lasted until the end of 1839. Faced with an economic crisis, the newly elected president, Martin Van Buren, was forced to either adhere to his predecessor's policy or modify it. A New York paper predicted the outcome, stating that Van Buren "feared the consequences of taking ground at so early a period of his administration in opposition to his political godfather [Jackson]." Concerned that Van Buren would make a change in policy, Jackson wrote to his successor on March 26, 1838:[20]

> I rejoice at the prospects of the divorce, or Treasury bill. . . . Permit me to assure you, that if the vote was now taken in this state upon the subject, two thirds of the people would vote in favor of separating the Government from the Banks. None but Bankers, and speculators, who all wish a second flood of depreciated paper, and a continued suspension of specie payments by the Banks, are in favour of any connection of the Government with Banks. . . . *Adhere to it, my friend,* and you land the vessel of state into a safe and pleasant harbour that will give you ease for the balance of your eight years.[21]

In the midst of a severe economic depression, Congress became more concerned about the cost of the Florida War. Questioning the demands for appropriations, Mr. Bond of Ohio reported, "The first appropriation . . . [was] made at a time when there was an immense surplus in the treasury, without attracting any notice. In a short time there was another appropriation called for of $1 million; and the ghost of this same Florida war was continually being brought to view . . . in the shape of a bill appropriating some millions of dollars for the suppression of Indian hostilities."[22]

Several problems associated with the war contributed to its escalating cost. First was the issue of inflated prices. Noting wasteful expenditures, Congressman Garland of Louisiana reported that "50 chords of wood cost the government $7,000." Also noting the personal gain of a steamboat operator, Garland remarked that the owner made enough on a single trip up a Florida river to pay for the boat.[23]

Another problem was the expense of volunteers and militia. The paymaster general informed the secretary of war that by the end of Armistead's command, $2,525,399.29 had been paid to regulars as compared with $3,461,622.15 to citizen-soldiers, who often served for only short periods of time. Those who feared a large standing army were quick to call for the use of more militia and volunteers. If nothing else, it was good politics.[24]

A third problem involved those who urged the war on for personal profit and security. Secretary of War Poinsett, reporting frauds committed by citizens against the government, wrote, "Many persons in Florida who are able to provide for themselves . . . are now drawing rations for themselves, families and negroes." Congress nevertheless continued to appropriate funds to bring the contest to a close, though in smaller amounts and with more strings attached.[25]

Although many congressmen complained about the cost of the war, few actually voted against the necessary appropriation bills. At that particular point in American history it was not politically safe for an elected official to be "soft" on hostile Indians. The best the Whigs could do was accuse Van Buren and Poinsett of gross mismanagement of the conflict. As far as most Americans were concerned, there was certainly a large element of truth to the statement.

In the spring of 1841, some notable personnel changes took place. First of all, a new president took office. William Henry Harrison was a Whig, and his election signaled a temporary end to the reign of the Jacksonian Democrats. To some extent, the unpopularity of the Seminole War helped Harrison defeat Martin Van Buren. Although the war was not the burning issue of the campaign, it certainly helped lend credence to the Whig argument that Van Buren was an incompetent leader. With the new President came a new Cabinet, including a new secretary of war, John Bell.

No sooner was the Cabinet in place then the unexpected happened: After only a month in office, President Harrison died. Vice President John Tyler, a Democrat turned Whig, assumed the presidency, but not with the wholehearted support of the nation or of his party. Once in office, the Whig acted more like a Democrat, but not nearly enough for the

Democrats. Before long, Tyler was a president without a party. Unhappy with the direction in which things were going, most of the Cabinet resigned later in the year, unwilling to serve under "his accidentcy."

The party change also affected things in Florida. Governor Robert R. Reid, appointed by Van Buren, was replaced by Richard Keith Call, the man Reid had earlier replaced. Call, who had left the Democrats to join the Whigs, was no doubt receiving his just rewards. During the election campaign, Call had traveled widely throughout the nation, speaking out against the administration's handling of the war. It was, after all, the Florida War that had brought about the estrangement of Call and his long-time friend, Andrew Jackson. Throughout the nation and the territory, the Whigs were getting their revenge for having long suffered under Jackson's "spoils" system.

As spring wore on, changes also took place in the military. In Washington, Commanding General Alexander Macomb passed away and was replaced by Winfield Scott. His longtime rival General Gaines was not happy about the change but was powerless to stop it. Scott had dabbled in Whig politics; Gaines stayed out of the political arena and was therefore relatively lacking in influence. Though more of a "hands-on" leader than Macomb, Scott does not seem to have taken an active role in directing the Florida War. He had been badly burned the first time; perhaps he wished to avoid the heat a second time.

In Florida, General Armistead felt that although the Indians had not been completely subdued, they were much less a threat than before. It was now only a matter of time until the final bands were rounded up. Florida, he thought, was secure enough to allow the discharge of the militia, an expensive force he felt was no longer needed. Feeling he had done his job well enough and long enough, Armistead asked to be relieved. According to Major Hitchcock, who seems to have considered himself the most influential man in America, it was on his recommendation that Armistead was relieved.[26]

On May 31, 1841, Armistead turned command over to Col. William Jenkins Worth. Worth was one of the army's rising stars. He had joined the service during the War of 1812 and had quickly become one of Winfield Scott's favorite proteges. Handsome, ambitious, and a bit vain, his performance in the Florida War would make him a general. Hard driving, he would gain fame in the Mexican War but lose the friendship of Scott, the most powerful man in the army.

FIGURE 20.
Col. William Jenkins Worth, by Charles Fenderich. Lithograph, 1844.
By permission of the National Portrait Gallery, Smithsonian Institution. #NPG.66.99.

The fact that Worth was not a general posed no real problem. With the militia disbanded, there was no longer the need for an officer who could outrank the militia's generals. All in all it was an indication that the war was slowly moving toward an inevitable conclusion. Although many people could not see it, the conquest of Florida was nearing completion.

The war may have been nearing an end, but was certainly not over. There were still several large bands of warriors operating throughout the territory. Halleck Tustenuggee and Tiger Tail were known to be in the northern part of the peninsula, along with smaller bands led by lesser chiefs. To the south, Billy Bowlegs and the aged but unstoppable Sam Jones were keeping the war alive. Most respected and feared was Coacoochee. After the death of Osceola and his own amazing escape from St. Augustine, Coacoochee had become the symbol of Seminole resistance. More than any other Seminole leader, Coacoochee was the man Colonel Worth wanted.

The Indian chief was well aware of the army's hope to win his favor; every commanding general since Jesup had let it be known that they were willing to negotiate. The chief had pushed these invitations to the limit. Several times he had come in to parley, made encouraging promises, then fled back into the hammocks after securing valuable supplies. The army was well aware of the trick but was in a quandary as to what to do about it. They wanted Coacoochee to be cooperative, to bring his people in. Killing him or taking him prisoner might accomplish little or nothing. Such tactics had already made a martyr of Osceola, and neither the army nor the government needed another larger-than-life legend.

Indeed, dealing with Indians who came in for a "talk" was proving a major embarrassment for the army. Although Armistead had ordered that every Indian carrying a white flag be taken prisoner, it was not that simple. The army wanted the entire band to come in, not just the chief or a solitary warrior. Locking someone in irons or quickly placing them aboard ship could eliminate a valuable messenger or a possible ally. It also tended to scare off other potential emigrants. The best an officer could do was hope that *this time* the Indians were sincere.

The Seminoles had learned to play the game with great skill. A chief would come in, promise to emigrate, but lament the fact that because of army actions, his band was scattered over a wide area. Collecting them would require time and provisions. To not supply those provisions would have been seen as bad faith on the part of the army, causing a distrustful Indian to reconsider his decision. Some chiefs would keep coming back, giving plausible excuses for why their bands had not yet arrived. Officers, often sympathetic to the Indians or under orders to cooperate, would hand out supplies, knowing full well it was a wasted effort. Suffering from a defeatist attitude, they may have reasoned that any chance of getting a large band to emigrate was worth the trouble.

The pitfalls and rewards of such a game become evident when we look at the capture and subsequent actions of Coacoochee. On March 5, 1841, the flamboyant chief arrived at Fort Cummings arrayed in costumes taken from the theatrical troop that had been waylaid near St. Augustine. Coacoochee met with Colonel Worth and promised to bring his people in. In a gesture of good faith, Worth released the Indian's twelve-year-old daughter, who had been captured the year before. In true Seminole fashion, the girl presented her father with powder and lead she had managed to gather while in the camp. The reunion brought tears to the eyes of the chief and to many of the white onlookers.

Coacoochee spent four days in Fort Cummings, discussing matters with Colonel Worth. Perhaps the costume of Hamlet made him ponder whether to stay or not to stay. "The white man comes; he grows pale and sick, why cannot we live in peace? I have said I am the enemy of the white man. I could live in peace with him, but first they steal our cattle and horses, cheat us, and take our lands. The white men are as thick as the leaves in the hammock; they come upon us thicker every year. They may shoot us, drive our women and children night and day; they may chain our hands and feet, but the red man's heart will always be free."[27]

The "talk" finished, Coacoochee departed, promising to return in ten day's time. True to his word, he came back at the end of the ten days and asked for an audience with General Armistead, who at this point was still in command. Three days later, March 22, he was at Fort Brooke. The meeting with Armistead went well, and it was agreed that the band would gather at Fort Pierce on the East Coast.

Optimism on the part of the whites slowly turned to mistrust. The old pattern seemed to reemerge. For all of April and most of May, Coacoochee would come to Fort Pierce and demand provisions, declaring they were needed for the far-flung members of his band. Maj. Thomas Childs, in command at the fort, had seen it all before. Warriors would show up, never women and children. The excuses were becoming less creditable with each telling. Not wishing to be made the fool, Childs requested permission to seize Coacoochee and the warriors in his company. Armistead agreed on May 21. Ten days later, Armistead's tour of duty was over and Colonel Worth took command.

At Fort Pierce, the patience of Major Childs had worn out. On the fourth of June, Coacoochee and several of his followers were taken into custody, quickly placed aboard ship, and embarked for New Orleans. For some reason, Worth did not receive word of the capture and removal until the fifteenth. Furious at the news, he quickly dispatched an agent to New Orleans, who caught up to the Seminoles on June 28. Worth may have wanted Coacoochee taken out of action, but he did not want him out of the territory.

Bringing the famous chief back to Florida was a bold and controversial move. If Coacoochee were to escape, Worth's career would suffer tremendously. The colonel obviously believed the rewards would greatly outweigh the risks. To prevent any chance of the cunning warrior escaping again, Worth kept the ship far from shore and the Indians shackled.

On July 4, Worth sailed out into Tampa Bay and boarded the prisoner's ship. The colonel was respectful but firm: "Coacoochee, I take you by the hand as a warrior, a brave man; you have fought long and with a true and strong heart for your country. . . . You love your country as we do, it is sacred to you. . . . Like the oak, you may bear up for many years against strong winds; the time must come when it will fall; this time has arrived."

Worth then got to the point. Coacoochee would have to call his followers in. If the entire band did not give themselves up, the chief and those warriors with him would be hung from the ship's yardarm. Worth made it clear that it was not an empty threat: "I say what I mean, and I will do it. . . . This war must end, and you must end it."[28]

The captive chief, his voice subdued, spoke of his lifelong struggle against the white man. Chained and with no chance of escape, he began to accept his defeat. "I asked but for a small piece of these lands, enough to plant and to live upon, far south, a spot where I could place the ashes of my kindred, a spot only sufficient upon which I could lay my wife and child. This was not granted me. I was put in prison; I escaped. I have been again taken; you have brought me back; I am here; I feel the irons in my heart."[29]

The irony of the moment was not lost on John Sprague, a witness to the proceedings. "Here was a chief, a man whose only offence was defending his home, his fireside, the graves of his kindred, stipulating on the *Fourth of July*, for his freedom and his life."[30]

The leadership of Coacoochee could not be denied, even when it came from a man in chains aboard a ship anchored far off shore. By the end of July all but twenty of his followers had given themselves up. Worth then showed his true respect for Coacoochee by letting the chief freely travel the countryside in an effort to convince other, more militant chiefs to end the war. By October, several hundred more Seminoles had gathered, ready for the trip west. Fearful that his people would become restless, Coacoochee asked that the ships be allowed to sail. The request was granted. Winter found Coacoochee and his followers in a new home, far from the swamps and hammocks they had fought so long to stay in.[31]

• • •

While Coacoochee had been talking, Worth's men had been in the field, keeping continual pressure on the more intransigent Seminoles still at large. Worth concurred with Armistead in the belief that the troops should be kept in motion during the summer. The colonel firmly believed that the high rate of sickness that occurred during the summer was due to the boredom, unhealthy diet, and easy availability of alcohol that was part of life when soldiers were confined to their posts. It was better, he thought, to keep the men in the field, where the exercise of the march and the excitement of battle would do their constitutions good. The common soldier no doubt had a different opinion on the matter.

Even after the departure of Coacoochee, Worth did not let up. The Everglades and Big Cypress Swamp had been explored enough to allow operations to take place all over southern Florida. New posts and depots were set up, and long, grueling expeditions scoured the swamps and hammocks, forcing the Indians to abandon fields and villages that had once been secure havens. After spending more than two exhausting months on patrol in the Everglades, an officer wrote in his journal, "Thus ended the Big Cypress campaign, like all others: drove the Indians out broke them up, taught them we could go where they could; men and officers worn down; two months in water; plunder on our backs; hard times; trust they are soon to end. Hear of good success at Fort Brooke. Tiger-Tail and Nethlockemathlar surrendered. Coacoochee and Hospetarke gone. Indians asking for peace in all quarters. The only reward we ask is the ending of the Florida War."[32]

The army, frustrated and hopeless, suffered from sickness, extreme heat, and the toll of war. Three hundred officers had resigned since the beginning of the war. This, in an army that had started the war with only a little more than 600 officers. Even high-ranking, experienced officers were not immune to mental and physical fatigue. After an especially grueling march, Col. John F. Lane had gone into his tent and run a sword through his right eye and into his brain. The official cause of death was listed as "disease unknown."[33]

Commenting on low morale, Sprague said, "Fatal paralysis, neither peace nor war, prostrated every exertion and crushes the ardent anticipation of officers and men." Hopelessness and despair brought out the worst in some men, including the officers. Describing a personal incident, Bartholomew Lynch wrote in his diary, "Captain Fowler struck me with a rifle and cut me without reason. I went to Gen. Taylor with my blood flowing. He laughed at me. It is no use to sue a devil if the Court be held in hell."[34]

The conditions in Florida were worse than even the most experienced soldiers had endured. Describing the intense heat and lack of water, Surgeon Motte noted in his journal, "We suffered very much during this march from the scarcity of water, every part of the ground being parched by the excessively hot sun. Our only mode of procuring it on many occasions was to dig holes in the ground, it being generally found at a depth of one or two feet from the surface; but of the colour and consistency of ink. We had to drink that or go without."[35]

Later, Capt. George McCall was faced with the opposite extreme. "We were marching through water from six inches to three feet deep, forty-eight days. . . . No more than two hundred men of the eight hundred could be mustered for duty; fevers, diarrheas, and swollen feet and ankles . . . having laid up in the hospital three-fourths of the command."[36]

Summing up the frustration felt by much of the army, McCall wrote, "Florida is certainly the poorest country that ever two people quarreled for. It is in fact a most hideous region to live in; a perfect paradise for Indians, alligators, serpents, frogs, and every other kind of loathsome reptile. . . . Then why not in the name of common sense let the Indians have kept it?"[37]

Civilians, disappointed that no brilliant and decisive victories had been achieved, blamed the soldiers. McCall complained of the "abusive comments of some civilians . . . vomited forth reproaches, sneers, and condemnation . . . assailing the characters of those who . . . were compelled to remain in this inglorious war . . . and finally, when worn out by arduous service, sent home with ruined constitutions."[38]

For the soldiers, sailors, and militia men, for the civilians living in fear of random attacks, for the people throughout the nation who paid for and argued over it, and for the hounded Seminoles, the war continued to drag on.

The war may not have been over, but the War Department had certainly tired of paying for it. In the orders issued to Worth upon his taking command, the secretary of war had told the officer to "diminish, in a spirit of sound economy, all unnecessary drains upon the treasury, by discharging all persons employed in a civil capacity, whose services you shall not deem indispensable to the duties of your command." Worth, in turn, called for special reports from all his junior commanders, listing the resources available. It was time to trim the fat.[39]

Cutting expenses meant cutting well paid civilian jobs. As Sprague pointed out, "The employment of clerks, and mechanics of all kinds, teamsters, laborers, &c., for so long a time, drawing their monthly pay with regularity, at exorbitant rates, induced many to look upon the Florida war as . . . a state of things which would secure employment profitable and lasting."[40]

At the top of Sprague's list of people who would prolong the war for personal profit were the black interpreters. Spanish fisherman living along the Gulf Coast also had an interest in keeping the war going. For many, fishing was often a pretense for smuggling arms and ammunition to the Seminoles. Even wealthy slaveholders profited from the war by hiring their slaves out as laborers to the army. For all these people the continuation of the war meant a steady paycheck, and many would do whatever they could to keep the conflict going.

One of Worth's first economy measures was to halt expenditures for maintenance on the army's many buildings. He was going to end the war and saw no reason to waste money on buildings that were soon to be abandoned. Next came the cuts in civilian employees. More than 1,000 civilians worked for the army in Florida, whose total strength in *fighting men* was slightly more than 3,000. Needless to say, Colonel Worth was not a popular man with many a Floridian.

Another expense that had been eliminated was the militia. The governors or Florida and Georgia both attempted to force these civilian troops upon Worth, but he and the War Department would have none of them. Every Indian scare brought out another appeal for the mustering of a company of militia. Some reports turned out to be nothing more than willful fabrications. One overly zealous militia officer reported to Governor Call, "Yesterday, about ten in the morning, the Indians made an attack on Mr. Osteen's house . . . killed Mrs. O., and were still firing on the house when the express left."

An army contractor disputed the claim. "I learned there that she was not killed, but it was generally supposed that she *might* have been shot at by an Indian. I reached Mrs. Osteen's the same day, found her in good health, and learned that she had not been shot. I was told by her neighbors that she had not even been fired on, and there was great doubt expressed whether any Indians had been in the vicinity."[41]

Worth continued to pursue the war, both militarily and through negotiations. Realizing how valuable the aid of Coacoochee had been in convincing many of the Indians to emigrate, the colonel asked that some influential chiefs be returned from Arkansas in an attempt to persuade others to join them. One of those who returned was Alligator, who was able to talk Tiger Tail into surrendering. This action alone brought in more than 150 Seminoles.

For every advance, however, there was a setback. Two of Alligator's associates were murdered when they tried to make contact with a group of intractables. Depredations by small bands of warriors continued throughout the territory, often in places that had been considered safe. As the sixth year of the war ended, people were still wondering if Florida would ever know peace.

Colonel Worth was not among them. Early in 1842, he began to believe that it might be possible to end the war. By his estimates, there were approximately 300 Seminoles left in Florida, only a third of them warriors. Pointing out that it would be almost impossible to catch those still at large, Worth suggested to Washington that for the time being, these people should be allowed to remain in the extreme southern portion of the peninsula. The suggestion was rejected. Of those who were consulted on the decision, only General Jesup supported the idea of ending the war. It was, after all, the same recommendation he had made four years earlier.[42]

Although his plan had been turned down, Worth began to implement as much of it as he could. He had been given full discretion to run the war as he saw fit, and scaling back operations was what he saw fit to do. He saw no use in keeping large numbers of men in the field. The only thing such a tactic seemed to accomplish was to further disperse the Indians, making them even harder to catch.

Of the several bands still at large, the one led by Halleck Tustenuggee was the most dangerous. In December 1841, Halleck and about twenty warriors struck the settlement of Mandarin, south of Jacksonville along the St. Johns River. Having experienced no Indian trouble for more than three years, the town was totally unprepared for the attack. The atrocities committed by Halleck's braves struck fear into all of North Florida and South Georgia.

Worth realized that if he could capture Halleck, the last serious threat would be eliminated and the war would be over. Most of the other large Seminole bands, including those of Sam Jones and Billy Bowlegs, were hiding in the Everglades, doing their best to avoid the whites. Every available unit was put in search of Halleck and his men.

About a month after the Mandarin attack, two companies of infantry caught up with the fugitive Seminoles. After a long exchange of gunfire, the Indians escaped. The Seminoles were then able to elude the army until mid-April, when Worth finally located the chief and forty followers near Lake Ahapopka. The Seminoles, outnumbered ten to one, made a stand in a well-defended hammock. Inevitably, the army was able to come in on the Indian's flank, and, as usual, the warriors were able to disappear undetected into the thick foliage.[43]

It was the last battle of the Second Seminole War. Halleck and his followers may have escaped, but the army had managed to capture his camp and most of his group's supplies. His people were now totally destitute, without the basic necessities needed to survive. At the end of April, Halleck came to Colonel Worth's camp to have a talk.

Not that the fierce warrior intended to surrender. He was, as was the habit, hoping to play the army for a fool, to gather supplies, then once again disappear. Worth let the chief have his way for a few days, then asked him to accompany him to Fort King. After the two men had left, Halleck's people, lured to the white camp by the promise of some sort of festivity, were taken prisoner. Word was immediately sent to Worth, who took Halleck prisoner at Fort King. The fighting was over.[44]

There had, since February, been a change of heart in Washington. The government was tired of the war and wanted it over. On May 10, Secretary of War John C. Spencer informed Worth that President Tyler wanted hostilities ended as soon as possible. Worth sent word to the remaining Seminoles that they would not be molested if they removed themselves to the area south of the Peace River. As the summer progressed, most of the Indians quietly drifted south. By August, it was all but over. The navy squadron that had been assisting in the war was taken off duty, and several units of the army were sent to other parts of the country.

Colonel Worth now met with the chiefs who remained in the territory. Those who wanted to stay would be allowed to, at least temporarily, while those who wished to emigrate would be given a sum of money, a rifle, and rations when they arrived in Arkansas. Some went west, others went south, while others took time to decide. Worth was satisfied that the hostilities were, for all practical purposes, over, and on August 14, he declared the war at an end.[45]

Worth, after receiving a brevet promotion to general, took a much deserved leave. Although the war was officially over, there were still scattered incidents of violence committed by several small bands that remained at large. Colonel Vose, who was temporarily in charge, was ordered to round up the remaining Indians in the northern part of the territory. Realizing that these Seminoles were no threat, he decided to ignore the order, believing it might reignite the war. The War Department later concurred with his decision.[46]

As 1842 drew to a close, the final stage of emigration was taking place. Aboard one of the ships was Tiger Tail, the last of the major chiefs to leave his homeland. Sickened, he died in New Orleans, midway between the old home and the new. In a final show of respect, he was buried with full military honors. For seven long, desperate years he had fought to remain on the soil of his birth. The will to continue had finally left him. He, and his homeland, were now at peace.[47]

10 Remnants and Resurrections

▲▲▲ ▲▲▲▲ ▲▲▲▲ ▲▲▲▲ ▲

The Second Seminole War was forgotten almost as soon as it ended. There were no banner headlines, no parades for the returning victors, and very little reflection upon what may have been learned. It had been an unpopular, dirty little war, and no one wanted to talk about it. For many Americans, the war in Florida was simply part of a long, continuous struggle with the Native Americans. The end of hostilities in Florida certainly did not signal the end of the nation's "Indian problem." The famous Indian wars of the American west were just beginning.

It is instructive to note that in an age when many Americans were fascinated or obsessed with literature and history, only one chronicle of the war was written. Several of the participants left diaries or accounts of their experiences, but only Capt. John T. Sprague made an effort to tell the whole story and to analyze what had happened. Others may have made the attempt, but no doubt found little encouragement. Samuel Forry, an army surgeon, went as far as to contact a publisher in New York. The bookseller replied that "the Florida war is so unpopular that any work on the subject, however interesting and well-written, would fall still-born from the press." If there were any lessons to be learned from the war, no one seemed willing to find out what they were.[1]

For many Americans the war could not be forgotten. Thousands of people were forced to live with the emotional and physical scars that had been dealt out over seven years of desperate conflict. At the top of the list were the soldiers who had suffered grievous wounds that would never heal, and would, in time, prove fatal for some. Many more had contracted one of the ever-present tropical diseases and were never able to fully recover. Others bore the inevitable emotional scars resulting from what they had experienced on the field of battle. For many soldiers, the extreme hardship of duty in Florida had been more than their constitutions could bear.

One such example was John Bemrose. A sixteen-year-old Englishmen who lied about his age and was technically too short for the army, Bemrose joined the service in late 1831, almost immediately after arriving in this country. Having been apprenticed as a pharmacist, he was sent to St. Augustine to fill a position as a hospital orderly. A likable, hard-working young man, he soon became a favorite of his immediate superior, Dr. Richard Weightman, and of General Clinch. When war broke out, Bemrose worked valiantly to save the wounded and those who had taken sick. Surrounded by the dead and near-dead, the young orderly took fever in May 1836. Although he survived, he could not regain his strength and was given a disability discharge in late July. Impressed by the young man's intelligence and dedication, Weightman had offered to assist Bemrose in getting into the College of Surgeons at Philadelphia. Grateful but too weak to attend class, the young Englishman booked passage for home, feeling the need to return to his "native air."[2]

The number of men killed in the war was low by today's standards but high for the time. The official tally for the army was 1,466 dead, a significant number for such a small army, and nearly everyone in the service had lost a friend. The biggest killer was not Seminole bullets but disease. More than 1,100 men fell to some sort of sickness, usually dysentery, diarrhea, or fever. One died from hiccups. A large number succumbed to "disease unknown." A surgeon in the Eighth Infantry classified the vast majority of his losses as being due to "disease incident to climate and severe service in Florida."[3]

All in all, the Seminoles were not very impressive as battlefield killers. One reason was the type of weapons used. Although their muzzle-loading rifles were accurate, they also took over a minute to load. Very often, one good shot was all a warrior would get. After that, sloppy loading and shooting on the run caused most Seminole bullets to miss their mark. Disciplined soldiers, who took the time to properly load and aim their weapons, even under fire, proved more deadly. Indians also tended to avoid hand-to-hand combat. Not that they lacked the skill or the courage, but with a limited number or warriors and no reserves, they simply had no choice.

The Dade Battle, the Battle of Lake Okeechobee, and the Harney Massacre accounted for almost half the army's losses to Seminole warriors. All in all, the Indians managed to kill 269 of the army's officers and enlisted men. Just *serving* in the army could be dangerous. Accidental or violent deaths took 85 lives, most from drowning. It was, after all, a land of rivers, lakes, and swamps. Murders and accidental shootings were also high on the list. Surprisingly, snake bite is never mentioned as a cause of death, even though encounters with the venomous reptiles are frequently mentioned by diarists. What we can never know is the number of suicides. Personal accounts mention several, but none are officially recorded. As with the case of Colonel Lane, it was kinder to list the cause of death as "disease unknown."

We must also remember that the numbers given above are only for the United States Army. The U.S. Navy and Marine Corps officially lost 41 men, though the squadron commander, Lt. John T. McLaughlin, added that he sent 125–150 men north as "incurable." By far the biggest gap in our knowledge of casualties is in the militia and volunteer units. Because these were "state" troops, the army did not keep track of their losses. Nor has anyone taken on the monumental task of searching through the various state archives to ascertain those numbers.[4]

Soldiers are not the only people affected by war. What of the uncounted widows and orphans? What of the parents, spouses, and siblings who were forced to care for those who returned with some form of disability? It was, after all, a time when social welfare systems were almost totally nonexistent. Jacksonian democracy was, more than anything else, an every-man-for-himself political system. Pensions were miniscule and there were no disability benefits.

And what of the people of Florida? How many had lost their homes and livelihoods to the war? How many had lost loved ones to Indian depredations? How had the war affected the growth of the territory in general? It took more than twenty years for Florida to achieve the status of statehood. Had the threat and reality of Indian hostilities forced potential immigrants to look elsewhere for a new home? There are, of course, two sides to every coin. There can be little doubt that in the process of hunting down the Seminoles, the government was forced to explore a large territory that previously had been almost totally unmapped. As would happen throughout the expanding nation, army posts often became magnets for settlement. Many Florida towns owe their names, if not their existence, to the Seminole Wars.

As high as the price of war had been for the Americans, it was higher still for the Seminole Nation. More than 3,000 Seminoles had been forced from their homes at gunpoint, kept in detention camps, loaded aboard ships, and deported to a strange land that was nothing like the one they had left. The number of Seminole deaths is impossible to estimate. Enemy casualty reports turned in by army officers tended to err on the high side or drift into the realm of exaggeration. Rarely would anyone think to report Seminole civilian casualties, either accidental or intentional. Although better adapted to the Florida climate, Indians were certainly not immune to tropical diseases and were often more susceptible to infection when held in detention camps prior to deportation. If nothing else, life on the run, living in inhospitable hideouts, and the inevitable stress of war all served to weaken the Seminoles' constitutions. And who can measure the emotional toll taken by the death of loved ones or the pain of having families torn apart when members were captured and shipped west? At times we wonder how any survived.

Yet survive they did. While the tale of the hardships of emigration and the struggles to survive in their new homes are important stories to tell, it would do injustice to the sufferings of these people to attempt such a thing in the limited space available here. The subject has been treated well and often, most notably by Grant Foreman in his books *The Five Civilized Tribes* and *Indian Removal*. We will, in this work, barely scratch the surface of the extremely sad tale of the emigrating Seminoles.

The first trial for those who were emigrating was simply getting to their new homes. Each group that traveled west was escorted by an army officer, and it is to their credit that many of these officers did everything within their power to make the trip as comfortable and safe as possible. Unfortunately, their power was very limited. Actual arrangements were made by low-bid private contractors who placed profit above the Indian's survival. To turn a profit, corners were cut and standards lessened. When the inevitable delays and shortfalls occurred, contractors would shrug their shoulders and Indians would suffer.

Even when supplies were plentiful and fit for human consumption, the trail could still be fraught with dangers. Disease could break out in overcrowded vessels. The weather could, and often did, turn bad. Rain could fall in torrents for days on end. Snow could fall, something native Floridians were totally unprepared for. Flooded streams would have to be forded. For the sick, the old, and the very young, the trip to Arkansas was often more than their frail bodies could endure.

Even those Indians who had willingly consented to emigration did not fare well. The bands of Holahte Emathla and Black Dirt had gathered at

Fort Brooke when the war commenced, deciding to emigrate rather than fight. More than 400 of their people left Tampa Bay in mid-April 1836. It took less than four weeks by sailing ship and steamboat to reach Little Rock, but in the process, twenty-five lives were lost. Then the trip became difficult. For another month the group labored across 127 miles of unsettled wilderness. It rained heavily almost every day, making the few primitive roads impassible and the numerous streams impossible to ford. Deaths averaged about two a day. Black Dirt lost his wife and daughter. On the night of June 3, Holahte Emathla died, just two days from his promised land. Of the 407 Seminoles that had left Florida, only 320 survived the passage. How many later died as a consequence of the trip is not recorded.[5]

Being in their new homes did not mean automatic prosperity. In Florida, the Seminoles had been surrounded by hostile whites. In Arkansas, they were surrounded by hostile Indians and were under the political control of the hated Creeks. Not surprisingly, many of the promises the government had made to them were never kept. Annuities were either delayed or not paid at all. Subsistence was cut off at a designated time, even though it was still desperately needed. Farm implements and promised services were often not delivered. No one knows how many Seminoles died of starvation or exposure while trying to adjust to their new homeland. It is a testament to the tenacity and strength of the Seminole people that, in time, they were able to thrive in their new surroundings and retain their identity.

The end of war and a new homeland did not bring peace to a number of Seminoles. One group that felt especially threatened were the black Seminoles. Despite having been promised their freedom, the threat of being sold into slavery was ever-present. Unscrupulous slave traders made deals with the Creeks to capture and turn over many blacks. Others were simply kidnaped. Blacks who had either escaped slavery or had never known it were now faced with the prospect of losing the freedom they had fought so hard to preserve.

In addition to the blacks, there were many Seminoles who did not feel safe on their new reservation. Some of the chiefs who had fought longest to remain in Florida found themselves with very little political power when they arrived in Arkansas, while those who had emigrated years earlier had been accumulating a measure of wealth and influence. The later emigrants found themselves left with the scraps from what was already a lean table. The best land was taken, and the best political positions were already occupied. In addition, there was often a measure of resentment between those who had left early and those who had stayed behind. Angry words had been said before the war, and violent deeds had been committed. Some warriors could not, or would not, forget. The Seminoles had always been a collection of tribes that often did not see eye-to-eye. Old animosities had been put aside for the sake of the war effort. The pressure of trying to survive in a strange new land often brought those ill feelings to the surface once again.

If Congress thought that the conclusion of the war would bring a halt to the costs associated with the conflict, they were sorely mistaken. Floridians blamed Washington for starting the war and for the gross mismanagement of it. No one seemed willing to admit that the Indians had been removed primarily for the benefit of white Floridians. People in other states also had claims against the government, the most common being charges for horses lost while serving in volunteer or militia units during the war.

With the war over, government officials hoped Florida would soon join the Union. Several factors served to conspire against this, however. Financially, the territory was extremely poor and controlled by antibank Democrats, which limited the amount of capital available for development. If Florida were to become a state, a portion of the expenses for the costly Seminole War would have to be paid by Tallahassee. There was also a degree of mistrust between the people of East and West Florida, which led to proposals for the entry of two separate states or to not entering the Union at all.

Such divisions helped slow the move toward statehood but could not stop it. In 1838, while the war was going strong, a constitutional convention had met to draft the document that would be required for entry into the Union. After that, all that was required were a sufficient number of residents. In 1830, there were less than 35,000 people in Florida, about half of them slaves. By 1840, the number had increased by only about 20,000, mostly in the extreme north. In contrast, Michigan, another frontier territory, went from about 31,000 to 212,000 people in the same period, and few of them were slaves. It was not until after the Seminole War ended that the population of Florida began to swell significantly. By 1850, the census showed almost 90,000 people living in Florida.[6]

In August 1842, as the war was drawing to its conclusion, Congress passed the Armed Occupation Act, designed to help populate Florida. In exchange for setting up and defending a homestead for five years, a family would be given title to 160 acres of land. The intention was for well-armed settlers to bravely defend their homes against what few Indians were left in the territory. As it turned out, most of the homesteaders did not even own a rifle, and at the first rumor of Indian trouble they quickly fled to the safety of the nearest military post. Fortunately for the settlers, the few Indians that remained in Florida were doing their best to stay clear of the white population.

In order to boost population, leaders in the territory began the difficult task of "selling" Florida to wary settlers. One of the territory's most enthusiastic proponents was congressional delegate David Levy. In a letter to the *National Intelligencer,* Levy laid forth, in the most glowing terms, all the advantages of life in Florida: "To the wealthy planter, Florida is eminently inviting. . . . But to the poor and the moderate in circumstance, it is, beyond comparison, the paradise of earth. There are no freezing winters to be provided against by close houses, magazines of supplies for embargoed and shivering families. . . . The means of subsistence are obtained with less labor, and labor is more productive, and industry more quickly blessed with accumulation and plenty than is conceivable to the inhabitants of a less fortunate region."[7]

It was a tough sell. Years of "negative press" had made people wary of Florida. The independent nation of Texas and lands just west of the Mississippi were far more attractive than Florida. Nonetheless, settlers trickled in. Statehood finally came on March 3, 1845, in conjunction with Iowa, the required free state needed to counterbalance the influence of adding another slave state to the Union. Although the ascension to equal status with the rest of the Union was cheered throughout Florida, it was not without some reservation: the new flag was emblazoned with the motto "Let Us Alone."

The same motto might well have suited the Seminoles of Florida. By 1843, the vast majority of Indians in Florida were living in the remote southern portion of the peninsula and were content to be there. Primary leadership of the Seminoles had fallen to two men. The aged Sam Jones (Abiaca) was near ninety and somewhat infirm but still commanded great respect among the Mikasukis. Among the remnants of the Alachua Seminoles, Billy Bowlegs (Holata Micco) had become the principal chief. A member of the Seminole "Royal Family," Billy was the hereditary tribal leader and well suited for the job. Intelligent and moderate, he was also one of the few chiefs who spoke English. Because he was more accessible than the reclusive Sam Jones, whites erroneously considered him the representative of all Seminoles in Florida. Billy was not, however, bow-legged. The name had been "in the family" for several generations and was corrupted from the common Seminole name Boleck.[8]

For the better part of six years Florida remained at peace. Although most whites still wanted the Seminoles totally removed, there seemed no great urgency to do it. True to their promise, the Seminoles generally kept to their South Florida reservation. They would, on occasion, make hunting trips north of the line, but they endeavored to keep a low profile and avoid whites. A trading post was set up on the shores of Charlotte Harbor that proved more convenient to the Indians than the one at Tampa Bay.

Other than the traders, the only whites who seemed to have much contact with the Indians were Capt. John T. Sprague and Capt. John C. Casey. Sprague was officer in charge of Indian Affairs until he left Florida in 1849, while Casey often assumed the role of Indian agent. Billy seems to have held both men in high regard. More than any other man, the Seminoles trusted Casey, and it was largely through his efforts that peace was maintained.[9]

The peace that all these men had fought to maintain was violated in July 1849. A band of five outlaw Seminoles left the reservation and committed several murders in quick succession on opposite coasts of the peninsula. The first occurred near Fort Pierce, where one man was killed, another wounded, and some houses were destroyed. The next assault occurred a few days later at the trading post on Charlotte Harbor, where two men were killed and another wounded.

Not realizing that the attacks were carried out by the same small band, frontier residents assumed a general Indian uprising was taking place. Alarmed, many of the settlers who had taken advantage of the Armed Occupation Act fled in panic to the military fortifications. These, of course, were the people who were supposed to have taken up arms to defend their homes. Before anyone could ascertain the truth, 1,400 federal troops had been dispatched to Florida and the militia had been called out.[10]

Billy Bowlegs and his followers realized the gravity of the situation. The Indians had been allowed to remain in Florida only upon the promise of being totally unobtrusive neighbors. Three violent murders put the whole tribe in jeopardy. Acting swiftly and with great tact, the chief dis-

FIGURE 21.
Chief Billy Bowlegs (Holata Micco).
By permission of the Florida State Archives. Image #RC03537, DBCN#AAM-1617.

patched warriors to apprehend the outlaws. The murderers were quickly captured and three of them turned over to the army. A fourth was killed while trying to escape; his severed hand was turned in as evidence of his capture. The fifth member of the band managed to get away.[11]

Billy's swift action in punishing the outlaws quieted things for a time, but an act of Congress in 1850 served to undermine all his best efforts. The Swamp and Overflowed Land Act gave to the states all federal lands that were more than half covered with water and that might be drained and made useful. In Florida, that was a considerable amount of territory, some 20 million acres. Normally, the development of federal lands tended to be slow and sporadic. Under state control, those same lands might be made available for immediate sale. Suddenly, land that was considered totally worthless fell under the gaze of speculators and developers. Extravagant plans for draining the Everglades were formulated and submitted to the state legislature. Our present arguments over Everglades restoration stem from this 1850 law.[12]

In the eyes of many people there were fortunes to be made in southern Florida, and the only thing standing in their way was the annoying presence of a few hundred Seminole Indians. Pressure mounted on politicians in both Tallahassee and Washington to remove the remaining Seminoles. The first efforts were simple and worth a try. Several old forts were reactivated and old friends were brought from the western Indian Territory to try and convince the Florida Seminoles to move. Agents met with Billy and representatives of Sam Jones and offered modest cash payments to all Indians that would emigrate. A few of the Seminoles took the offer, but most politely refused.

Rebuffed, the government tried harder. A highly paid special agent named Luther Blake was appointed. Blake again brought a delegation from the West, and larger sums of money were offered to the Seminoles. A few were convinced, but the majority held fast.

Blake then made an attempt to impress the Seminoles with the power and determination of the United States. In 1852 Billy and several other chiefs were taken to Washington, where they met President Millard Fillmore. They then went to New York, where they were treated like minor celebrities. The amount of money the government was willing to spend on peacefully removing those few remaining Seminoles amounted to hundreds of thousands of dollars. Unfortunately, the tactics failed. Try as they may, the government could not convince the Seminoles to move west.[13]

From a twenty-first-century perspective, this is hard to understand. Today there are several thousand Seminoles living in a much more crowded Florida, and Floridians are proud to have them in the state. Why were so few seen as such a great threat a century and a half ago? The most obvious reason is that the Seminoles' reputation was considerably more threatening back then. Seven years of war had cost the government dearly. The War Department did not want to spend millions of dollars in a long, embarrassing war in Florida. For the people of Florida, it was more a matter of fear than money. In 1849, it had only taken five warriors to clear the frontier. Speculators knew that as long as the Seminoles were in South Florida, settlers would not move in.

Washington decided to increase the pressure. More forts were erected, with several of them in the Big Cypress Swamp where many of the Seminoles lived. If that alone was not a strong enough warning to Billy Bowlegs, the presence of survey parties served to drive the point home. Companies of soldiers marched and boated over southern Florida, noting the locations of the Seminole camps and trails. In 1854, Billy Bowlegs was once again treated to a trip to Washington and New York. Like it or not, the Seminoles knew that the wave of white expansion was about to break over them again.

Clearly, Washington had hoped the increased pressure would force the Indians to admit that life in Florida was no longer possible. As had happened in 1835, these officials did not understand just how determined the Seminoles and Mikasukis were to remain upon their land. Instead of submitting, the Indians attempted to avoid conflict by avoiding the whites. Villages were abandoned as the Seminoles moved to ever more remote locations. The Seminoles had managed to elude the white men for seven long years in the previous conflict; perhaps they could do it again.

According to legend, it was a rather trivial incident that sparked the explosion. In December 1855, a small survey detachment under Lt. George Hartsuff had come across one of Billy's villages and found it deserted. Upon leaving, one or more soldiers cut one or more bunches of bananas from some of Billy's trees, or may have destroyed the entire grove. Whether or not this incident really happened is open for debate; the primary account seems rather romanticized. One thing is for certain: in the early morning hours, as the soldiers slept, a war party of about thirty Seminoles attacked. After killing four soldiers and wounding another four, the Indians melted away. Hartsuff, grievously injured, made his way painfully back to Fort Myers. The government had been pushing; Billy Bowlegs had at last shoved back.[14]

Despite the buildup of troops, the army was unprepared for war. Companies of militia and volunteers were quickly organized but proved ineffective. The civilians soldiers, too proud to walk on foot, insisted on forming mounted companies. These forces tended to stay close to home and generally kept to the open roads. If the army intended to drive the Seminoles from Florida, it would have to leave the populated, well-traveled areas and take to the swamps and hammocks. The militia, more interested in tending to their crops or rounding up their cattle, showed little inclination to invade the Everglades.

For the first part of 1856, the Seminoles seemed to strike at will throughout the state. Small parties of warriors assaulted whatever vulnerable targets presented themselves. On January 7, three white men tending a coontie flower mill near Fort Dallas (Miami) were attacked. Only one of them managed to escape with his life. On the opposite side of the peninsula, five soldiers were killed near Fort Denaud on the Caloosahatchee River. Further south, a party of patrolling soldiers was attacked, resulting in two fatalities.[15]

In late March, Floridians were shocked to hear that a dozen warriors had attacked the home of state senate president H. V. Snell in Sarasota, killing one man and freeing a number of slaves. Fortunately, the senator was not at home. Another attack took place a bit north of Sarasota at the home of Dr. Braden. The attack turned sour for the Indians a week later when the party was located and surprised by a company of Florida volunteers. Two Indians were killed in the ambush, and two more were killed as they fled into a nearby creek. Seven slaves were recovered along with three mules. Two of the Seminoles were scalped, one while he was still alive.[16]

No one in South Florida could feel secure. In February, two oystermen were killed in Charlotte Harbor. They appeared to have been attacked in their boats at night; the vessels were looted and set aflame. Farther east, near the Peace River, a wagon train carrying supplies for the militia was attacked, resulting in the death of two men and a young boy. A Florida Militia officer concluded, "Doubtless the Indians are scattered along our entire frontier, and we must be active in our duties, or the settlements will suffer."[17]

As with the latter part of the Second Seminole War, we again run into to a problem of perspective. This third war would last two and a half years, but little action would take place. Most Floridians, living in the far north of the state, were completely untouched by the fighting. Except for the problem of having to supply militiamen and having to pay taxes to support the war effort, the fighting did not affect them. For the thinly settled southern peninsula, it was an altogether different matter. Homesteaders,

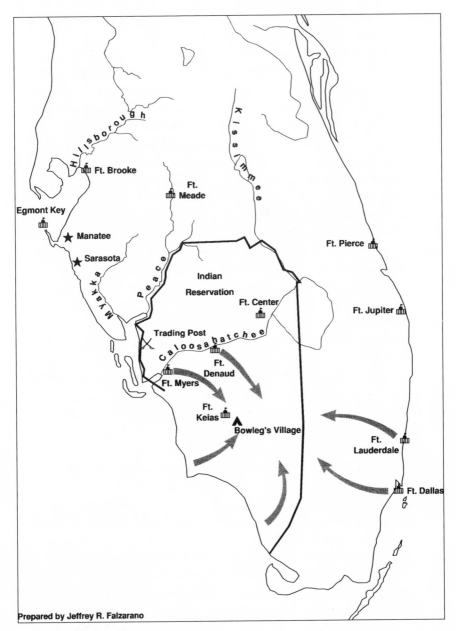

MAP 7. Third Seminole War, 1855–1858.

poorly informed and totally unaware of where the next attack might come from, fled the countryside.

Although attacks on settlements were few and far between, Floridians could not rest easy until the fighting had ceased. The Seminoles' reputation for cunning and savagery was so great that the *news* of them being on the warpath was enough to throw the countryside into panic. With so many frightened constituents, politicians were forced to act. Thousands of troops had to be dispatched to round up fewer than a hundred Seminole warriors. Nor could the troops be withdrawn until the task was complete. Small as the war might have been, its effect on Florida was large indeed.

For the most part, the Third Seminole War was a guerrilla conflict. Rarely did the Indians take on the army in open battle, and then only when the advantage was with them. The first such instance occurred on April 7, 1856, as an army patrol of more than 100 men was approaching Bowlegs Town. Choosing their defensive positions well, the Seminole warriors held the white men off for the better part of six hours, inflicting seven casualties, one of them fatal.[18]

Unhappy with the government's preparations for or prosecution of the war, Floridians began to let their feelings be known. The editor of the *Tampa Peninsular* complained that "depredation has succeeded depredation, until the public mind is worked up to such a pitch that we are constantly on the tip-toe of anxiety, expecting every hour to hear of some horrible massacre of our fellow citizens—some inhuman butchery of defenceless unprotected women and children, or the burning of their habitation." He then asks, "What has been done to remove or exterminate the Seminoles? We answer *nothing!*"[19]

In mid-June 1856, one of the more noteworthy engagements of the conflict took place. Just south of Fort Meade, along the Peace River, about a dozen Indians attacked the homestead of the Tillis family. The whites, surrounded in a crude shack, were able to hold the attackers off until a small detachment of militia arrived from the nearby fort. The militia unit, numbering only seven men, immediately gave chase to the Seminoles. As the Indians took up defensive positions in a dense hammock, the militiamen divided up into two groups and charged the hammock from two sides. Fighting at close quarters, three of the whites were killed in exchange for one Indian life.

On the following day a detachment of nineteen men set out after the Seminole warriors. A day later, the soldiers discovered the Indian camp

FIGURE 22.
Brig. Gen. William S. Harney, by Mathew Brady.
By permission of the National Archives. NWDNS-III-B-4693.

and attacked, catching the warriors by surprise. In the ensuing battle, several Indians and two whites were killed. Among the dead Indians was Oscen Tustenuggee, the leader of the war party. Fleeing to the opposite shore of a creek, the Indians were able to return fire and eventually escape.[20]

The battle at the Tillis farm marks a turning point in the war. With the death of Oscen Tustenuggee, the Seminoles lost their primary war chief in the central portion of the state. From this time on, most of the fighting would take place farther south. A small group to begin with, the Seminoles simply did not have the manpower that would allow them to effectively carry the war to the whites.

The war continued through the remainder of 1856 with small engagements at various places throughout the lower portion of the peninsula. A blockhouse at the mouth of the Caloosahatchee River was attacked, resulting in the death of one soldier and the wounding of another. In other parts of the state, the Seminoles were visiting old haunts. In late August, Indian signs were found near Bradenton, and in September, the Indians once again visited the Tillis home near Ft. Meade. In response to such threats, the Florida Militia concentrated its efforts in the Peace River area. Although signs of an Indian presence were abundant, no Indians were found.[21]

Although the United States had learned few lessons from the Second Seminole War, the army certainly had. Veterans of the earlier war knew that the only way to defeat the Seminoles would be to chase them out of their Everglades hiding places. Such a task would take time, special equipment, and a lot of hearty men. Slowly, regular forces and militia units began to gather near Fort Myers and Fort Dallas. Special shallow draft boats were purchased and supplies were gathered and stored at fortified depots located in the heart of the Seminole homeland.

To direct the campaign, the army sent Gen. William S. Harney, veteran of the Second Seminole War and a man with the reputation of being able to deal with Indians. Harney spent the final months of 1856 attempting to negotiate with the Seminoles, while at the same time gathering men and supplies for an offensive campaign into the Everglades. The Indians, forever wary of the white man's flag of truce, did not respond.[22]

Having received no replies to his peace feelers, Harney commenced offensive operations in January of the new year. It was a slow, laborious campaign. Throughout the winter and into the spring and summer of 1857, numerous companies of soldiers moved throughout the southern portion of the state, never giving the natives a chance to rest. Outnumbered and with families to protect, the Seminoles were forced to move from one hideout to another as the soldiers discovered their camps and destroyed their farms. Occasionally, a small group of women and children were found and taken prisoner. These individuals were then taken to Egmont Key off Tampa Bay to await removal to the west.[23]

As always, it was the worst of duty for the soldiers. Companies would travel on foot or in small boats for weeks at a time, braving disease, insects, and the occasional Seminole bullet. Skirmishes with the Indians were few, but to the men being shot at, it was as dangerous as the Battle of Lake Okeechobee. The will to fight had not left the Seminoles. In May, two soldiers were killed and another two wounded while fetching water for their camp. In another skirmish, the Indians killed one soldier and captured about 500 rounds of ammunition.[24]

Capt. Abner Doubleday, who would one day be falsely credited with inventing baseball, reported on a scouting mission in the area of Fort Lauderdale. "This proved by far the most wearisome toil I had ever undertaken," he wrote. "The men soon sank up to the middle in slimy mud and their progress became slow and laborious. . . . The men were often obliged to cross floating islands which could hardly bear their weight. In some cases they fell through and would have been drowned were it not for the prompt assistance of their comrades. . . . Our labor now became, if possible, more severe, the water being deeper, floating islands more frequent, and the roots of the trees imbedded in slime."[25]

Throughout 1856, the Indians and their few black allies had managed to do a respectable job of eluding the army. Some Seminole camps and fields were located and destroyed, but the number of Indians killed or captured was small. In 1857, things were different. More and more soldiers pushed ever deeper into the Everglades, making it difficult for the Seminoles to survive. The number of Indians captured or killed was on the rise, but not swiftly. James Buchanan, the newly elected president, and the incoming secretary of war, John B. Floyd, began to discover what several of their predecessors had: it was going to be very expensive to drive the Seminoles from Florida.

Both sides of the conflict lived in fear of the other. The Seminoles had divided into small groups, living off the land or planting small fields that were well hidden. Still, no place could be completely concealed. In April 1857, two companies of volunteers scouting east of Lake Okeechobee came upon an Indian trail that led them to a small encampment. The soldiers charged the camp, killing one warrior and a boy and capturing a twelve-year-old girl.[26]

Just as the campaign was beginning to take effect, the administration decided that Harney's experience was needed in Utah, where Brigham Young and his Mormon followers were defying federal authority. Although he was miffed at having to leave the job unfinished, the general packed his bags and left the scene. Command fell to Col. Gustavis Loomis, who continued Harney's campaign into the summer.[27]

With August came a change in tactics, made necessary by the climate.

The heat, humidity, and continual rains were all taking their toll on the men in uniform. In order to give them some rest, it was decided to once again bring in a delegation of chiefs from Arkansas. Hopefully they could convince the Florida natives to emigrate. The westerners traveled up the rivers and along the coast, but Billy and his compatriots refused to respond. Their will to remain in their homeland was not yet broken. As ever, it was a war of wills: which side would give up first?

Frustrated and wanting a quick end to the conflict, the War Department authorized the employment of additional companies of Florida militia. At the commencement of the conflict the militia had been disorganized and slow to respond. Now, after months of toil and discipline, the civilian soldiers were beginning to act like professionals. Most effective were the "boat companies" of Capt. R. B. Turner and Capt. Jacob Mickler. Taking to the waters of the Everglades and the Kissimmee River, they were able to harass the Indians and capture a number of women and children.[28]

For many soldiers, it was a chance to explore a territory few men had seen. One of the boat companies reported finding an unusually large oak tree measuring thirty-seven feet in circumference and shading an area forty-five yards in diameter. The officer in charge noted that his entire company of eighty-eight men and their horses were able to take their noon meal under the shade of the giant tree.[29]

The Seminoles were soon running out of places to hide and were finding it difficult to stay well fed. As more companies of volunteers and regulars entered the Everglades, they inevitably come upon Seminole camps. In November, the camp of Billy Bowlegs was discovered. Taken were Billy's shot bag and turban, a gift from the president when the chief had been in Washington. Also seized was a photograph of Billy taken during the same trip. More telling was the amount of supplies lost: 500 bushels of pumpkins, 100 of rice, 50 of corn, and numerous utensils and tools.[30]

The fighting continued as the Seminoles took revenge for their losses. Unable to attack a large force of soldiers, the Indians vented their anger upon the soldier's horses, killing thirty-six of them in a single night. In another engagement, near the island of Chokoloskee in the Everglades, Captain Parkhill was killed and several of his men were wounded while crossing a stream. Elsewhere, a volunteer was killed while gathering palmetto cabbage near a camp filled with 500 soldiers.[31]

At the same time, events in other places were working toward bringing the war to a conclusion. One of the primary obstacles to Seminole removal in 1835 had been the Indians' objections to being placed under Creek domination. In the Indian Territory, those who had emigrated during the Second Seminole War were finding their fears of Creek oppression realized. Black Seminoles were being stolen and disputes over land were common. Coacoochee and John Cavallo had been forced to flee to Mexico, while other Seminoles were living under the protection of friendly Cherokees. Faced with problems at both ends of the Seminole spectrum, Washington began to show some uncharacteristic flexibility. In August 1856, the government reached a new agreement with the western Seminoles. In the new treaty, the Seminoles received their own reservation and political autonomy from the Creeks. A trust fund of half a million dollars was set up, but as an inducement to end the fighting in Florida, half of it was withheld until the eastern Seminoles migrated.[32]

A year and a half had passed since the signing of the treaty, and the western Seminoles were anxious to get their money. Because Billy Bowlegs and Sam Jones had refused to acknowledge any of the flags of truce the army had put out, there was good reason to believe the Florida Indians were unaware of the new situation out west. Once again, a large party of Seminole chiefs was brought from Arkansas to attempt a meeting with their eastern brethren. Weakened by war, perhaps the Florida Indians would be willing to talk.[33]

For everyone concerned, the time had finally come to end the Seminole Wars. In March 1858, Billy Bowlegs came out of the swamp to have a parley with the white officials and the Arkansas Seminoles. His people, hunted and pursued to exhaustion, were at last willing to emigrate. The words of his old friends who had returned from the West helped convince him that it was now to Billy's advantage to take his people to the new reservation in what would come to be known as Oklahoma.[34]

The fighting in Florida was over. Most, but not all, of Billy's people accompanied him to the West. The white offensive had been so successful in scattering the Seminoles that several bands could not be located and were left behind. A few other bands steadfastly refused to leave, no matter what the inducements. Perhaps 150 Seminoles did not go west, and the approximately 2,500 Seminoles who now reside in Florida are descendants of these tenacious warriors and their wives. Sam Jones and a good many of the intractable Mikasukis were among those who stayed behind. He alone had been able to survive the three Seminole Wars and die peaceably in his chosen homeland.[35]

Today, it all seems such a waste. Forty years, tens of millions of dollars, and thousands of lives. For what? Were the Seminoles really such an immense threat? Well, yes, they were, or at least they were *perceived* to be. Perhaps what troubles us the most today are the *reasons* for their being seen as such a threat. The Seminole Nation, as with every other Indian nation, stood in the way of white expansion. Americans were intent on controlling (and selling) every square inch of the North American continent. The nation saw it as a destiny ordered by God. Are we really any different today?

At times it looks as if the motive for all this suffering was nothing more than greed. Yet what appears as greed to a far-removed observer would have been seen as simple survival to the nineteenth-century citizens of whom we are being critical. Can we truly fault the common farmer who was struggling to raise enough grain to feed his family? Did he really want anything more than a better life for his children? And in that respect, was he really any different from us? Food on the table and a secure home are the two most basic of human needs. The solitary homesteader drove American expansion, and the vast majority of them were good, hard-working people. They simply wanted a better life.

It is easy to blame the speculators who bought and sold Indian lands, sometimes for a very large profit. Weren't they intentionally stealing from the natives and reselling at exorbitant prices? Not really. They were purchasing land that had been legally (though not always morally) obtained from the Indians and often were taking a great financial risk. These people made the land suitable for habitation and sold it at a price that people were willing to pay. Were they really any different from the developers of today? And while it is certainly fashionable to blame developers for many of Florida's present environmental ills, we must keep in mind that a good many of us are living in large, comfortable houses that we purchased from those same developers.

We must also bear in mind that the proceeds from the sale of the former Indian lands were used, in large part, to pay off the massive national debt left over from the American Revolution. One of the reasons the United States was able to survive the Republic's formative years is that it had a wealth of land to sell and to settle. Other nations that had gained their independence in the same era were saddled with staggering debts they were unable to pay off. The American people and their trading partners were glad to extend credit to the young nation because they knew it possessed millions of acres of good collateral. Cheap land also offered the American people hope. There was, just over the horizon, a place where a family could make a new start. For a young nation, trying to find its political way, hope was all-important. In a way, the Indians' loss helped ensure the nation's future. Obviously, they were not the beneficiaries.

There were other reasons the Seminoles posed a great threat to white society, and foremost was the matter of slavery. We can, with little trouble, forgive the struggling homesteader; for the most part he meant no one any harm. Can we do the same for the slave-owning planter? Slavery is always a tough issue to understand, and explaining it is certainly not within the intended scope of this work. Yes, slavery was a great evil. No, not all slave owners were the devil incarnate. Many southerners knew that "the peculiar institution" was often more trouble than it was worth and would have liked to have been rid of it. But how? Just free all the slaves? Easy for us to say; we are not faced with all the problems associated with such a move. With all our experience and accumulated knowledge, we Americans have yet to solve our present-day racial problems.

It would be very convenient if we could point to one or two individuals and say they were to blame for all the woe heaped upon the Native Americans. We cannot. Andrew Jackson might seem a good target for our twenty-first-century wrath, but in the final analysis, he comes across as nothing more than a superpatriot, very much like Osceola. Both men loved their homeland and were willing to risk everything for it. We can fault them, but we should also admire them.

If we want to blame anyone, we might start with the person who stares back at us when we look in the mirror. How many of us live in homes that stand on land that once belonged to an Indian nation? How many of us are in a profession that is somehow tied to such lands? (Real estate, building trades, surveyor?) If we are not, what about our ancestors? How many of them were pioneers or served in the militia? In the end, we all share a small portion of the responsibility for what happened to the Seminoles and other native peoples. We cannot, however, go back and change the past or make it go away. The best we can do is work to see that it does not happen again. Justice, equality, and tolerance will always be "works in progress."

And what of the ways in which the wars were conducted? As every soldier knew, there was little chance for glory in the Seminole Wars. And, as every Seminole warrior would eventually discover, their dream of a peaceful life in Florida was a lost cause. In all three wars there were very few winners. Yes, Andrew Jackson drove the Seminoles away from the border with Georgia and devastated their economy, but he did not drive them out of Florida. Yes, he captured St. Marks and Pensacola, but they had to be returned. In the end, diplomacy brought Florida to the United States, as it probably would have, Jackson or no Jackson.

The Second Seminole War was brimming over with empty achievements. The Dade "Massacre" was a great victory that started a war that proved disastrous for the victors. General Clinch took pride in being called "Old Withlacoochee," yet in truth, he had been forced to retreat across that river. Gaines declared the war over, yet the fighting continued for six more years. Winfield Scott moved his large army at will throughout the territory yet never engaged the enemy. Governor Call had the Seminoles within his grasp at the Wahoo Swamp but did not follow through. Jesup captured most of the important leaders of the Seminole resistance and was vilified for it.

The longer the war continued, the worse it seems to have gotten. In winning the Battle of Lake Okeechobee, Zachary Taylor suffered excessive casualties and failed to crush the Seminoles. At least he eventually won the presidency. Whole nations fared no better than individuals. The United States had won the war after two years but refused to let it end, forcing Floridians on both sides to suffer for another five years. The Seminoles achieved what they wanted in 1839, then threw it all away in the Harney Massacre. Hollow victories, every time.

The tragedy continued to the very end. How much did it cost Billy Bowlegs and his people to remain in Florida for another two years? How triumphant did the government feel when it realized that after all that effort there were still Seminoles living in Florida? Was it worth the cost? In the crudest of simple calculations the answer seems almost ridiculous. It cost roughly $10,000 to send each Seminole to the new Indian Territory, a princely sum at the time. It certainly would have cost a lot less to have done the job right in the first place. Worse yet, for every two Seminoles shipped west, one American soldier died.

Was everyone a loser? Of course not. Sam Jones got what he wanted. The United States got what it wanted, albeit at an astronomical price. It was certainly not a poor investment. Today, Florida is one of the richest, most dynamic states in the Union. Even the most wildly enthusiastic Floridians of the 1840s would be astounded at how well we have done. They would also be surprised at how well the "defeated" Seminoles have done.

Could the whole Seminole experience have been handled better? Obviously. Treaties were necessary; there could be no hope of peace for either side without them. Had they been fairly negotiated the Seminoles would have been much less likely to have ignored them. Had *both parties* adhered to the stipulations they had made, they might have established a mutual trust that would have turned enemies into good neighbors. Had there been just a little tolerance and respect for the rights of the Indians, the whole fiasco might have been avoided. Unfortunately, it was not going to happen. America was young; the nation still had a lot of growing up to do. We still do.

Perhaps what strikes us as most tragic about the Seminole Wars is that if the United States had simply let the Indians be, Florida would not be very different today. Americans of all races would have flocked to the Sunshine State for the very same reasons they always have. A small number of Seminoles would not have stopped them. No matter what amount of territory they started with, various pressures would have caused the Seminoles to sell most of it to wealthy speculators and developers. As perfectly normal humans, the Seminoles would have assimilated those aspects of American culture that suited their needs. They would have kept mostly to themselves and retained those aspects of their own culture that made them feel proud to be a Seminole. In short, they would have been what they are today.

The Seminole Wars, like all the other Indian wars, were clashes between cultures. As much as we might lament the fact from today's perspective, there was simply no way the two cultures could coexist. Today they can, but only because both cultures have changed. Indians are no longer hunters who require vast hunting grounds and live by the warrior's code. Most Americans no longer seek to develop every square inch of the continent. We have learned to appreciate what we have lost, and we try to protect what is left. In the early nineteenth century, neither culture was willing to change.

Native Americans were faced with the classic evolutionary imperative: adapt or die. White Americans should not feel guilty for placing the Indians in this situation; it was a natural occurrence. Sooner or later the crowded nations of Europe were going to discover the Americas. Settlers were bound to arrive and come in contact with those who were already in place. If the nation should feel guilty about anything, it is that it did so little to help the natives adapt. America gave them little time, little support, and precious little space to live in. Worst of all, the nation did not give them the opportunity to join in American society even when they did adapt.

Fortunately, the American Indian *has* adapted. Today, for good or bad, the Seminoles are often viewed as just another of Florida's many tourist attractions. Instead of hiding out in the Everglades, the Seminoles have erected billboards along I-75 beckoning people to visit the Big Cypress Reservation and to take a ride on "Billy's Swamp Safari." Instead of companies of soldiers leaving Fort Myers in search of war parties, tour busses run from Fort Myers to the Seminole Indian Casino, where white- haired retirees are invited to "play Indian games." The descendants of those few last survivors, those who were left alone in the swamps and hammocks, have learned to prosper in the land their ancestors once fought so doggedly to remain in. Most Floridians cannot imagine a great war taking place in this most inviting of states. Yet there was a time, not really that long ago, when true fear stalked the land and names such as Osceola, Coacoochee, Sam Jones, and Billy Bowlegs stirred emotions throughout the entire continent.

Notes

Preface

1. Sprague, 101; Mahon, 326; *Congressional Globe* 3:11 and 4:2.
2. Survey of articles in *Niles' Weekly Register* (hereafter referred to as *Niles*), 1836–39.

Chapter 1. Newcomers

1. Covington, *Billy Bowlegs War*, 29, 37.
2. Brown, 4; Milanich, 1, 80, 93; U.S. Bureau of the Census.
3. Wright, 3, 16.
4. Ibid., 59.
5. Mahon, 10; Covington, *Seminoles*, 6; Wright, 29.
6. Giddings, 79.
7. Porter, *Black Seminoles*, 28.

Chapter 2. Americans

1. Sprague, 509.
2. Ibid., 59.
3. Weinberg, 85, 73.
4. Hudson, 27.
5. Ibid., 107.
6. Cherry, 65; Stephanson, 21.
7. Smith, 61, 66.
8. Patrick, *Florida Fiasco*, 4.
9. Smith, 200, 232.
10. Holland, 9–10.
11. Ibid., 21–22; Heidler and Heidler, *Old Hickory's War*, 19.
12. Heidler and Heidler, 26; Mahon, 22; Holland, 37.
13. Holland, 37.
14. Heidler and Heidler, 17.
15. Parton, 492–93.

16. Heidler and Heidler, 38–50.

17. Ibid., 54–55, 60; Aptheker, 50.

18. U.S. Congress, H. Doc. 122.

19. Ibid.; *American State Papers Foreign Relations* (hereafter referred to as *ASP.FR*), 4:556.

20. U.S. Congress, H. Doc. 122.

21. Ibid.; *Niles* 17:187.

22. *Niles* 17:187; Heidler and Heidler, 70–71.

23. *Niles* 17:186–87.

24. *Niles* 17:187; Heidler and Heidler, 73.

25. *Niles* 17:187.

26. Ibid.; Heidler and Heidler, 73–74.

27. Milligan, 17; *Army and Navy Chronicle* (hereafter referred to as *A&NC*), 2:116; *Niles* 17:187.

28. Heidler and Heidler, 74.

Chapter 3. The First Seminole War

1. Knetsch, "Range War in the East," 108.

2. *American State Papers Military Affairs* (hereafter referred to as *ASP.MA*), 1:685.

3. Much of the background information on the First Seminole War was gathered from letters published in *Niles* for 1817–19.

4. *ASP.FR* 4:607–8.

5. Heidler and Heidler, 152.

6. *ASP.MA* 1:686; Heidler and Heidler, 100.

7. *ASP.MA* 1:686.

8. Ibid. 1:688.

9. Ibid. 1:687.

10. Ibid. 1:748; Silver, *Gaines*, 71; Heidler and Heidler, 104.

11. *ASP.MA* 1:687.

12. Ibid. 1:690.

13. Heidler and Heidler, 119–20.

14. *Niles* 13:413 and 14:31, 104.

15. *ASP.MA* 1:698.

16. *ASP.FR* 4:574; *ASP.MA* 1:703.

17. *ASP.MA* 1:699.

18. Ibid. 1:704.

19. Ibid. 1:703; Heidler and Heidler, 145–46.

20. *ASP.MA* 1:700, 703.

21. Ibid. 1:703.

22. Ibid.

23. Ibid. 1:700.

24. Ibid. 1:734.

25. Ibid. 1:709.

26. *ASP.MA* 1:713.

27. Ibid. 1:708.

28. *Niles,* supplement to 15:138; U.S. Congress, H. Doc. 82.

29. U.S. Congress, H. Doc. 82.

30. *Niles* 7:257, 14:64, supplement to 15:118; *ASP.MA* 1:703.

31. *Christian Observer*, Feb. 1819, 18:134.

32. *Niles* 15:131.

33. Bucholzer.

34. *Niles* 15:367–68; *ASP.FR* 4:539–612.

35. *Niles* 14:399.

36. Heidler and Heidler, 206.

37. Ibid., supplement to 15:131, 134.

38. Ibid., supplement to 15:114.

39. Ibid., supplement to 15:136, 142.

40. Ibid., supplement to 15:169.

41. Ibid., supplement to 15:154–55.

42. *Niles* 28:370.

43. Heidler and Heidler, 229–31.

Chapter 4. Coming to Terms

1. *Portsmouth Oracle,* 13 Nov. 1819.

2. Mahon, 29; *ASP.FR* 4:623–25.

3. *Niles* 20:96.

4. Carter 22:237; Mahon, 30; *New York Spectator,* 6 Nov. 1821.

5. Carter 22:26–27, 169–71.

6. Ibid., 219–22.

7. Ibid., 205–8.

8. Ibid., 205–10.

9. Ibid., 210–13, 409–10; Mahon, 34.

10. Mahon, 35; Sprague, 19.

11. Carter 22:463–65.

12. Ibid., 495–97.

13. Ibid., 552–53, 560–63.

14. Ibid., 552–56, 560–63.

15. Ibid., 597–98.

16. Ibid., 193–96.

17. Ibid., 497, 533–34, 563.

18. Ibid., 169–71.

19. Ibid., 471–72.

20. Ibid., 495–97.

21. Ibid., 501–2.

22. Ibid., 501–2, 504.

23. Ibid., 533–34.

24. Ibid.

25. Ibid., 533–34, 556–60.

26. Ibid., 532–33, 597–98.

27. Ibid., 556–60.

28. Ibid., 577–79.

29. Mahon, 45.

30. Ibid.

31. Friedberg, 53.

32. Sakolski, 135–37.

33. Ibid., 232–35.

34. *National Intelligencer,* 7 Apr. 1821.

Chapter 5. Disagreement and Defiance

1. Carter 22:784–85, 795–96, 802, 841–43.

2. Ibid., 841–46.

3. Ibid., 918–19, 968–71.

4. Ibid., 922–23; 23:13–17.

5. Ibid. 23:22–23.

6. Ibid.

7. Ibid., 78–80, 88–91.

8. Ibid., 88–91.

9. Ibid., 115–16, 163–64, 177, 323–24.

10. Ibid., 273–75, 293–96; *Niles* 29:4.

11. Carter 23:335–37.

12. Ibid., 358–59.

13. *Niles* 30:37.

14. Ibid.

15. Carter 23:423–25.

16. Ibid., 443–44; *Niles* 30:29.

17. Carter 23:432–35; *Niles* 30:226.

18. Carter 23:545–47.

19. Mahon, 62; Carter 23:535–37.

20. Carter 23:539–41.

21. Ibid., 548–51.

22. Ibid.

23. Ibid., 500–501.

24. *Niles* 31:312; Carter 23:822–23.

25. Carter 23:757–59, 807–8.

26. Ibid., 801–2, 816–18.

27. Ibid., 867–901.

28. Ibid., 898–901.

29. Ibid., 911–12, 1059–61; 24:6, 8, 22.

30. Ibid. 23:1066–67.

31. Ibid. 24:282–85, 297–98, 319–21, 339–40.

32. Ibid., 94–97, 114–15, 203–5.

33. Ibid., 164–65, 197–98, 203–5, 209–10, 230–31, 381.

34. Ibid., 392–93, 450.

35. Ibid., 392–93, 450, 454–55, 461–62, 479–80, 528.

36. Mahon, 72.

37. Ibid.; *Register of Debates in Congress* 6:1026–27, 1030, 1038–40, 1045.

38. *Register of Debates in Congress* 6:1026–27.

39. Ibid., 1038.

40. *Niles* 38:260.

41. *U.S. Reports*, 30:1–80; 31:515–97.

42. Carter 24:740–41.

43. Ibid., 713–14, 719–20, 727–28, 734, 740–41, 752–54, 829–30, 833–34, 858–61, 988–89.

44. Sprague, 74–75.

45. Carter 24:873, 876, 916–18.

46. Knetsch, "Wiley Thompson," 87; Mahon, 87.

47. Carter 25:58–63.

48. Coe, "Parentage of Osceola," 202–5.

49. Carter 25:90–91, 99–101.

50. Sprague, 82.

51. Ibid., 83.

52. Ibid., 84–85; Bemrose, 17–26; Potter, 79–81.

53. Sprague, 86.

54. Bemrose, 30.

55. Carter 25:182–84, 186–189.

56. Ibid., 200–201.

Chapter 6. Shock and Aftershock

1. Carter 25:198–99, 208–9; *Congressional Globe* 3:484.

2. Carter 25:214–15, 217–18, 294.

3. Ibid., 300.

4. Ibid., 209–10.

5. Potter, 100–101; Carter 25:216–17.

6. Carter 25:224–26; Mahon, 102.

7. The foremost work concerned with the Dade Battle is Laumer, *Dade's Last Command*. Accounts of the battle by Ransom Clarke, the only white survivor to tell about it, can be found in Potter, 102–107; McCall, 300–306; *Niles* 50:419; *A&NC* 2:55 and 4:369. For the Seminole account of the battle, see Sprague, 90.

8. Potter, 108.

9. Carter 25:218–19.

10. Patrick, *Aristocrat*, 47, 66, 81, 214.

11. For several different accounts of the battle refer to Bemrose and Potter; Clinch's official report published in *Niles* 49:366; Clinch's defense of his actions in *Niles* 52:315–18; Call's response to Clinch in *Niles* 52:395–98.

12. *Niles* 49:366; Bemrose, 59.

13. Mahon, 112, 138.

14. Bemrose, 42.

15. President's annual messages to Congress of 1833, 1834, and 1835, printed in the *Congressional Globe*, vols. 1, 2, and 3.

16. Horn, "Tennessee Volunteers" 1:347.

17. Sprague, 102.

18. Patrick, *Aristocrat,* 192–93.

19. *New York Observer,* 30 Jan. 1836; *New York Herald,* 16 Feb. 1836; *Mobile Chronicle,* 27 Jan. 1836.

20. *Congressional Globe* 3:74, 142; *Niles* 49:333; Mahon, 138.

21. Mahon, 138–39.

22. Bemrose, 73; McCall, 308.

23. McCall, 308–9; Potter, 133–34.

24. Potter, 140–41; McCall, 309–10; Croffut, 88–89.

25. Potter, 138.

26. Bemrose, 73–74; McCall, 321–22; Potter, 138; Croffut, 89–92.

27. Bemrose, 74; McCall, 320–24, 323; A&NC 2:227, 380.

28. Bemrose, 74; Potter, 141–42.

29. Potter, 142–44; McCall, 326.

30. For reports on Gaines's campaign, see Sprague, 110–13; A&NC 2:225–27; Potter, 139–64; McCall, 314–22.

31. Croffut, 95.

32. Bemrose, 76; Porter, *Black Seminoles,* 51; Croffut, 95.

33. Bemrose, 77; McCall, 329–30; Potter, 154–57; Croffut, 93–94; Porter, *Black Seminoles,* 51.

34. Silver, "Counter-Proposal," 207–15.

35. Bemrose, 76; McCall, 330; Potter, 162–63.

36. Bemrose, 78–79; Croffut, 95–96.

37. For various reports on Scott's campaign, see Sprague, 114–57; A&NC 2:253, 293–94; Cohen, 158–92; Potter, 166–80; Laumer, *Amidst,* 35–39.

38. Bemrose, 88–89.

39. Cohen, 166; Potter, 170–72, 175, 178; A&NC 2:293–94.

40. Cohen, 166–67, 173–74; Potter, 172–73, 177.

41. Cohen, 175, 177–80; Potter, 174, 178–79; A&NC 2:293–94.

42. Sprague, 157–58.

43. *Niles,* Jan. 1836–Aug. 1836, 4th ser., vols. 13 and 14, and Sept. 1836–Dec. 1836, 5th ser., vol. 1.

44. Bemrose, 90; Mahon, 158.

45. Bemrose, 92–96; Mahon, 159.

46. Journal of Col. Wm. S. Foster, 6 Dec. 1836, Special Collections, Univ. of Florida; Foster to Lindsay, 29 Apr. 1836, Foster Collection Folder 39, McClung Collection, Knox County Library.

47. Bemrose, 103–4.

48. Ibid., 97; Sprague, 158–59; Mahon, 173–74.

49. *A&NC* 2:76.

50. Ibid. 2:124; *Niles* 51:181.

51. *A&NC* 3:172.

52. Mahon, 162; Bemrose, 96; Carter 25:283.

53. Carter 25:279, 314–15.

54. For debates on the war in early 1836, see *Congressional Globe* 3:385, 402, 468, 480; Appendix: 430, 573, 709.

55. For Governor Call's report of his campaign and his explanations for its failure see Carter 25:344. For a different view of Call's campaign, see Horn, "Tennessee Volunteers" (Sept. 1942–Sept. 1943).

56. *Congressional Globe* 4:6; Carter 25:339–41; Mahon, 181–82.

57. *Niles* 51:196.

58. Porter, *Black Seminoles*, 63–65.

Chapter 7. The Destruction of Trust

1. Kieffer, 29, 34, 67.

2. Ibid., 70.

3. Ibid., 119, 152.

4. *Niles* 50:382.

5. Mahon, 195–96; *National Intelligencer*, 19 Dec. 1836; *Niles* 51:340.

6. Eisenhower, 251; Mahon, 225–26.

7. *Niles* 51:401; Mahon, 197; *National Intelligencer*, Feb. 1837; *St. Augustine Florida Herald*, 28 Jan. 1837.

8. *ASP:MA* 7:820–21; Mahon, 197.

9. *Niles* 51:401.

10. Ibid. 52:80; *A&NC* 4:110.

11. *Niles* 52:31.

12. *A&NC* 4:215.

13. *Niles* 52:133, 146.

14. *National Intelligencer*, Mar. to June 1837.

15. Ibid., 21 June 1837.

16. Sprague, 180.

17. *A&NC* 4:163; *Niles* 7:73.

18. *A&NC* 4:168.

19. *Niles* 52:71.

20. Ibid.52:120–24; *A&NC* 4:241–46.

21. *Congressional Globe* 5:142, 148; Carter 25:411.

22. Giddings, 158.

23. Ibid., 161.

24. Sprague, 181–86.

25. Ibid., 186, 216.

26. Ibid., 216.

27. *A&NC* 5:270.

28. Ibid. 5:284–85.

29. Boyd, "Asi-Yaholo or Osceola," 303–5.

30. Coe, *Red Patriots,* 114.

31. Axelrod, 146.

32. DeLorme.

33. *A&NC* 5:222; *A&NC* 5:347.

34. Sprague, 184–97.

35. Ibid.

36. Porter, *Black Seminoles,* 86; Coacoochee's account of the escape in Sprague, 325–27.

37. Motte, 149; Peters, 153; Sprague, 191.

38. Sprague, 213, 203; *A&NC* 6:81.

39. Porter, *Black Seminoles,* 91–92.

40. *A&NC* 6:125.

41. Ibid. 6:159; Sprague, 198.

42. *A&NC* 6:172.

43. Sprague, 193; 200.

44. Ibid., 200.

45. Mahon, 236–37; Motte, 209.

46. Sprague, 201–2.

47. Ibid.

48. Carter 25:494–96.

49. Rippy, 86, 167; Poinsett, 19.

50. *St. Augustine Florida Herald,* 17 Feb. 1838; Coe, *Red Patriots,* 134–35.

51. Remini, 436; Jackson to Poinsett, 14 Aug. 1837, *Poinsett Papers.*

52. Bassett 5:512, 522; Wilson, 184.

Chapter 8. Wedded to War

1. Sprague, 195; Porter, *Black Seminoles,* 96.

2. Porter, *Black Seminoles,* 96; Sprague, 195.

3. Sprague, 221; *A&NC* 6:332; Mahon, 247.

4. *A&NC* 6:397; 7:44–45.

5. Wik, "Captain Nathaniel Wyche Hunter," 67.

6. Brown, 123.

7. Bassett 5:512.

8. Sprague, 221–27.

9. *Niles* 54:386.

10. Ibid.

11. Sprague, 104.

12. Ibid.

13. Ibid., 221–24.

14. Ibid., 224.

15. Ibid., 225.

16. *Congressional Globe* 7:214, 322.

17. Everest, 9, 16.

18. Ibid., 24.

19. White, "Macomb's Mission," 192.

20. Ibid., 144, 165.

21. *A&NC* 8:330.

22. Ibid. 8:346; White, 144.

23. *A&NC* 8:364.

24. Ibid. 8:364.

25. White, 175–86.

26. *A&NC* 8:377, 394; 9:9.

27. Ibid. 9:121.

28. Ibid. 9:140–41.

29. Ibid. 9:138–39.

30. Ibid. 9:235.

31. Ibid. 9:236.

32. Ibid. 9:309–10.

33. Ibid. 9:189.

34. Ibid. 8:364; 10:61.

35. Ibid. 9:289.

36. Ibid. 9:132.

37. Ibid. 9:146.

38. Ibid. 10:115.

39. Ibid. 10:187, 221.

40. Ibid. 10:114–16.

41. Ibid. 10:173, 221, 239.

42. Giddings, 264.

43. Ibid.; Covington, "Cuban Bloodhounds," 117; *A&NC* 10:220.

44. Remini, 303.

45. Coe, *Red Patriots*, 127.

46. *A&NC* 10:186.

47. Chamberlain, 263; Leckie, 83.

48. *A&NC* 9:280.

49. Ibid. 9:364.

50. Ibid. 9:365.

51. Ibid. 10:117.

52. Ibid. 10:142.

53. Ibid. 10:366.

Chapter 9. "I Feel the Irons in My Heart"

1. Porter, *Black Seminoles*, 113.

2. Sprague, 459.

3. Porter, *Black Seminoles*, 113–14, 128.

4. *Congressional Globe* 9:346–51.

5. Mahon, 274; Heitman, 169; Kersey and Peterson, "Was I a Member of Congress" 450–51.

6. *A&NC* 10:348.

7. Ibid. 11:93, 106, 155.

8. *A&NC* 10:364; Sprague, 437, 538.

9. *A&NC* 10:394; 11:13–14, 41.

10. Ibid. 11:139–40, 153–54; 26: 194–95.

11. Ibid. 11:331; *Niles* 60:63.

12. *A&NC* 11:395.

13. *Niles* 59:322.

14. Ibid. 59:322.

15. The best accounts of the navy's role in the Second Seminole War can be found in Buker; Sprague, chap. 9; and *A&NC*.

16. Croffut, 123; Carter 26:243, 250; Sprague, 250.

17. *Congressional Globe* 6:125–26.

18. Ibid. 3:7.

19. Wilson, 3, 11–12, 44–47.

20. Ibid., 52.

21. Bassett 5:546.

22. *Congressional Globe* 5:43.

23. Ibid.

24. Mahon, 293.

25. Carter 25:613.

26. Croffut, 131.

27. Sprague, 259–60.

28. Ibid., 287–88.

29. Ibid., 289.

30. Ibid.

31. Ibid., 258–59, 263, 267, 299–303, 320–23.

32. Ibid., 376.

33. Laumer, *Amidst,* 61; Sprague, 526.

34. Sprague, 248; Knetsch, "Airy and Comfortable," 31.

35. Motte, 222.

36. McCall, 397.

37. Motte, 199.

38. Ibid., 144.

39. Worth's efforts to cut expenses are detailed in Sprague, 266–69, 275, 305–308.

40. Ibid., 268.

41. Ibid., 418–19.

42. Mahon, 307; Sprague, 441–45.

43. Sprague, 396, 399–400, 456–60.

44. McCall, 402, 406–8, 413, 463–67.

45. Sprague, 485–86.

46. Ibid., 485–86, 488, 494–97.

47. Mahon, 318; Sprague, 500–502.

Chapter 10. Remnants and Resurrections

1. Forry, 99.
2. Bemrose, 98, 105.
3. Sprague, 526–47.
4. Ibid.
5. Foreman, 332–41.
6. U.S. Bureau of the Census.
7. *National Intelligencer,* 1 Oct. 1842.
8. Porter, "Billy Bowlegs," 219.
9. Covington, *Billy Bowlegs War,* 79; Knetsch, "John Darling," 6.
10. Covington, "Indian Scare," 55.
11. Ibid., 58.
12. Knetsch, "John Darling," 6–17.
13. Covington, *Billy Bowlegs War,* 19–23.
14. Horgan and Wynne, 29; Canova, 6.
15. Covington, *Billy Bowlegs War,* 41–42; *Tampa Peninsular,* 2 Feb. 1856, 12 Apr. 1856.
16. *Tampa Peninsular,* 8 Mar. 1856, 12 Apr. 1856; *Tallahassee Floridian and Journal,* 15 Mar. 1856, 19 Apr. 1856.
17. *Tallahassee Floridian and Journal,* 15 Mar. 1856, 12 Apr. 1856, 31 May 1856.
18. *Tampa Peninsular,* 19 Apr. 1856; *Tallahassee Floridian and Journal,* 26 Apr. 1856.
19. *Tampa Peninsular,* 26 Apr. 1856.
20. Covington, *Billy Bowlegs War,* 49–51; *Tampa Peninsular,* 21 June 1856, 5 July 1856.
21. *Tampa Peninsular,* 9 Aug. 1856, 6 Sept. 1856, 15 Nov. 1856.
22. *Tallahassee Floridian and Journal,* 3 Jan. 1857.
23. Ibid., 25 Apr. 1857, *Tampa Peninsular,* 2 May 1857.
24. *Tampa Peninsular,* 9 May 1857.
25. Knetsch, "Southeast Florida," 28-31.
26. *Tallahassee Floridian and Journal,* 25 Apr. 1857.
27. *Tampa Peninsular,* 22 May 1857; Adams, 156.
28. *Tampa Peninsular,* 25 July 1857, 29 Aug. 1857.
29. *Tallahassee Floridian and Journal,* 29 Aug. 1857.
30. Covington, *Billy Bowlegs War,* 72; *Tampa Peninsular,* 12 Dec. 1857.
31. *Tampa Peninsular,* 12 Dec. 1857, 19 Dec. 1857.
32. Ibid., 6 Dec. 1856.
33. Covington, *Billy Bowlegs War,* 76; *Tampa Peninsular,* 23 Jan. 1858.
34. *Tampa Peninsular,* 10 Apr. 1858, 17 Apr. 1858.
35. Ibid., 1 May 1858, 19 Mar. 1859.

Works Cited

Adams, George R. *Gen. William S. Harney, Prince of Dragoons*. Lincoln: University of Nebraska Press, 2001.

American State Papers: Foreign Relations. 6 vols. Washington, D.C.: Gales and Seaton, 1834.

American State Papers: Military Affairs. 7 vols. Washington, D.C.: Gales and Seaton, 1832–61.

Aptheker, Herbert. *American Negro Slave Revolts*. New York: Columbia University Press, 1943.

Army and Navy Chronicle. Washington, D.C. Jan. 1835–May 1842.

Axelrod, Alan. *Chronicle of the Indian Wars*. New York: Prentice Hall General Reference, 1993.

Bassett, John Spencer, ed. *Correspondence of Andrew Jackson, 1833–1838*. 7 vols. Washington, D.C.: Carnegie Institution of Washington, 1926–35.

Bemrose, John. *Reminiscences of the Second Seminole War*. Edited by John K. Mahon. Gainesville: University of Florida Press, 1966.

Boyd, Mark F. "Asi-Yaholo or Osceola." *Florida Historical Quarterly* 33, nos. 3 & 4 (Jan.–Apr. 1955): 303.

Brown, Robin C. *Florida's First People*. Sarasota: Pineapple Press, 1994.

Bucholzer, H. "The Little Magician Invoked." Political print. Call No. PC/US-1844.B157, no. 17. Library of Congress.

Buker, George E. *Swamp Sailors: Riverine Warfare in the Everglades, 1835–1842*. Gainesville: University of Florida Press, 1975.

Canova, Andrew P. *Life and Adventures in South Florida*. Tampa: Tribune Printing, 1906.

Carter, Clarence Edward, ed. *Territorial Papers of the United States*. Vols. 22–26, *Florida Territory*. Washington, D.C.: Government Printing Office, 1956–62.

Chamberlain, Samuel. *My Confession: Recollections of a Rogue*. Edited by William H. Goetzmann. New York: Harper, 1956.

Cherry, Conrad. *God's New Israel: Religious Interpretations of American Destiny*. New York: Prentice-Hall, 1971.

Christian Observer. vol. 18. Boston, Mass.: William Wells and T.B. Wait and Co.,1802–66.

Coe, Charles H. "The Parentage of Osceola." *Florida Historical Quarterly* 33, nos. 3 & 4 (Jan.–Apr. 1955): 202.

———. *Red Patriots: The Story of the Seminoles.* Cincinnati, 1898; facsimile reproduction, Gainesville: University Press of Florida, 1974.

Cohen, Meyer M. *Notices of Florida and the Campaigns.* Charleston, 1836; reprint with an introduction by O. Z. Tyler Jr., Gainesville: University of Florida Press, 1964.

Congressional Globe Containing the Debates and Proceedings of the Congress. Washington, D.C.: Blair and Reeves, 1833–73. Vols. 1 (23d Cong., 1st sess., Dec. 1833), 2 (23d Cong., 2d sess., Dec. 1834–Mar. 1835), 3 (24th Cong., 1st sess., Dec. 1835–July 1836), 4 (24th Cong., 2d sess., Dec. 1836–Mar. 1837), 5 (25th Cong., 1st sess., Sept. 1837–Oct. 1837), 6 (25th Cong., 2d sess., Dec. 1837–July 1838), 7 (25th Cong., 3d sess., Dec. 1838–Mar. 1839), 9 (26th Cong., 2d sess., Dec. 1840–Mar. 1841).

Covington, James W. *The Billy Bowlegs War.* Chuluota, Fla.: Mickler House Publishers, 1982.

———. "Cuban Bloodhounds and the Seminoles." *Florida Historical Quarterly* 33, no. 2 (Oct. 1954): 117.

———. "The Indian Scare of 1849." *Tequesta* 21 (1961): 55.

———. *The Seminoles of Florida.* Gainesville: University Press of Florida, 1993.

Croffut, W. A., ed. *Fifty Years in Camp and Field: Diary of Major General Ethan Allen Hitchcock.* New York: G. P. Putnam Sons, 1909.

DeLorme. *Street Atlas 4.0.* Geographic software program.

Eisenhower, John S. D. *Agent of Destiny: The Life and Times of General Winfield Scott.* New York: Free Press, 1997.

Everest, Allan S. *The Military Career of Alexander Macomb.* Plattsburg, N.Y.: Clinton County Historical Association, 1989.

Foreman, Grant. *Indian Removal: The Emigration of the Five Civilized Tribes of Indians.* Norman: University of Oklahoma Press, 1972.

Forry, Samuel. "Letters of Samuel Forry, Surgeon, U.S. Army 1837–38, Part III." *Florida Historical Quarterly* 7, no. 1 (July 1928): 88.

Friedberg, Daniel M. *Life, Liberty and the Pursuit of Land.* New York: Prometheus Books, 1992.

Giddings, Joshua A. *The Exiles of Florida: or, the Crimes Committed by Our Government Against the Maroons, Who Fled from South Carolina and Other Slave States, Seeking Protection Under Spanish Law.* Columbus, Ohio, 1858; reprint with an introduction by Arthur W. Thompson, Gainesville: University of Florida Press, 1964.

Heidler, David S., and Jeanne T. Heidler. *Old Hickory's War: Andrew Jackson and the Quest for Empire.* Mechanicsburg, Pa.: Stackpole Books, 1996.

Heitman, Francis B. *Historical Register and Dictionary of the United States Army, 1789–1903.* Washington, D.C.: Government Printing Office, 1903.

Holland, James W. *Andrew Jackson and the Creek War: Victory at the Horseshoe.* Tuscaloosa: University of Alabama Press, 1990.

Horgan, James J., and Lewis N. Wynne, ed. *Florida Decades: A Sesquicentennial History, 1845–1995.* Saint Leo, Fla.: Saint Leo College Press, 1995.

Horn, Stanley F., ed. "Tennessee Volunteers in the Seminole Campaign in 1836: The Diary of Henry Hollingsworth." *Tennessee Historical Quarterly* 1 (Sept.–Dec. 1942): 347; 2 (Mar., June, Sept. 1943): 61.

Hudson, Winthrop S. *Religion in America.* New York: Macmillan, 1977.

Kersey, Harry A., Jr., and Michael Peterson. "Was I a Member of Congress . . . : Zachary Taylor's Letter to John J. Crittenden, January 12, 1838, Concerning the Second Seminole War." *Florida Historical Quarterly* 75, no. 4 (Spring 1997): 447–61.

Kieffer, Chester L. *Maligned General: The Biography of Thomas Sidney Jesup.* San Rafael, Calif.: Presidio Press, 1979.

Knetsch, Joe. "Airy and Comfortable: Or Life in the Forts During the Second Seminole War." *Tallahassee Historical Society* 11 (1996): 31.

———. "John Darling, Indian Removal, and Internal Improvements in South Florida, 1848–1856." *Tampa Bay History* 17, no. 2 (Fall/Winter 1995): 6.

———. "Range War in the East: Conflict Over Cattle and Land on the Georgia-Florida Borderlands." *Proceedings of the 90th Annual Meeting of the Florida Historical Society,* 1992, 108.

———. "Southeast Florida in the Third Seminole Wars: Roads, Scouts and Expeditions, Part II." *Broward Legacy* 22, nos. 1–2 (Winter/Spring 1999):28–31.

———. "Wiley Thompson and the Origins of the Second Seminole War." Presented to the Marion County Historical Society, 20 Apr. 1991, 1.

Laumer, Frank. *Amidst a Storm of Bullets: The Diary of Lt. Henry Prince in Florida, 1836–1842.* Tampa: University of Tampa Press, 1998.

———. *Dade's Last Command.* Gainesville: University of Florida Press, 1995.

Leckie, Robert. *From Sea to Shining Sea: From the War of 1812 to the Mexican War, the Saga of America's Expansion.* New York: HarperCollins, 1993.

Letters Sent, Register of Letters Received and Letters Received by Headquarters, Troops in Florida, and Headquarters, Department of Florida: 1850–1858. Roll 7, Letters Received by Headquarters, Dept. of Florida, Registered, A–G, 1857, Microfilm M1084, National Archives.

McCall, George A. *Letters from the Frontiers.* Philadelphia, 1868.

Mahon, John K. *History of the Second Seminole War, 1835–1842.* Rev. ed. Gainesville: University of Florida Press, 1992.

Milanich, Jerald T. *Florida Indians and the Invasion from Europe.* Gainesville: University Press of Florida, 1995.

Milligan, John D. "Slave Rebelliousness and the Florida Maroon." *Prologue* 6 (Spring 1974): 10.

Motte, Jacob Rhett. *Journey into Wilderness: An Army Surgeon's Account of Life in Camp and Field During the Creek and Seminole Wars, 1836–1838.* Edited by James F. Sunderman. Gainesville: University of Florida Press, 1953.

Parton, James. *Life of Andrew Jackson*. New York: Mason Brothers, 1860.

Patrick, Rembert W. *Aristocrat in Uniform: General Duncan L. Clinch*. Gainesville: University of Florida Press, 1963.

————. *Florida Fiasco: Rampant Rebels on the Georgia-Florida Border, 1810–1815*. Athens: University of Georgia Press, 1954.

Peters, Virginia Bergman. *The Florida Wars*. Hamden, Conn.: Archon Books, 1979.

Poinsett, Joel R. *The Objects and Importance of the National Institution for the Promotion of Science*. Washington, D.C.: P. Force, 1841.

Poinsett Papers. Philadelphia: Pennsylvania Historical Society, 1837.

Porter, Kenneth W. "Billy Bowlegs (Holata Micco) in the Seminole Wars." *Florida Historical Quarterly* 45, no. 3 (Jan. 1967): 219.

————. *The Black Seminoles: History of a Freedom-Seeking People*. Revised and edited by Alcione M. Amos and Thomas P. Senter. Gainesville: University Press of Florida, 1996.

Potter, Woodburne. *The War in Florida, Being an Exposition of Its Causes and an Accurate History of the Campaigns of Generals Clinch, Gaines, and Scott*. Baltimore, 1836.

Register of Debates in Congress, 1825–1837. 29 vols. Washington, D.C.: Gales & Seaton, 1825–37.

Remini, Robert V. *Andrew Jackson: The Course of American Democracy, 1833–1845*. Baltimore: Johns Hopkins University Press, 1984.

Rippy, J. Fred. *Joel R. Poinsett, Versatile American*. Durham, N.C.: Duke University Press, 1935.

Sakolski, A. M. *The Great American Land Bubble: The Amazing Story of Land Grabbing, Speculations, and Booms from Colonial Days to the Present Times*. New York: Harper & Brothers, 1932.

Silver, James W. "A Counter-Proposal to the Indian Removal Policy by Andrew Jackson." *Journal of Mississippi History* 4 (1942): 207.

————. *Edmund Pendleton Gaines: Frontier General*. Baton Rouge: Louisiana University Press, 1949.

Smith, Joseph Burkholter. *The Plot to Steal Florida*. New York: Arbor House, 1983.

Sprague, John T. *The Origin, Progress and Conclusion of the Florida War*. New York, 1848; Gainesville: University Press of Florida, 1964.

Stephanson, Anders. *Manifest Destiny*. New York: Hill and Wang, 1995.

United States Reports. Washington, D.C. "Cherokee Nation vs. Georgia," 30:1–80 and "Worchester vs. Georgia," 31:515–97.

U.S. Bureau of the Census. *1990 Census of Population and Housing*. Washington, D.C., "1990 Population and Housing Unit Counts: United States":38–39.

U.S. Congress. *United States Congressional Serial Set*. Washington, D.C. "Information in Relation to the Destruction of the Negro Fort, in East Florida," 15 Cong., 2d sess., 2 Feb. 1819, H. Doc. 122, and "Report of the Committee on Military Affairs," 15 Cong., 2d sess., 12 Jan. 1819, H. Doc. 82.

Weinberg, Albert K. *Manifest Destiny: A Study of Nationalist Expansionism in American History.* Gloucester, Massachusetts: Johns Hopkins Press, 1935.

White, Frank F., Jr., ed. "Macomb's Mission to the Seminoles." *Florida Historical Quarterly* 35, no. 2 (Oct. 1956): 192.

Wik, Reynold M. "Captain Nathaniel Wyche Hunter and the Florida Indian Campaigns, 1837–1841." *Florida Historical Quarterly* 39, no. 1 (July 1960): 67.

Wilson, Major L. *The Presidency of Martin Van Buren.* Lawrence: University Press of Kansas, 1984.

Wright, J. Leitch, Jr. *Creeks and Seminoles: The Destruction and Regeneration of the Muscogulge People.* Lincoln: University of Nebraska Press, 1986.

Newspapers

National Intelligencer (Washington D.C.). 19 Dec. 1837, Feb. 1837, Mar.–June 1837, 21 June 1837, 1 Oct. 1842.

Niles' Weekly Register (Baltimore). 1811–39: vols. 12 (Mar.–Sept. 1817), 13 (Sept. 1817–Mar. 1818), 14 (Mar.–Sept. 1818), 15 and supplement to 15 (Sept. 1818–Mar. 1819), 17 (Sept. 1819–Mar. 1820), 20 (Mar.–Sept. 1821), 28 (Mar.–Sept. 1825, 29 (Sept. 1825–Mar. 1826), 30 (Mar.–Sept. 1826), 31 (Sept. 1826–Mar. 1827), 38 (Mar.–Sept. 1830), 49 (Sept. 1835–Mar. 1836), 50 (Mar.–Sept. 1836, 51 (Sept. 1836–Mar. 1837), 52 (Mar.–Sept. 1837), 54 (Mar.–Sept. 1838), 50 (Mar.–Sept. 1841), 59 (Sept. 1840–Mar. 1841).

St. Augustine Florida Herald. 28 Jan. 1837 and 17 Feb. 1838.

Tallahassee Floridian and Journal. 15 Mar. 1856–14 June 1858.

Tampa Peninsular. 29 Dec. 1855–19 Mar. 1859.

William and Sue Goza Collection of Historical Newspapers. Microfilms obtained through University of Florida, Gainesville. *National Intelligencer* (7 Apr. 1821), *New York Herald* (16 Feb. 1836), *New York Observer* (30 Jan. 1836), *New York Spectator* (6 Nov. 1821), *Mobile Chronicle* (27 Jan. 1836), *Portsmouth Oracle* (13 Nov. 1819).

Manuscripts

Journal of Col. William S. Foster, Special Collections, University of Florida, Gainesville, Florida.

Foster Collection, Folder 39. McClung Collection, Knox County Library, Knoxville, Tenn.

For Further Reading

The intent of this volume is to view the Seminole Wars much as one would view a distant planet through a telescope: a general, overall picture but necessarily lacking in detail. For those who would draw out a microscope instead and look deeper, we recommend the following books as a starting point.

For a more personal view of the war, we highly recommend the diaries and journals of the following individuals: John Bemrose, Meyer Cohen, Ethan Allen Hitchcock, George McCall, Jacob Rhett Motte, Woodburn Potter, and Henry Prince.

Most of these writings are available from the Seminole Wars Historic Foundation, 35247 Reynolds Street, Dade City, Florida 33523.

George E. Buker, *Swamp Sailors*. An engrossing look at the navy's unusual role in the Florida War.

James W. Covington, *The Billy Bowlegs War*. The only well-researched book available concerning the Third Seminole War.

David Heidler and Jeanne Heidler, *Old Hickory's War*. The most comprehensive work available concerning the First Seminole War.

Frank Laumer, *Dade's Last Command*. A fascinating reconstruction of the battle that became known as Dade's Massacre.

John K. Mahon, *History of The Second Seminole War 1835–1842*. The only authoritative modern history of the war, Mahon's book is considered the benchmark in Seminole War studies.

Kenneth W. Porter, *The Black Seminoles*. The intriguing story of the escaped slaves whose quest for freedom brought them into an alliance with the Seminoles.

John T. Sprague, *The Florida War*. Written by an officer who served in the war, it is the only contemporary history of the Second Seminole War.

Index

Quakers, 173
Quartermaster general, office of, 122–23

Racism, 182
Read, Brig. Gen. Leigh, 119
Red Sticks (Upper Creeks), 21, 41, 70, 137
Reid, Gov. Robert, 175, 192
Religion, 15–16, 25, 30, 222
Richards, Stephen, 60
R. K. Call (steamboat), 168
Rochefoucauld, duc de la, 67
Ross, John (chief), 141

St. Augustine, 4, 20, 69, 76, 93, 104; attacks near, 71, 100, 126, 177, 184, 194
St. Augustine Herald, 149, 167, 172
St. Johns River, 63, 138, 200
St. Marks, 40–42, 51, 60–63, 70, 93, 120, 224
Sanderson, Lt. James, 184
Sandy (interpreter), 167
San Felasco Hammock, 154
Sanford, 127
Santa Fe River, 157
Sarasota, 214
Savannah Georgian, 184
Scare of 1849, 210–11
School: for Indians, 65, 75, 79
Scott, Fort, 28, 35–37, 39–40
Scott, Lt. Richard W., 37
Scott, Maj. Gen. Winfield, 25, 78, 87, 117, 122, 125, 140, 224; becomes commanding general, 192; campaign, 104, 111–14; and Court of Inquiry, 130–31; in Creek war of 1836, 123; dispute with Gaines, 80, 107–9, 162–63
Scott Massacre, 37–38, 41, 51
Segui, Bernardo, 63
Seminoles, 1, 26, 31, 53, 131, 137–38, 140, 224; and Armistead, 183–87; attitudes toward blacks, 11, 86, 179–82; and Battle of Lake Okeechobee, 142–46; and "capitulation," 126–30; and Clinch, 97–100; culture, 9–10, 68; and Dade, 95, 97; early negotiations, 54–55; before First War, 31–32; during First War, 40–42; and Gaines, 107–9; and Harney Massacre, 165–69; and Jesup, 151–52;

and Macomb, 160–65; origins, 3–7, 24; during Patriot War, 20; population, 55; present-day, 225–26; and Scott, 111–14; before Second War, 88–92, 198–202, 205, 209–13; sent west, 151, 153, 206–8; in summer of 1836, 114–17; sympathy for, 173–76; and Taylor, 154–60, 176–78; and Third War, 213, 222; at Treaty of Moultrie Creek, 63–66; at Treaty of Payne's Landing, 81–86; as warriors, 41, 98, 107, 114, 204
Seminole Wars Historic Foundation, 109
Semmes, Lt. Raphael, 119
Seven Years' War (French and Indian War), 7
Sherwood, Lt. Walter, 186
Sickness, 56, 115, 176–77
Sitting Bull (chief), 137
Sixth Infantry, 143
Slavery, slaves, 3, 10–12, 24, 61, 74–75, 90, 124, 151, 207, 214; and bloodhounds, 169–73; fear of insurrection, 20, 26, 89, 91, 94, 104, 126; influence on wars, 41, 78, 86, 104, 128, 132–33, 149, 179–82, 199, 223
Smith, Col. Persifor, 138, 144
Smith, Lt. Constantine, 97
Smith, Sen. Alexander, 49
Smithsonian Institution, 148
Snell, Sen. H. V., 214
Snodgrass, Col. (militia), 138
South Carolina, 104
Spain, Spaniards, 13, 199; cedes Florida to U.S., 52–53; conquest of Florida, 2–3; and First War, 38, 46–47; and Negro Fort, 28; and Patriot War, 18–20; in War of 1812, 20
Spanish Indians, 166–67, 185–86
Specie Circular, 190
Speculation, speculators, 67–68, 189, 212–13, 222–23, 225
Spencer, Sec. of War John C., 201
Sprague, Capt. John T., 15, 163–64, 179, 196, 199, 203, 210
Sprague, Pvt. Joseph, 97
Squatters, 15, 18, 31, 70
Stewart, Elizabeth, 37, 41
Stiles, Ezra, 16

John and Mary Lou Missall serve on the board of directors of the Seminole Wars Historic Foundation, and are currently editing the letters and journals of Col. William S. Foster, an officer who served in the Second Seminole War. They also serve as consultants and researchers for an upcoming documentary film on the Seminole Wars.

THE FLORIDA HISTORY AND CULTURE SERIES
Edited by Raymond Arsenault and Gary R. Mormino

Al Burt's Florida: Snowbirds, Sand Castles, and Self-Rising Crackers, by Al Burt (1997)

Black Miami in the Twentieth Century, by Marvin Dunn (1997)

Gladesmen: Gator Hunters, Moonshiners, and Skiffers, by Glen Simmons and Laura Ogden (1998)

"Come to My Sunland": Letters of Julia Daniels Moseley from the Florida Frontier, 1882–1886, by Julia Winifred Moseley and Betty Powers Crislip (1998)

The Enduring Seminoles: From Alligator Wrestling to Ecotourism, by Patsy West (1998)

Government in the Sunshine State: Florida Since Statehood, by David R. Colburn and Lance deHaven-Smith (1999)

The Everglades: An Environmental History, by David McCally (1999), first paperback edition, 2001

Beechers, Stowes, and Yankee Strangers: The Transformation of Florida, by John T. Foster, Jr., and Sarah Whitmer Foster (1999)

The Tropic of Cracker, by Al Burt (1999)

Balancing Evils Judiciously: The Proslavery Writings of Zephaniah Kingsley, edited and annotated by Daniel W. Stowell (1999)

Hitler's Soldiers in the Sunshine State: German POWs in Florida, by Robert D. Billinger, Jr. (2000)

Cassadaga: The South's Oldest Spiritualist Community, edited by John J. Guthrie, Phillip Charles Lucas, and Gary Monroe (2000)

Claude Pepper and Ed Ball: Politics, Purpose, and Power, by Tracy E. Danese (2000)

Pensacola during the Civil War: A Thorn in the Side of the Confederacy, by George F. Pearce (2000)

Castles in the Sand: The Life and Times of Carl Graham Fisher, by Mark S. Foster (2000)

Miami, U.S.A., by Helen Muir (2000)

Politics and Growth in Twentieth-Century Tampa, by Robert Kerstein (2001)

The Invisible Empire: The Ku Klux Klan in Florida, by Michael Newton (2001)

The Wide Brim: Early Poems and Ponderings of Marjory Stoneman Douglas, edited by Jack E. Davis (2002)

The Architecture of Leisure: The Florida Resort Hotels of Henry Flagler and Henry Plant, by Susan R. Braden (2002)

Florida's Space Coast: The Impact of NASA on the Sunshine State, by William Barnaby Faherty, S.J. (2002)

In the Eye of Hurricane Andrew, by Eugene F. Provenzo, Jr., and Asterie Baker Provenzo (2002)

Florida's Farmworkers in the Twenty-first Century, text by Nano Riley and photographs by Davida Johns (2003)

Making Waves: Female Activists in Twentieth-Century Florida, edited by Jack E. Davis and Kari Frederickson (2003)

Orange Journalism: Voices from Florida Newspapers, by Julian M. Pleasants (2003)

The Stranahans of Ft. Lauderdale: A Pioneer Family of New River, by Harry A. Kersey, Jr. (2003)

Death in the Everglades: The Murder of Guy Bradley, America's First Martyr to Environmentalism, Stuart B. McIver (2003)

Jacksonville: The Consolidation Story, from Civil Rights to the Jaguars, by James B. Crooks (2004)

The Seminole Wars: America's Longest Indian Conflict, by John Missall and Mary Lou Missall (2004)